NATIVE ROOTS

NATIVE ROOTS

ROOTS

HOW THE INDIANS
ENRICHED AMERICA

JACK WEATHERFORD

FAWCETT COLUMBINE

NEW YORK

A Fawcett Columbine Book
Published by Ballantine Books
Copyright © 1991 by Jack McIver Weatherford

All rights reserved under International and Pan-American Copyright Conventions. Published in the United States by Ballantine Books, a division of Random House, Inc., New York, and simultaneously in Canada by Random House of Canada Limited, Toronto.

This edition published by arrangement with Crown Publishers, Inc.

Library of Congress Catalog Card Number: 92-90072

ISBN: 0-449-90713-9

Cover design by Kristine V. Mills

Manufactured in the United States of America
First Ballantine Books Edition: October 1992
10 9 8 7 6 5 4 3 2 1

For
Roy Pearce Maybank

CONTENTS

NATIVE ROOTS

1

THE ROAD TO TUKTOYAKTUK

America ends at Tuktoyaktuk. There the land yields to the Arctic Ocean and the polar ice cap. Except for a few distant islands, human habitation stops. The frozen world beyond Tuktoyaktuk belongs to the seal-hunting polar bears that eternally wander the ice, and to the small herds of caribou and wild musk oxen that inhabit the most northern islands of the earth.

The treeless, nearly barren Tuktoyaktuk Peninsula juts hesitantly from the Canadian mainland into the cold Arctic waters, but for most of the year the ice covering the land of frozen bogs and lakes looks much like the ice covering the ocean. The only landmarks separating Tuktoyaktuk Peninsula from the Arctic Ocean are the scattered pingos, the small, round ice volcanoes that poke up out of the earth like ruptured navels. In contrast to the frozen sea, the frozen land also serves as home to a band of nine hundred native Inuvialuit who built their village around a rocky bay at the base of the peninsula.

Tuktoyaktuk also hosts a second settlement, a radar station

huddled within its own fence and protected by its secretive domes. The United States military operates the station as part of the DEW line, the Distant Early Warning system, across the Arctic. No two cultures could seem more different than this native village of polar bear and beluga hunters next to a compound of radar technicians, electronics specialists, and computer personnel. One group belongs to the frozen land where it has lived for millennia, and the other is totally alien and composed of rotating cadres of young men and a few women from a much different environment. If cut off from outside contacts and supply lines, the people of the radar station would probably die as soon as they exhausted their food, gasoline, and ammunition, but the Inuvialuit could continue to survive on the peninsula alone for another thousand or so years, just as they have done in the past.

America ends in Tuktoyaktuk not merely because the road ends there, but because Tuktoyaktuk represents the final stages of a process of social and cultural contact that has taken five centuries to unfold. Tuktoyaktuk straddles the continent's last frontier, where the radically different worlds of native Inuvialuit and modern Americans face each other. In Tuktoyaktuk there seems to be no today; one sees only yesterday on one side and tomorrow on the other.

Despite their differences, the two communities, so far from other human habitation, hug up against each other for mutual protection and warmth against the Arctic wind and the eternal night of winter. The military station provides a few jobs and goods for the local Inuvialuit. The Inuvialuit hunters share caribou with the men stationed at the radar station, and sometimes the technicians get sconelike bannock from the village women, or buy their souvenir moccasins and dolls made from seal fur.

I had experienced this same symbiosis of dramatically different cultures in several special places, before coming to Tuktoyaktuk. I had seen it among the Bedouin herding their sheep and camels across the Egyptian desert, living at once in permanent contact with the cities of the Nile, and yet maintaining a vast cultural distance from them. I had seen the same cultural gap in the fearful face of a Chinese boy soldier nervously watching an elderly Tibetan women throw herself forcefully and repeatedly in the dirt to prostrate herself before the barred doors of the Jokhang, the holiest temple of Tibetan Buddhism. I had seen it in the mild flirtation and haughty withdrawal of nearly naked tribal women crossing the Sahara on the back of a truck and separated from the blue-veiled Tuareg warriors by a wall of desert salt slabs being hauled to market in Timbuktu.

William, a hunter from Tuktoyaktuk, running with his dogs and sledge past the radar station fence, appeared much like Abdul the Badu walking his camels at a respectful distance from the pyramid of Meidum near al-Faiyum oasis. But there was also a major distinction that separated the cultural mix of Tuktoyaktuk from that which I found in all those other places. The nomadic Bedouin have lived beside the stone cities of the Nile for thousands of years. The scene of the Badu driving his herds and flocks past the pyramids could have been the same three thousand years ago as it is today. The Chinese and the Tibetans have lived side by side for thousands of years, sometimes at war and sometimes peacefully sharing religion, tea, and, in marriage, each other's children. The Bororo, the Bambara, and the Tuareg of the Sahel have visited the salt market of Timbuktu for as long as the city has existed.

These ancient cultures have maintained their cultural and spatial distance and yet interacted with one another for millennia. In Tuktoyaktuk, the interaction has just begun within the lifetime of the people still living there. The mixture of the other cultures I had seen across the globe had been allowed to work itself out slowly through thousands of years, but in America, disparate cultures have clashed more quickly and intensely than ever before in human history.

In the fourteenth century, the North African historian and social philosopher Abd-al-Rahman Ibn Khaldun became the first scholar to analyze the importance of the relationship between tribal and urban nations. In his lengthy study the *Muqaddamah,* the preface to world history, he recognized that the key to understanding Mediterranean and even world civilization lay in this dynamic tension between the tribal peoples and the cities. The cultural contact of such different groups added vitality to their political systems, their economic ties, and their religious beliefs. Most of the world's great empires have arisen when small states conquered surrounding tribes or when nomadic tribes such as the Mongols, Huns, Tartars, or Arabs conquered settled nations. During times of peace, tribal peoples often controlled the commerce between major urban areas such as the salt, gold, and ivory routes across West Africa or the Silk Road that connected the ancient Mediterranean with India and China. By controlling the lines of commerce, they also controlled the flow of ideas and the spread of world religions. Without the tribal people, the urban people remained isolated and stagnant.

Ibn Khaldun died in 1406, the century of Spain's "discovery" of America, but the ensuing history of North America has proven the accuracy of his analysis. With the arrival of explorers followed by traders and settlers, a chain reaction of cultural explosions ripped across North America.

The coming together of the varied native cultures of North America with the rest of the world generated a long list of superlatives. The United States became the world's first federal democracy and, together with Canada, made North America the largest democratic area in the world. Later it became the most potent military power in the world, and the technological leader in the exploration of outer space. As the largest producer of agricultural and industrial goods, the United States and Canada became the world's largest common market and one of its most powerful economic engines.

The great achievements of North America in economics, politics, technology, and agriculture have resulted from the rich diversity of peoples and cultures that have come together in this continent, a mixture that has created new social systems and a uniquely American culture. Beneath the surface of each of these American accomplishments lie indigenous roots. The settlers grafted their civilization onto the native American roots, and together they produced a hybrid civilization of unprecedented vigor.

Only a historical moment ago, a mere thousand years, the first European settlers arrived from Scandinavia, ready to make new settlements on the Atlantic Coast of Canada. After the thorough and decisive defeat of this Viking colony, the Europeans did not return for five hundred years, until the accidental arrival of three Spanish ships lost in the Caribbean in 1492. Yet another century passed before arrival of the first permanent European settlers and their African slaves in what was to become the United States and Canada.

This cultural transformation that started with the voyages of Leif Eriksson and his followers to North America around A.D. 1000, accelerated with the English settlement of Jamestown in 1607 and reached a frenzy as it moved westward toward the Pacific coast in the nineteenth century, has now reached distant Tuktoyaktuk, where it is winding down on the Arctic shore. The process of change through cultural contact and the mixture of various populations will probably continue as long as humans live on earth, but it will probably never again attain the dramatic proportions that it did in North America in the last few centuries.

All of America was once Tuktoyaktuk. At some time in the last five hundred years every valley, every beach, every river, every lake, every mountain, every island, every plain, every forest, and every community has stood on the cutting edge of the frontier where the old world encountered the new, where the civilizations of incoming settlers encountered the civilizations of native America. The American frontier mixed together Pilgrims with Pequots, Frenchman with Hurons, Spaniards with Choctaws, Africans with Seminoles, Germans with Dakotas, Basques with Navajos, Chinese with Haida, Jews with Kiowas, Russians with Aleuts, Vietnamese with Menominees, Scandinavians with Inuit, Hmong with Ojibwas, and Dutch with Dene. The scramble of peoples and cultures in North America has created a cultural mixture that probably will not be repeated in world history until we encounter life on another planet.

2

PYRAMIDS ON
THE MISSISSIPPI

A climber ascending the worn slope of the great pyramid sees the river plain slowly stretching out to the horizon. The top of the pyramid soars a hundred feet in the air, the equivalent of a ten-story building, and provides the highest viewpoint on the plain. Unlike the pointed top of the Egyptian pyramid, this truncated pyramid is capped by a massive field large enough to host a football game.

On each side of the pyramid, lumps in the earth mark the sites of smaller pyramids, burial mounds, large open plazas, or perhaps markets and other buildings that surrounded the main pyramid. Faint traces remain visible in the soil showing the line of a stockade that surrounded the entire ceremonial complex.

With more than twenty thousand residents, Cahokia was the largest city in America north of ancient Mexico. During its most prosperous period, around A.D. 1250, Cahokia was larger than London and ranked as one of the great urban centers of the world. Even the colonial cities founded by European settlers across North America did not surpass ancient Cahokia's population until the eighteenth century, when Philadelphia grew to twenty thousand inhabitants.

From the top of the great pyramid at Cahokia, one can see the river to the east, just beyond which loom modern skyscrapers surrounded by residential areas. Gleaming on the distant bank of the river rises the great arch of St. Louis, which seems small and barely visible from the top of the Cahokia pyramid.

Cahokia lies in southern Illinois, just across the river from St. Louis, Missouri. Of all the great pyramids built in the world—in Egypt, Mexico, Guatemala, and Peru—this is the most northerly. Cahokia and the other earthen pyramids of the United States are the world's only pyramids built in a temperate zone.

Climbing any of the world's great pyramids is much the same experience. The climbers mostly watch their feet and the immediate area, searching for the next firm foothold. On some pyramids, such as those of Egypt, it is a little harder because the pyramid was not made for climbing. On others, such as at Cahokia, or at Teotihuacán in Mexico, the climb is a little easier because the pyramid comes equipped with stairs or ramps for that purpose. What varies from one pyramid to the next is not the climb to the top, but what the climber sees from the top.

From the pyramids of Giza and Saqqara in Egypt, the climber sees only desert for a thousand miles to the west; to the east lies a glimpse of the green Nile and its narrow band of cultivated fields. The desert usually beckons open and clear, while the nearby inhabited areas choke in a cloud of dust, diesel smoke, and noxious gases that obscure the view of the city. From the pyramids at Meroe, built during the first millennium before Christ in the ancient kingdom of Kush, along the middle Nile in the modern Sudan, one sees only the ruddy stones and sand of a desert that stretches out like a rusting landscape of taconite ore.

The pyramids of Teotihuacán look out over low scrub and small houses of the central Mexican highlands; approximately a mile above sea level, they were built at the highest altitude of any pyramids in the world. From atop the pyramids of Chichén Itzá and Uxmal in the Mexican Yucatán, one sees a low-lying jungle that looks almost like a carpet unrolled over the earth.

The most spectacular pyramid view must be that from the tops of the steep pyramids of Tikal in Guatemala. The pyramids poke up above the surrounding jungle like the heads of turtles looking out over a green ocean. Only the great pyramids of Tikal qualify as truly jungle pyramids. Monkeys screech and play in the branches adjacent to the pyramid as well as on the pyramids themselves. Iridescent green turkeys strut noisily around the lower levels of the pyramid. The pyramid seems to be less a human artifact than a part of nature itself.

Cahokia does not occupy a monumental setting today. The largest pyramid in the United States sits adjacent to the horseradish capital of the world, Collinsville, Illinois. It occupies an unincorporated urban niche, a virtual no-man's-land tucked between the cities of St. Louis, Collinsville, and East St. Louis. Collinsville Road, which cuts across the foot of the Cahokia mound, long ago became a night strip of honkytonks. Cheap motels sprang up around nightclubs and liquor stores that took advantage of the more liberal Illinois laws to cater to the nocturnal appetites of the greater St. Louis urban area, directly across the Mississippi River in Missouri. A drive-in theater moved onto the flattened ground around the Cahokia mound. Within a few miles, entrepreneurs erected the Fairmount Park racetrack for horses and the St. Louis International Speedway for cars.

Today, even the seedy night strip has deteriorated. One motel still advertises rooms for eight dollars a night, but many of the buildings have been cleared away. They have given way to the next stage in urban blight, an even less dramatic collection of salvage yards and treatment plants.

In the summer, the thick leaves of the trees obscure much of the view from the top of Cahokia mound, but when the leaves drop in the cool fall air, the surrounding area comes more clearly into focus. An asphalt and cement company on the eastern edge of the site often fills the air with the strong smells of asphalt and petroleum. The pond behind it hosts a collection of old tires, chunks of cement, and discarded industrial junk.

Across the street a battered cinder-block nightclub without windows now has become a discount butcher outlet surrounded by hand-lettered signs:

TURKEY WINGS OR NECKS—5 LBS.—$2.49
RHIND-ON SLAB BACON—99¢

Close by the butcher shop lies a dump for some two hundred rusting hulks of wrecked and worn-out city buses with broken windows and dented sides. The buses lie pell-mell around the site like butchered dinosaurs that have been skinned and left where they fell in some bizarre hunting ritual.

Monk's Mound, the largest of the Cahokia pyramids, covers 16 acres; it rests on a base 1,037 feet long and 790 feet wide, with a total volume of approximately 21,690,000 cubic feet, a base and total volume greater than that of the pyramid of Khufu (or Cheops), the largest in Egypt. The pyramid of Khufu is 756 feet on each side (an area of 571,536 square feet), but the base of the Cahokia pyramid is nearly 250,000 square feet larger than the Egyptian pyramid. In all the world, only the pyramids at Cholula and Teotihucán in central Mexico surpass the Cahokia pyramid in size and total volume. No other structure in the United States approached the size of the Cahokia pyramid until the building of airplane hangars, the Pentagon, and skyscrapers in the twentieth century.

The top of Monk's Mound served as the place for now-unknown ancient rituals and as the home of a chief or priest, but it was clearly an uncomfortable place to live. In the summer the sun shines directly onto the top of the mound without the mitigating effects of trees or hills. Standing on top of the pyramid in August is like standing in the middle of a large, desolate parking lot. The wind merely redistributes the stifling heat without offering relief. At the end of a long, hot day, storm clouds frequently blow overhead and cast giant shadows across the pyramids like rapidly moving ink blots.

In the cooler months, icy winds swoop down from the north and blast the top of the mound. Nothing stands between the top of the mound and the Arctic but the long, flat plains of the North American interior. Thick air from the Gulf of Mexico brings enough moisture to make the area around Cahokia very humid, but it does not bring enough tropical warmth to defeat the winter cold. Only a few minutes in that wind can leave one with an earache, a runny nose, and small particles of ice dangling from eyelashes and hair ends.

The ruins of approximately 45 smaller pyramids and burial mounds still stand clustered around Monk's Mound; these alone survive from the 120 originally constructed by the Indians. For decades, European-American settlers used the mounds as quarries for dirt, and obliterated 75 of them. Farmers slowly cut down the pyramids through repeated years of tilling the soil. Especially the horseradish farmers have loosened and damaged the archaeological remains by cutting into the earth the eighteen inches that they need for their deep-root crop.

Despite the losses and degradation of the site, Cahokia still ranks as the largest collection of pyramids ever constructed in one place anywhere in the world. In addition to Cahokia, ten other large urban areas occupied this stretch of the Mississippi River, and scattered between them were another fifty smaller villages (Fowler).* The present city of St. Louis now occupies the site of one such suburb of ancient Cahokia. The white settlers of St. Louis nicknamed their settlement "Mound City" in recognition of the twenty-six Indian mounds they found there, but those mounds have since been cleared away to make room for the modern city.

Little is known about the people who made this city. Even the name *Cahokia* comes from the name of the Indians living in the area when the French arrived in the eighteenth century. For lack of a more accurate name, anthropologists generally call the people who built it "Mississippian," and the site of Cahokia is in a twenty-five-mile stretch of the river called "American Bottom" in anthropological literature. The name of the largest pyramid, Monk's Mound, derives not from ancient Indian priests who lived on it, but from Christians, namely the Trappist monks who owned it and farmed it in the nineteenth century.

The city plan of Cahokia closely followed a common pattern of urban Mississippian sites, but Cahokia achieved a scale that surpassed all others. A collection of temple pyramids, mounds for chiefs' houses, and burial mounds bordered an open, rectangular plaza that was probably used for religious and civic ceremonies as well as athletic events and markets. The cities and towns that we now call Mississippian were concentrated along the Mississippi, Ohio, and Arkansas Rivers in the central part of the United States and across the entire width of the Southeastern United

---

* Names in parentheses refer to works listed in the bibliography.

States from St. John's River along the Atlantic Coast of Florida and Ocmulgee in the uplands of Georgia to Spiro, Oklahoma.

Archaeological investigations reveal that settlement began between A.D. 600 and 800 at Cahokia and grew steadily to its greatest size a few centuries before the arrival of the Europeans. The city started before the foundation of the Holy Roman Empire and persisted through the time of the Middle Ages and the Renaissance in Europe.

In the 1960s, archaeologists made an unexpected discovery when a freeway was about to be built within a half-mile of Monk's Mound. They found a large circle that had once consisted of a series of large poles, which they named Woodhenge after its similarity to England's Stonehenge. The ancient Cahokians erected Woodhenge about A.D. 1000. The circle measures 410 feet in diameter, with the largest post in the center. The structure apparently served as a giant solar calendar for determining the solstices and equinoxes of the year, important information for an agricultural civilization.

The origins of the Mississippian culture coincide with the introduction of the hoe, which replaced the smaller digging stick in the eighth century (Fowler), and with the introduction of new types of maize from Mexico around the tenth century, and it seems to have been steadily reinforced by the introduction of new types of beans and the domestication of native plants. A great variety of squashes, maize, and beans formed the "three sisters" that typified agriculture throughout North America. Indian cooks knew how to make virtually every corn dish that we know today, including corn on the cob, hominy grits, stew, and cornmeal. They also grew pumpkins, Jerusalem artichokes, nuts, persimmons, sunflowers, marsh elder, and a number of seed plants that now grow wild in the Mississippi area.

Even though today we do not know who the people were who founded Cahokia, we can easily imagine why they located it where they did; it was a transportation, trade, and communications hub, the evidence and noise of which still deafens visitors. From atop Monk's Mound today, one can hardly escape the noise of the surrounding area. Planes fly overhead, going into and out of St. Louis International Airport. Automobile traffic on Collinsville Road seems reasonably light between rush hours, but the trains that crisscross it frequently stop the cars until they form queues even longer than the passing trains. The trains connect the city north to Chicago, south to New Orleans, and east and west to the Atlantic and Pacific coasts.

Barges churn up and down the Mississippi River, but the constant whine of cars on the adjacent freeways drowns out the comparatively silent engines of even the largest chain of barges. No matter in which direction one looks from the top of Monk's Mound, one sees a freeway. Three cross-country freeways and a major urban loop intersect, leaving Cahokia marooned on an island in the middle of them. Interstate 55 passes Cahokia on its path from Chicago to New Orleans; Interstate 70 joins it there in its run from Pennsylvania to Denver and out into the middle of Utah. Interstate 64 terminates there after starting at Norfolk, Virigina. Interstate 255 circles the site as part of the outer loop around the greater St. Louis area.

Ancient Cahokia arose where it did for much the same reason that St. Louis arose, because both straddle a major nexus on the Mississippi River, halfway between its origins in Minnesota and its effluence from Louisiana into the Gulf of Mexico. Cahokia sits at the continental hub of North America. It was an ideal place for trade, commerce, and communication.

Whether measured by length, width, volume of water, or size of the total area drained, the Mississippi River ranks as one of the great rivers of the world. Its tributaries, including the Missouri, Arkansas, and Ohio, would be major rivers in their own right if they stood alone in another part of the world. With a length of 3,740 miles, the Mississippi-Missouri system is the fourth-longest river, since it is a few hundred miles shorter than the Nile, Amazon, and Yangtze. But if we examine the total drainage area, only the Amazon and the Congo surpass the 1,255,000 square miles drained by the Mississippi system. This dwarfs the 733,400 square miles of the Nile system or the 454,000 square miles of the Yangtze. The Mississippi and its tributaries drain an area equal in size to India, or more than one and a quarter times the size of the Mediterranean Sea.

The builders of Cahokia selected their city just to the south of where the Missouri and Illinois rivers empty into the Mississippi and to the north of where the Meramec River drains into the

Mississippi from the Ozark Mountains. Only 150 miles south of Cahokia, the Ohio joins the Mississippi at Cairo, where the modern states of Kentucky, Illinois, and Missouri converge. Virtually no other spot on this planet can claim a more favorable location for long-distance travel by river in every direction.

Travelers along the waterways of the Mississippi can reach the southern areas of what are now Alberta and Saskatchewan provinces in Canada. They could reach Montana and Idaho in the northwest, or New Mexico in the southwest. Toward the east, the Ohio and Tennessee rivers lead to the edge of the Appalachian Mountains and the borders of Pennsylvania and the Carolinas. In addition to this massive area drained by the rivers, the Mississippi and several of its tributaries reach within only a few miles of the Great Lakes, providing easy access into the largest freshwater lakes in the world, and from there into the St. Lawrence River system, the next largest in North America.

At its southern terminus, the river spills into the Gulf of Mexico, which is virtually an inland sea surrounded by land on all sides except where it opens into the Atlantic Ocean and the Caribbean Sea with a line of islands stretching across the open water between the peninsulas of the Yucatán and Florida. In the midst of all this stood Cahokia, at the center of a water network stretching effectively from the Carribbean to Hudson Bay and uniting peoples with vastly different cultures, economies, and languages.

Even though we have no ancient writing from the city of Cahokia, no carved friezes, no illustrated manuscripts or records, we do know, from the trade items found in their burials, that the citizens of Cahokia utilized the full diversity of this area through trade. Archaeologists have found rolled sheets of copper imported from the Great Lakes, arrowheads made from the black chert of Oklahoma and Arkansas, ornamental cutouts of mica from North Carolina, worked shells from the Gulf of Mexico, salt from southern Illinois, lead from northern Illinois, and worked stone from around what is now Yellowstone National Park in Wyoming (Fowler). Cahokia itself probably controlled the entry into this network of chert deposits that were mined extensively in nearby quarries and controlled a major source of salt.

Cahokia united a trading empire larger than the combined area of France, the United Kingdom, Spain, Germany, Austria, Italy,

Belgium, the Netherlands, Ireland, Greece, Denmark, Romania, Switzerland, Czechoslovakia, Yugoslavia, Portugal, Luxembourg, and Bulgaria. Its trade stretched along routes longer than from London to Constantinople, from Madrid to Moscow, or from Paris to Cairo. We have no evidence that Cahokia controlled a political empire, but it certainly controlled the nexus of a trade empire that surpassed in geographic size the empires of ancient Rome and Egypt.

Another interesting fact about Cahokia emerges when we examine the distribution of North American languages at the time of European contact. We find that Cahokia straddled the boundary of the three great language families of eastern North America. The southern Muskogean languages of the Gulf Coast, the eastern Iroquoian languages, and the western Siouan languages all converged in this area. In this regard, Cahokia may have played an important intermediary role as a channel of trade, information, and the regulation of social or political relations among these three major groups.

We know very little about the civilization of Cahokia. The Indian record was not written, and no European explorer ever saw Cahokia at its height and lived to record it. By the time the explorers arrived at Cahokia, the area had already suffered two centuries of Old World diseases that traveled overland much faster than did the European explorers. The civilization of Cahokia had already withered and died. Some evidence points to destruction from indirect contact with the whites, while other evidence indicates that with a fluctuation in climate, the focus of Mississippian culture shifted to southern sites in the Gulf states from Louisiana to Georgia.

Of the three primary cultural areas of the Americas—the Andes of South America, where the Incas flourished; Mesoamerica of the Maya and Aztecs; and the Mississippian area of North America—we know today the least about the Mississippian area. As they conquered Mexico and Peru so quickly, the Spanish conquistadores saw those civilizations at their zenith, and even though they destroyed the cultures, they recorded some information about them. We can read Spanish documents and capture a faint vision of the Mexican and Peruvian civilizations, but we have no such picture of the ancient people of Cahokia, whose very name for themselves has now been lost in the blood of conquest and the dust of colonization.

Ancient America may be thought of as a cultural continuum as well as a geographic one, from Mexico to Canada. Mexico represented the densest population organized into a sedentary civilization based primarily around agriculture, but controlled from cities that served as political, mercantile, and religious centers. The nations and empires of Mexico resembled in many respects the nations and empires of the ancient Mediterranean.

At the other end of the geographical and cultural continuum, Canada and Alaska contained a sparse population devoted almost exclusively to foraging—living by hunting, gathering, and fishing. In the far north the Inuit (Eskimo) hunted sea mammals; on the Atlantic and Pacific coasts the natives fished and gathered seafood. In the plains they hunted buffalo, and around the Great Lakes they hunted deer and fished. None of these people had cities, and most of them pursued highly mobile if not nomadic lives that precluded the accumulation of large amounts of material goods or the production of large artifacts such as buildings, bridges, and pyramids.

The area we now call the United States served as the transition zone between the foraging nations of Canada and the settled empires of Mexico. Some of the ancient peoples of what would become the United States led foraging lives much like those of their Canadian neighbors.

The modern states of New Mexico and Arizona were home to farmers whose influence spread as far east as Kansas and Texas. The peoples of the Mississippi River valley also farmed and lived in settled communities. In the Northeastern United States the peoples of New York and New England pursued an agricultural life pattern that included many aspects of their neighboring foragers.

The aboriginal peoples of one half of the United States hunted and gathered wild foods, and the peoples of the other half devoted themselves primarily to agriculture. The dividing line did not run east to west through the United States but rather ran in a diagonal from the Northeast to the Southwest. This imaginary line ran from Quebec in the Northeast to Arizona in the Southwest, or, more precisely, from the mouth of the St. Lawrence River in the North Atlantic to the mouth of the Colorado River in the Gulf of California. To the east or south of the line, most Indians lived by agriculture; to the north or west of the line, most lived by foraging.

The highest concentrations of people lived east and south of the line, in agricultural areas. These people and their descendants we now know as the Iroquois and Huron of the Northeast; the Algonquian tribes of the Great Lakes and the Atlantic Coast; the Five Civilized Tribes of Creek, Cherokee, Choctaw, Chickasaw, and Seminole—most of whom were removed from the Southeast to Oklahoma; and the settled pueblo people of New Mexico and the Hopi, Papago, and Pima of Arizona.

The foraging side of the line included the Plains nations of the Dakota, Lakota, Assiniboin, Crow, Kiowa, Arapaho, and Cheyenne, as well as the southern nations of the Comanche, Apache, and Navajo. It also included the Cree of Canada and all the Pacific Coast people from the Aleuts of the north to the Chumash and Diegueno Indians of the southern California coast.

Cahokia lay just to the south of this diagonal line that separated foraging peoples from agricultural peoples. By growing corn and other crops from Mexico, the people of ancient Cahokia established at least an indirect connection with the Maya and Aztecs of the south. By trading for minerals and metals from the north, the ancient Cahokians maintained a similar tie with the nomadic tribes. Cahokia stood at the hub of these two important and strikingly different cultures and modes of life.

Anyone who digs into the substructure of St. Louis will discover Cahokia, just as anyone who digs in any city of North America will find some stratum of Indian life. The foundations of modern North America rest firmly on a solid bed of ancient civilization. This past deserves our attention not merely for the sake of antiquarian curiosity, but because our culture and society today descend from ancient Cahokia as much as from medieval London, Renaissance Rome, and ancient Athens.

When the European adventurers and settlers explored North America, they did not find monuments of antiquity awaiting them such as existed in the Old World. North America offered no great Coliseum, no Parthenon, no Tower of London, no Louvre, no Temple of Jerusalem, no Great Wall as in China. They found no giant statues of men dotting the landscape, and no monuments to great conquerors. North American history did not speak to them; the continent seemed silent.

The settlers coming into America believed that the land contained no civilization, so they steadfastly saw none. Alexis de Tocqueville, representing the common European view, erred egregiously when he wrote in his *Democracy in America* that "North America was inhabited only by wandering tribes, who had no thought of profiting by the natural riches of the soil; that vast country was still, properly speaking, an empty continent, a desert land awaiting its inhabitants." For him the Indians had merely "occupied without possessing" America. They were prevented from developing a civilization by their "implacable prejudices, their uncontrolled passions, their vices, and still more, perhaps, their savage virtues."

The continent did not speak to the newcomers because the civilizations of North America did not always speak in loud stone. They spoke in earth and wood, in fiber and textile, in bead and shell. Even when they did choose to speak in stone, they selected small images that could be carved from softer stone, such as the carved animal pipes of the ancient Hopewell people, or the polished red pipestone of the Plains. Even the stone buildings at Chaco Canyon in New Mexico or Mesa Verde in Colorado spoke in a softer tone, without triumphant arches, expansive domes, soaring pillars, or other modes of imperial adornment and ostentation.

The ancient people of North America built civilizations that only now we begin to see, but that we still do not understand. North America is the land of great and mysterious civilizations whose roots grow deep into the soil; yet, compared to the other continents of the world, America is still the great enigma. When Columbus arrived in the New World, he thought that he was off the coast of India or Japan or China. After four voyages and a decade exploring the Caribbean, he still could not see where he was; he insisted that he was in Asia.

Even though today we no longer share Columbus's folly of thinking that we are in Asia, we still do not adequately know where we are. We have built cities and cleared farms across the continent, but we do not know the story of the land on which we live. We take nourishment from this soil, but because we cannot see our roots down deep in the American dirt, we do not know the source of that nourishment.

Our cultural roots as a modern people lie buried in Cahokia and a thousand similar historical sites and surviving Indian reservations across the continent. These ancient and often ignored roots still nourish our modern society, political life, economy, art, agriculture, language, and distinctly American modes of thought.

3

WOMEN (AND A FEW MEN) WHO LED THE WAY

The Mississippi River has one of the least dramatic sources of any great river in the world. The Ganges and the Mekong thunder down from the Himalayas, the Amazon begins at a glacier high in the Andes, the Nile starts in the headwaters of Lake Victoria and in the highlands of Ethiopia, over a mile above sea level, and the Rhine begins in the snowy Swiss Alps. Even the Missouri River splashes to life among the dramatic peaks of the Rockies, and the Ohio begins in the rolling mountains of Appalachia. The Mississippi River gently gurgles out of Lake Itasca in north central Minnesota. At a mere 1,475 feet above sea level, even its birth occurs as a gentle, seemingly insignificant event.

By comparison to the headwaters of other rivers, the terrain at the source of the Mississippi lies relatively flat, but compared to the prairie of Minnesota, it might be called a zone of rolling hills. It is the sprawling domain of Christmas-tree farms and medium-sized forests where the three-hundred-year-old white pines and red Norway pines barely attain a hundred feet in height.

The stream that begins the Mississippi seems hardly different from thousands of other gentle streams passing around rocks and under fallen trees in North America. The point where the Mississippi leaves Lake Itasca stretches no more than twenty feet wide and less than a foot deep. In the summer, children eagerly wade across the mouth, while proud parents snap pictures and make videos of the momentous event. In the dead winter, cross-country skiers pass by, and if there were there no signs posted to announce the importance of the spot, they might easily miss it in the heavy snow and ice that coat the region. Local people visit the spot frequently and vacation around Lake Itasca, but the area lies too far from a major airport or an interstate highway to draw a big international, or even national, crowd of visitors.

Almost the only time that the local people do not use the park around Lake Itasca for something is during a blizzard. Particularly during a wet spring snowstorm that drops snow too slushy for skiers, the source of the Mississippi stands alone and deserted. The large, greasy snowflakes fall into the barely moving water and slowly dissolve. Other snowflakes congregate on a twig, a leaf, or any buoyant matter to make a small floating island of ice and snow.

As soon as the snows and pounding northern wind subside, the forest comes alive with the animals that seem to know that despite four inches of snow, winter has been once again defeated by the lingering sun of spring. A large red-headed woodpecker drums away at a dead tree, sending bark flying into the air in its search for bugs and other tasty insects. The ducks patrol across the lake. White-tailed deer bravely wander into new areas in search of ever-scarcer food before the spring snows yield to new growth. A still-healthy and well-fed beaver inspects the long shoreline of the lake after its deep winter's rest in its lodge.

The snows of spring hang heavy on the trees, bending them toward the ground like overladen Christmas trees. The sudden snap of a breaking branch on an old tree rips through the air like the report of a rifle and reverberates through the woods, leaving a strange, ringing aftertone that transfixes every animal, including a human.

Flowing at the leisurely rate of only a mile and a half an hour, it will take the snowflakes that fall around Lake Itasca an average of ninety days to make the journey to the mouth of the Mississippi in the Gulf of Mexico, 2,552 miles to the south. A May snowflake falling in Minnesota arrives in New Orleans as a drop of water on a humid and hot August day.

Around Lake Itasca, one can still see two native burial mounds from the Woodlands Indians about five hundred years ago. Nearby, on the other side of the lake, archaeologists found an even older site where some ancient Americans butchered a giant *Bison occidentalis* eight thousand years ago.

Today, Ojibwa people still live all around the source of the Mississippi. The White Earth Reservation flanks it on the west, and the Leach Lake Reservation on the east. Despite all the Indian ruins and the abiding native communities, plaques around Lake Itasca proclaim that Henry Rowe Schoolcraft discovered the source of the Mississippi River in July 1832. For the Indian people who have lived here so many thousands of years, Lake Itasca was obviously not "lost" or "undiscovered" before 1832. They knew it well, albeit under another name. Schoolcraft "discovered" the source of the Mississippi only because an Ojibwa chief guided him and his small expedition to the site.

Oddly, this was not the first time Schoolcraft "discovered" the source of the Mississippi. In 1820 he claimed to have discovered the source in another lake, and as evidence to support that claim, he published a book in 1821 with the ungainly title *Narrative Journal of Travels from Detroit Northwest Through the Great Chain of American Lakes to the Sources of the Mississippi River in the Year 1820.*

Schoolcraft sent the book to John C. Calhoun, the Secretary of War, who had sponsored the expedition. The book contains a rather dull accumulation of random observations and tidbits crammed into journal form. The only thing that saved it from total obscurity was the claim loudly stated in the title of having discovered the sources of the Mississippi River, which the explorers located in what is now northern Minnesota, in Lake Cass (or "Cassina" as they called it), named for the expedition's leader.

Newspapers such as the *American* in New York, and the *Detroit Journal and Michigan Advertiser,* eagerly published accounts of Schoolcraft's expedition, including excerpts from his journals. The great search for the source of the Mississippi rivaled in intensity and color the search for the source of the Nile, which gained international attention later in the nineteenth century, after the development of an increasingly important press tool, the telegraph. As soon as Schoolcraft's first book appeared to claim the honor of discovering the Mississippi's source, the Italian explorer Giacomo Constantino Beltrami put forth a rival claim by locating the river's source in 1823 in another lake, which he named Julia.

Despite publication of his first book, Schoolcraft apparently recognized that that the Cass expedition had not found the true source of the Mississippi River, since a small stream fed into Cass Lake. In 1832, with the help and guidance of his wife's Ojibwa relatives, Schoolcraft set out on his second expedition to find the true source of the Mississippi.

Schoolcraft had married Jane Johnston, an Ojibwa woman with a white trader father. Jane Johnston's twenty-six-year-old brother, George, served as interpreter for Schoolcraft's expedition. Ozawindib, or Yellow Head, an Ojibwa chief, guided the group into Minnesota, where they soon found the true source of the Mississippi River in Omushkos, an Ojibwa name meaning Lake of the Elk; it was known by fur traders as Lac La Biche, which also meant Elk Lake. With his penchant for making new names and claiming credit, Schoolcraft renamed the lake Itasca, which he derived from the final letters of the Latin words *veritas* (true) and *caput* (head). This expedition became the subject for Schoolcraft's next book, *Narrative of an Expedition Through the Upper Mississippi to Itasca Lake* (Savage, p. 232).

Schoolcraft brought to a close a three-hundred-year chapter of American history obsessed with the search for the source of the Mississippi, a search that began with Hernando De Soto's claim of having discovered the lower reaches of the Mississippi in 1541.

In the annals of American exploration, the name of Schoolcraft comes late and is relatively minor compared to Coronado, De Soto, Joliet, and Lewis and Clark. The names of the Indians who already lived in these areas and guided the explorers appear far less commonly. Aside from a few highly romanticized guides, such as Sacajawea, the names of Indian guides like Ozawindib rarely occur, and many of the names seem now lost for eternity.

As soon as the European explorers arrived in the Caribbean, they needed the guidance of Indians to get them from island to island and to the mainland. This need intensified when the European explorers came to the mainland, because most of the explorers had only maritime backgrounds, and thus found themselves poorly prepared for exploring the land.

Indians made some of the earliest maps for the explorers. Their personal knowledge of the land allowed them to draw maps with precise and accurate detail at the request of the whites. The use of forced Indian guides and Indian mapmakers by whites began with Christopher Columbus on his fourth voyage along the coast of Mayan country on the Yucatán Peninsula, in 1502. He encountered a trading party in a canoe propelled by twenty-five paddlers. Among the crew was an old man who knew how to make maps and diagrams. After dismissing the other men, Columbus kept the old man and had him make coastal charts (Winsor, p. 442).

After landing in Mexico in 1519, Hernando Cortez depended on the Aztec woman Malinche (also called Marina or Malintzin) to interpret and to guide him from the coast to Tenochtitlán, capital of the Aztec empire. Because of her knowledge of the various Mexican cultures as well as the languages, her role surpassed that of mere interpreter or guide; she gained Cortez's confidence to become his chief negotiator and strategist. She hammered and welded together the native coalition of dissatisfied Indian nations that finally battered down the Emperor Montezuma and destroyed the Aztec Empire. As Mexican writers frequently note, Malinche deserves as much of the credit or blame for Spanish success as do Cortez and all his horses and artillery. Malinche would never have brought down the empire without Cortez, but Cortez may never have brought it down without her.

The Mexican writer Octavio Paz wrote at length in *The Labyrinth of Solitude* about the psychological and cultural role that La Malinche played in shaping the cultural psyche of the Mexican people. She spanned the transition from the ancient Indian society to the modern Indian-Spanish mestizo nation of Mexico. Unlike the Aztec emperors and nobles who sank beneath the surface and disappeared from history, Malinche survived. The Mexicans of today continue to call themselves "the children of La Malinche."

Soon after Cortez conquered Mexico, the French explorer Jacques Cartier cautiously sailed his ships up America's North

Atlantic coast. In 1534 his expedition explored the coast of Canada, and like Cortez, he also wanted to venture inland in search of treasures and new cities. To prepare for the excursion into the interior, he kidnapped Taignoagny and Agaya, two coastal natives whom he took back to France with him to teach them to speak French. Cartier returned in the spring of the following year with the interpreters, whom he used to guide his ships up the St. Lawrence River to the Huron territory of Chief Donnaconna and on to the Huron village of Hochelaga, which became Montreal.

One of the guides, Agaya, acquired a special role in medicinal history because he was the one whom Cartier beseeched for a treatment for scurvy when the ailment began to decimate his crew. Agaya turned to the Huron women, who prepared a medicine from one of the evergreen trees. This medicine of the unknown Huron women reversed scurvy in every one of Cartier's men and prevented any more deaths that winter.

Rather than releasing the interpreters in appreciation for their services, Cartier kept them with him for his return voyage to France. Cartier also kidnapped Chief Donnaconna, who, along with both interpreters, died in France without seeing his homeland and family again.

The English explorer Martin Frobisher developed a novel technique for using the services of the Inuit as pilots for his ship during his first Arctic exploration, in 1576. When he sailed around Baffin Island, searching for a northwest passage to the Pacific, Frobisher watched for Inuit men out in their kayaks. When he saw one, he leaned over the bow of his ship and rang a bell, which he held out as though offering a gift to the passing native. When the friendly Inuit came closer and reached up for the bell, Frobisher grabbed him and forced him to pilot the large ship through the Arctic bays and inlets.

Kidnapping Indians and forcing them to become interpreters, guides, or slaves grew into a well-established cultural pattern among explorers. Such practices became a standard part of the business. By the time Samuel de Champlain made his first voyage up the St. Lawrence, in 1603, he did not need to do the kidnapping himself. He saved a whole trip to America by first securing in France the services of two Indians as guides. The men had probably been kidnapped by some other explorer or fishing expedition and abandoned or sold in France.

Champlain continued to rely on native help, and in 1610 he took an Indian boy with him from America to France for the purpose of teaching him the French language so that he could serve as a guide. Champlain also added a new dimension to this during the same year by persuading a French boy to live among the Indians and learn their language and culture while Champlain was away in France. Thus, when Champlain returned to Canada in 1611, he had a Huron-speaking French boy who could interpret, and a French-speaking Huron who could guide him.

The Spaniards lacked the well-established French custom of kidnapping Americans and taking them back to Europe for training guides. Like Cortez and Francisco Pizarro, most of the Spaniards seized translators and guides as they needed them. This lack of training by their guides may account for some of the more fantastical stories brought back by Spaniards about men of gold and cities of gold; maybe the Spaniards simply heard what they wanted to hear.

After joining forces with Pizarro in Peru, Hernando De Soto received a thousand pounds of gold as his share of the ransom of the Inca emperor Atahualpa in 1533. He then sailed back to Spain to petition the king for permission to invade the final unknown continent of North America, then called Florida. In granting De Sota his request, the king appointed him governor of Cuba and *adelantado* of all of America north of Mexico. The concession signed by the king charged De Soto "to conquer, pacify, and populate the lands there are from the Province of Rio de las Palmas [Texas] to Florida" (Buckingham Smith).

With the king's political endorsement, but with his own money, De Soto assembled the largest armada of ships and men yet to sail against the Indian nations of North America. De Soto intended to conquer and rule Florida. He sailed to America determined not to suffer the same fate as Pánfilo de Narváez, whose Florida expedition disintegrated, wandering aimlessly until some of his men reached Texas. De Soto had an advantage over Narváez in that he knew the value of local guides, and he knew ways to force them to cooperate.

After finding little of political or mercantile interest on the Florida peninsula, De Soto marched his army northward across what was to become Georgia and into South Carolina, searching for a civilized kingdom to conquer. He came closest to his goal when he met the exotic Lady of Cutifachiqui, the woman who ruled over a large portion of what is now South Carolina. Scholars argue over the precise location of her capital, but it probably lay in the middle of South Carolina's piedmont, quite possibly near the ancient ruins around modern Camden.

According to the memoirs of one of De Soto's men, the land of Cutifachiqui "was delightful and fertile," and "the forest was open, with abundance of walnut and mulberry trees." De Soto's private secretary, Rodrigo Ranjel, describes the country as possessing "many very fine fields and a pretty stream and a hill covered with walnuts, oak trees, pines, live oaks, and groves of liquidambar, and many cedars" (Bourne, p. 102). Since De Soto stayed in South Carolina in May, it is hardly surprising that all of the memoirs of the survivors of the trip speak of the beauty of the land and its fertility, for May is the most beautiful and pleasant month of the year in that region, and the land abounds with the bright green color of lush new growth and with the fragrant blossoms of a thousand flowering plants.

The Gentleman of Elvas, another of De Soto's companions, proclaimed the people as "more civilized than any people seen in all the territories of Florida." Rodrigo Ranjel portrayed them as "very clean and polite and naturally well conditioned" (Bourne, p. 99). Because the people of Cutifachiqui had no prior experience with Spaniards, they received De Soto with courteous interest and with minimal fear.

Even if the natives had wanted to resist the Spaniards, they had recently been weakened by strange, ravaging epidemics. European diseases had already traveled up from the coasts and had decimated the population. Many of their villages were now deserted, and grass and vines had taken over the central plazas. The mortuary temples overflowed with bodies and the goods buried with them.

The Cutifachiqui were ruled by a woman who sent her daughter, sister, or niece (the accounts vary) to meet De Soto. In a scene reminiscent of his encounter with the Inca emperor Atahualpa, De

Soto received her with Spanish pomp and formality, but the Lady of Cutifachiqui matched him in dramatic pageantry. She approached De Soto's encampment slowly, traveling in a large canoe, where she sat in the stern, proudly posed on large cushions and protected from the harsh sun rays by a billowing awning. Her warrior escorts surrounded her in adjacent canoes.

After she disembarked, her men carried her seated on a chair atop a litter that they bore on their shoulders. According to Rodrigo Ranjel, her litter was draped with a delicate white cloth that looked like linen (Bourne, p. 99), but was probably a finely spun cotton. Unlike the nearly naked people to the south in the Florida peninsula, her people were dressed in clothes and shoes, and she wore three strands of shining pearls that luxuriously draped her body down to her thighs.

The Lady presented a stunning parade of gifts to De Soto. She gave him furs, shawls, dressed skins, and blankets. In a gesture of great drama, which the writer Garcilaso de la Vega compares to Cleopatra's reception of Marc Antony when trying to save her dynasty, the Lady of Cutifachiqui slowly and dramatically unwound the strands of pearls from around her neck and held them out to one of De Soto's men to give to him. De Soto asked her to bring them to him herself, whereupon he removed from his finger a gold ring set with a ruby and presented it to the Lady.

After the genteel exchange of luxury gifts, the Lady of Cutifachiqui supplied the expedition with goods of more immediate need. A generous and regal hostess, she gave the Spaniards plentiful supplies of food, including bushels of corn, strips of dried venison, dry wafers, and the much-desired luxury of salt, for which the men lusted in the subtropical Carolina heat.

In addition to food and gems, De Soto wanted information. He grilled the Lady of Cutifachiqui to gain intelligence regarding the surrounding provinces—their produce, rulers, cities, and any other pertinent information—for his conquering caravan. The Spanish observers of this meeting marveled at how well informed the Lady seemed, and how eloquently she spoke. But we must wonder how much accurate information she gave De Soto regarding neighboring lands, and how much she embellished her descriptions to discourage De Soto and his men from lingering in her own lands.

Despite this great show of courtesy, cooperation, and hospitality from the Lady of Cutifachiqui, De Soto finally seized her and her court, just as he had seen Pizarro do so successfully in his capture of the Inca emperor in Peru. De Soto then looted her country. When he demanded gold, the Indians brought him copper, and when he demanded silver, they brought him silvery mica, which they mined in the North Carolina mountains, in sheets up to three feet wide and three feet long.

De Soto found little precious metal, but an abundance of pearls, especially in the mortuary temples. In one town alone his expedition found 25,000 pounds of pearls. The mortuary temples of the people of Cutifachiqui astounded the Spaniards, who had already seen the cathedrals of Spain, the mosques and fountains of the Arabs, the palace of Montezuma in Mexico, and the gold ransom of Atahualpa in Peru.

Outside the massive doors into the temple that housed the pearls, twelve wooden giants stood guard. The huge figures held over their heads massive clubs covered with strips of copper and studded with what appeared to the Spaniards to be diamonds, but may have been mica chips.

The Indians had decorated the roof of one temple with pearls and feathers so that it looked to the Spaniards like a building from a fairy tale. Along the sides of the roof, pearls had been suspended from threads so thin that the pearls seemed to be floating in the air around the temple. Inside the temples the Spaniards saw rows of chests, each filled with pearls of uniform size. The Spaniards could not carry all the pearls, but they selected out the best ones for themselves. Ironically, even though De Soto's expedition was the first into the area, his men also found in the temple some European trade goods—glass, cheap beads, and a rosary—indicating just how fast and efficiently the native trade systems operated.

After ravaging Cutifachiqui, De Soto marched away with the nation's wealth and a new supply of Indian slaves, including the Lady of Cutifachiqui herself. De Soto wanted her as his guide and as insurance against Indian attack. The troop set off toward the mountains, probably near the present border of North and South Carolina, to one of the Lady's provincial towns, called Xuala. When they neared the end of her territory and were about to cross over into the territory of Guaxule, the Lady and some of her servants escaped, taking the best of their pearls with them.

De Soto wanted to recapture the Lady, but his lust for treasure pulled him forward toward the next town, where, she had promised him, was much gold. He wandered on in his expedition of greed across the southern United States with a series of kidnapped and impressed guides. In May 1541, De Soto's guides took him to the Mississippi River, which he promptly "discovered."

De Soto's health began to fail after months of unrewarding pillage and conquest across America. Tortured by repeated disappointment in his search for riches, and racked by persistent fevers, he grew weaker and more depressed as his invasion lingered into its third unproductive year. On May 21, 1542, almost a year to the day after he first claimed to have discovered the Mississippi River, Hernando De Soto died, probably near the site of Ferriday, Louisiana. His men buried him, but fearing that the Indians would dig up his body and desecrate it, some of his followers secretly took the body to the middle of the Mississippi River and consigned it to the deepest part of the water. His followers auctioned off his possessions, which included two male slaves, three female slaves, seven hundred pigs, and three horses with saddles. His conquest and enslavement of the people of the Lady of Cutifachiqui, and his pillaging of their lands as well as the lands of Mauvila and so many other of the Southern nations, had produced nothing but suffering for the Indians and for his own men.

During the summer of 1541, while De Soto tramped around the southern Mississippi River, another Spanish explorer and would-be conqueror roamed only a few hundred miles northwest of him, also searching for the fabled rich cities. Francisco Coronado wandered lost somewhere in Kansas after trekking thousands of miles up from Mexico and across Arizona, New Mexico, Oklahoma, and Nebraska.

Even though both De Soto and Coronado served under the banner of the same Spanish king, they competed with each other to see who could discover and conquer the most valuable Indian kingdoms. Coronado sought to find, claim, and conquer anything of value in North America in the name of Mexico before De Soto could claim it for Florida. Neither one of them knew what riches North America might hold, but whatever these riches might be, each explorer wanted them for himself.

After a bloody conquest of the pueblos of New Mexico, Coronado wanted to conquer kingdoms of greater value. He wanted a *new* Mexico equal in value and glory to the old Mexico. His lust made him particularly susceptible to the tales offered by an Indian known to us simply as El Turco or "the Turk," so named because his appearance reminded the Spaniards of the Turks they had seen in the Mediterranean.

Coronado's men encountered the Turk at Pecos Pueblo in New Mexico, but he apparently came originally from somewhere out on the Great Plains to the east. He claimed that many days' journey to the east the Spaniards could find a great river six miles wide and filled with fish as large as horses. According to the Turk, the boats on this river required forty men to row them, and had canopies under which their lords reclined. On land the subjects carried their lords in litters. The ruler supposedly read from a sacred book and worshipped the Queen of Heaven.

The Turk called this place the land of Quivira, and he claimed that beyond it lay even larger and richer lands. He called one of these "Harahey" or "Arahe," now thought to be the Pawnee lands of Nebraska, and he referred to the other as "the Gaues," now thought to be the Kaws or Kansas of the Missouri River (Bolton, p. 233).

The reports left to us by the chroniclers depict a mythic and romantic image, in part because the descriptions have been filtered through the eyes of Spaniards and had to be translated from Indian languages to Spanish. With their poor ability to communicate even with their own guides, the Spaniards often translated their guides' words to fulfill their own fantasies. Today we have very little way of knowing what the Indian guides actually said; we have only the Spanish descriptions.

These reports are often dismissed as the mere fantasies of a man who made them up and lied to the Spaniards for whatever reason he may have had. Yet the substance of these claims rings true, and certainly seems to point toward the civilizations of the Mississippi River, which was a large enough body of water to fit the Turk's description. Even though it may not have fish the size of horses, it has giant catfish of over a hundred pounds swimming along its muddy bottom, and in its southern regions there were once alligators as long as horses.

Judging by the size of the war canoes encountered by De Soto along the Mississippi, the Turk's reference to boats of forty oarsmen was an understatement. The Turk may not ever have seen the Mississippi or any of these marvels he described, but his information possibly derived from hearsay based more on fact than conjecture. The reports seem too close to what we know of the Mississippi civilizations to be coincidental with the fantasies of a pathological liar or a lunatic.

The Turk embroidered his descriptions with tales of gold and silver, since that was what the Spaniards seemed most interested in hearing. Almost everything that he says about the gold we can dismiss as either a lie (if he was trying to deceive the Spanish or enhance his own importance) or a mistake, if the Turk did not know the difference between gold and copper or between silver and mica.

In April 1541, Coronado set out across the Great Plains in search of Quivira and its six-mile-wide river. The departing company must have made one of the most unusual spectacles to head out onto the American plains. Coronado departed with 300 mounted soldiers in armor and a marching infantry, which, together with the slaves and servants, amounted to about 1,500 people accompanied by 1,000 horses, 500 cattle, and a massive flock of 5,000 sheep (Horgan, p. 146). At the head of this caravan rode Coronado proudly atop his steed. In front of Coronado walked El Turco, leading the way but controlled by Coronado, who kept him on a long chain.

As Coronado traveled toward the east, it seemed that the plains would never end. All they saw were great stretches of sky and a land filled with "humpbacked cows," as they called the bison. He encountered Plains Indians who painted their bodies and lived in pavilions (tepees) made of many skins. They also had dogs that carried their masters' goods in packs like miniature saddles and dragged the tepee poles that served as a travois between encampments. This meeting marked the first European encounter reported with the Plains Indians, who would become internationally famous in the nineteenth century because of their prolonged struggle to defend their home from the increasing waves of white pioneers.

To hasten the discovery of Quivira, Coronado set out ahead of his main party with a smaller and faster party of thirty soldiers and a handful of Indian slaves and guides. The Turk obviously did not know how to get to the Mississippi, but he took them as far as Kansas, where they found twenty-five villages of tattooed Indians cultivating maize and living in straw houses. These people were possibly the Wichita or some related group, but precise identification today proves difficult. Whoever they were, the Spaniards obviously had not reached the land of the great river filled with giant fish and mighty boats.

The Indians encountered by Coronado told him of other white men like himself, wandering farther south. Assuming that this might be the rival De Soto expedition, Coronado tried to contact them by sending out couriers with letters, but nothing has ever been found of these communications. By a strange coincidence, however, one of the captive women in Coronado's expedition did make contact with the De Soto expedition. She escaped from the Coronado expedition, probably somewhere in the Panhandle of Texas. She hid herself from her Spanish master, Juan de Zaldivar, by taking refuge in an isolated canyon. Since the Coronado group was moving northeast, the Indian woman fled to the south, into the heart of Texas.

By a cruel twist of fate, after escaping from Coronado's group in the north of Texas, she then encountered the remnants of the De Soto expedition (by then under the leadership of Luis de Moscoso, following De Soto's death) on the upper branches of the Brazos River, nine days' journey south of where she had left Coronado's men. To get information about the country to the north, the Spaniards tortured the woman and the Indians with whom she had sought refuge. The woman first told them the story of the Spaniards in the north, but under more torture she recanted and said that she had lied.

Only years later did the accuracy of her story emerge when the Gentleman of Elvas wrote his account of the De Soto expedition and Pedro Castañeda wrote his account of the Coronado expedition. The fact that she had given De Soto's men correct details of the Coronado expedition, including the names of Coronado's officers, proved that the woman was the same one.

Explorers quickly forgot the tragic story of the Indian guide called the Turk, but for generations they continued to search in vain for his fabled Quivira. For the next two hundred years after the Coronado and De Soto expeditions, mapmakers had trouble locating the mythical land of Quivira on their maps. It showed up on maps in places as widely apart as the Great Lakes, Texas, and the coast of what would now be British Columbia.

In disgust at not finding a rich kingdom to conquer, Coronado had the Turk executed. Coronado's men garrotted him in much the same way that Pizarro had had the Inca emperor Atahualpa executed after he ceased to be of use to the Spaniards. Coronado and his convoy headed back to the pueblos of New Mexico, where they hardly found an enthusiastic welcome.

Coronado spent the winter in the pueblos, but in the spring of 1542, Coronado's great steed stumbled and threw him to the ground, leaving him with lifelong injuries. Defeated and humiliated, he began the long retreat back to Mexico; news had reached him of Indian rebellions in northern Mexico, and he feared being trapped in New Mexico with hostile natives on every side.

Over the centuries after the Spanish *entrada,* native guides continued to lead explorers, settlers, and pioneers across North America. One of the last great Indian guides was the Shoshone woman Sacajawea, who had been captured by the Hidatsa and sold to the French trapper Toussaint Charbonneau. In 1804 she encountered the Lewis and Clark expedition at a Mandan village near modern Bismarck, North Dakota. Sacajawea led the expedition across North Dakota and through Montana to the tribe of her brother Cameahwait, and then she accompanied them to the Pacific Coast and back again. Along the way, she had a healthy baby in the middle of the winter of 1805.

The era of North American exploration effectively opened with Malinche leading Cortez across Mexico in 1519, and ended when Sacajawea led Lewis and Clark to the northern Pacific Coast in 1805. Throughout these three centuries of exploration, women played an exceptional role as guides and interpreters. Because they had often been captured in raids or sold into a distant area as slaves, women frequently spoke several languages and knew the routes from one area into another.

Women also had excellent foraging skills that allowed them to live off the land by finding food even when animals were not around. Like the Huron women who saved Cartier's crew from scurvy, native women possessed the specialized knowledge of medicines derived from herbs, roots, and barks that proved so important for curing illness, treating cuts and wounds, binding sprains and splinting broken bones, and combating the effects of insect and snake bites. This knowledge often proved even more valuable to the explorers than did the women's linguistic and travel experience.

Indian women possessed other vital skills for long-distance travel. They knew how to make and repair the birchback canoes the explorers used in northern America, and they also knew how to track. On one occasion, after the Lewis and Clark expedition had traveled nearly a thousand miles from Mandan territory without seeing another Indian, they came across an abandoned campsite. Sacajawea immediately identified the territory and the makers of the camp by examining the distinctive sewing pattern on a discarded moccasin that she found at the site.

Although we know the names and the stories of a few of these women, such as Malinche, the Lady of Cutifachiqui, and Sacajawea, many of the others, such as the woman who escaped from Coronado's men only to be re-enslaved by De Soto's men, remain nameless. Many men who became known to us as trappers, traders, or explorers depended heavily on their Indian wives for much the same services of translation, counsel, and guidance in their dealings with other Indians in crossing the American land.

Most of these explorers and trappers, usually known pejoratively as "squaw men," left us few records to detail how their native wives helped them. They rarely shared credit with anyone else, much less with Indian women. Sometimes we know something about these women, such as Henry Schoolcraft's Ojibwa wife, who arranged for his trip to "discover" the source of the Mississippi, but Schoolcraft himself, even in mentioning his Indian guides, oddly omits the information that his guides were his in-laws, related to him through his wife.

The American natives proved to be such important guides not merely because they lived on the continent and thus knew where the next village or river was located, but also because they had specialized kinds of knowledge, much different from European knowledge. Nowhere did this prove more important than in the

Arctic region of North America, where European knowledge and technology proved inadequate.

A compass is of little use in the North American Arctic. The North Magnetic Pole actually lies within the northern islands of North America, and not out in the center of the Arctic Ocean with the geographic North Pole. When used in such places, the compass needle twirls and points in virtually any direction, with little regard for true north. Even if the compass did point at the North Magnetic Pole, the explorer could easily be east or west or even farther north of the magnetic pole.

The sun in the Arctic offers little help. For several months, depending on how far north the traveler goes, the sun fails to appear. In the summer, the explorer certainly cannot depend on the sun rising in the east or setting in the west; it circles tirelessly in a clockwise path just above the horizon for weeks on end. At any season of the year, fog or snow can cut off any view of the sun, moon, or stars for several successive days.

In such a context the Inuit developed completely different ways of travel that relied less on astronomical calculations than on earthly ones. Like Polynesian sailors who learn to "read the waves," the Inuit learn to read the waves on the ocean, rivers, and streams, but they must also learn to "read the snowdrifts" that occur much more frequently in their homelands. By studying the different kinds of winds and the patterns that they make, Inuit walk parallel or counter to the snow ridges to move in the desired direction, even when they have no dogs to help lead the way. Similarly, they know how to keep the wind hitting a particular quadrant of the body in order to steer them, even when a blinding snow destroys all visibility (Hall, p. 24).

Explanations of Inuit, Aleut, and Dene navigation methods become difficult in English because we lack adequate words to explain what they see and how they interpret it. Where we see only undifferentiated snow, they may have a dozen or more different words to describe what lies before them. Similarly, they have many more words to describe different kinds of ice, various shades of white, and the different colors of water and movement of ripples or types of animal tracks. All of these words come into play in deciding which way one can move with safety.

The Slave tribe of Dene, who live on the Mackenzie River near the Arctic Circle north of the Great Slave Lake, have a general word *te* meaning "ice," but they have thirteen categories of ice, which we could easily translate into English as "black ice" (*tetsidenit'le*), "white ice" (*tega*), "blue ice" (*tedeit'le*), "hollow ice" (*tevu*), "muddy ice" (*tetagot'le*), and so forth. English words, however, lack the full meaning conveyed in the Slave language. The Slave know which kind of ice can support the weight of a child, which can support the weight of a man on snowshoes, which can support a full dog team and sledge, and so forth. Such information frequently proves vital in the activities of daily life, when a Slave Indian must repeatedly make decisions on where and how to cross a river, lake, or stream (Basso).

The importance of American natives and their specialized knowledge about exploration continued right through the twentieth century. A Greenland native named Oodaq helped a series of international explorers of the Arctic in the early twentieth century, including Robert Peary, Knud Rasmussen, and Jean Malaurie. Even if one rejects the rigorously debated claim of Robert Peary to having reached the North Pole in 1909, all the polar explorers used Inuit assistance.

Even though Captain Cook sailed to Antarctica as early as November 1773, the continent resisted repeated attempts to be crossed. Because no people lived there, the area offered no ready-made technology or cultural patterns that the newcomers could appropriate for their explorations. The Europeans lacked the equipment and technology to travel across the land. Early explorers even tried using shaggy ponies to carry their supplies, but they failed.

In December 1911, the Norwegian explorer Ronald Amundsen became the first man to reach the South Pole. He did so by relying almost exclusively on Inuit technology. He wore only Inuit clothing, made by Inuit women in the traditional way and thus weighing about half as much as the clothes worn by his competitors. He traveled with four sledges, each drawn by thirteen Inuit dogs. As a Norwegian, he preferred to travel on Scandinavian skis rather than on Native American snowshoes. All subsequent explorations of Antarctica, from 1911 through the 1990 crossing by Will Steger with his dog teams, have continued to rely heavily on the technology, knowledge, and culture of the Arctic Inuit.

4

FIRESTORM

Thick birch forests cover much of south central Canada. Seen from a distance in the moonlight, the thin, straight birch trees, clustered tightly together, look as dense as the plains of elephant grass in northern Guinea, or the bamboo jungles of southern China. By growing close together, the birch, which appears to be a rather fragile tree, easily chokes out other trees and bushes by denying them a chance to get sunlight and grow. They leave no room for interlopers. Occasionally a single tall pine or fir juts up from a birch grove that invaded after it had already grown too tall to shield from the sun. The tall fir stands like a bear rearing up on its haunches, surrounded by baying dogs. The birches cannot kill the tall tree in their midst, but they surround it so densely that none of its seed will ever take root and spring to life.

A grove of birches has unique beauty, for the birches are the whitest of trees. The white bark peels back in spots to reveal mottled gray specks up and down the trunks and branches. Particularly in the winter, when snow hides the fallen birch leaves, the trees lure visitors with the purity of their color and with their diminutive size that does not overwhelm a person the way the large pines and other hardwoods can.

The view from inside a birch grove in the winter contrasts delicately with the vision of the grove from a distance. Once inside the grove, one sees that the white of the flaking paper bark is the same hue as the surrounding snow; it is hard to tell where the tree begins and the ground ends. When it starts to snow in a birch grove, there is no longer any up or down or sideways. An interloper can be overcome with a sensation of floating in a viscous white liquid, and must, like an insect caught in the sap of some mysterious, carnivorous plant, struggle to stay upright.

The birch is a special tree, and the native people of the Great Lakes and across southern Canada learned to live with the birch tree and to use it in constructing their homes and making fires, sewing boxes, and containers—and they used it to build canoes. Today, most of the native communities have disappeared from the birch belt; they have been replaced by small towns and farms. Those Indian communities that survive appear poorer than, but otherwise similar to, the nonnative communities.

Gull Bay is one small community that has survived in the forest, somewhat isolated from the modern city. It sits aside Lake Nipigon in western Ontario. Even though the name conjures images of a peaceful cove on the ocean, the town lies more than a thousand miles inland from either the Atlantic or the Pacific. To reach Gull Bay, one must drive north out of Thunder Bay for about a hundred miles over dirt roads that cut through the heart of some of the thickest forest left in North America.

Gull Bay is a settlement of about 450 Ojibwa who live in small wooden frame houses at the point where the small Gull River flows into Lake Nipigon. The road to the south is the only one that enters Gull Bay. To go east, north, or west, one must travel by snowmobile in the winter or by water in the summer. The people of Gull Bay live too far away to commute to industry and service jobs in Thunder Bay on Lake Superior, and they live too far north for productive agriculture. The people fish, hunt, and gather wild rice, but their frustration shows clearly in a hand-lettered sign in front of one of the houses: "Work, Not Welfare."

A few hopeful people opened small stores in the front rooms

of their homes, where they sell some basic items, but the settlement has too few people to support even one real store. Other homes offer haircutting or auto repair, but the only steady employment comes from the government and from the timber industry. The government has a small police force, a health clinic, a road maintenance crew, and a school that teaches in English. The road maintenance crew has a hard job keeping the road open all winter, when snowfall in a normal year can easily exceed fifteen feet.

Evidence of the timber industry appears all around Lake Nipigon. The loggers carve rough roads into the forest, and then clear sections by cutting all the trees within them. They haul the logs to Thunder Bay, where the world's largest paper mills spit out millions of pounds of newsprint for the daily newspapers of Canada.

Even today the forests of North America stretch the human powers of understanding. The bristlecone pines of the White Mountains in California reach back through history approximately 4,600 years, making them the oldest living trees on the planet. Approximately 750 species of trees grow wild on the continent, including a few Old World species that have acclimated themselves to the new climate and terrain. The native trees of North America range from the small pawpaw, which usually measures only a few inches in diameter, to the giant redwoods.

At one time forest covered America, and the Indians lived for the most part in or along the edges of forests. Both coasts contained large forests, and the enormous Atlantic Coast forest reached inland to the Mississippi River and as far north as Hudson Bay. The Southern states nourished large forests of magnolia, cypress, persimmon, pecan, hickory, long-leafed pine, live oaks, and the durable palmetto. The lower Missouri River sustained cottonwood, cedar, ash, hickory, oak, walnut, and willow. The Ohio River valley offered giant sycamores, cottonwoods, tulip poplars, and walnut trees. Birch and fir trees covered much of Canada, and large cedars grew on the Pacific Coast north of the redwoods. Pines grew wherever they found sufficient moisture in the Southwest, and some areas sustained large forests of the stately ponderosa pine.

Along with the jungles of Brazil, the Congo, and Indonesia,

North America was one of the most wooded places on earth. Elias Pym Fordham, an Englishman who settled in Indiana, wrote a complaint that was common to many newly arrived Europeans:

"There is too much wood; and when on the barren peak of some rocky hill, you catch a distant view, it generally is nothing but an undulating surface of impenetrable forest" (Blakeless, p. 272).

Except for the Great Plains and the desert areas of the Southwest, forest covered most of North America, and the Indians of all parts of the continent took advantage of the presence of such a plentiful and varied resource. They built homes and temples of wood, and protected their villages from animal predators and human enemies by erecting wooden palisades. They used wood for canoes, spears, bows and arrows, atlatls or spear-throwers, mortars and pestles, spoons, storage boxes, traps, travois, clubs, pipestems, bowls, harpoons, snow goggles, cradles, blowguns, digging sticks or dibbles, and a wide variety of other tools.

The concepts of Stone Age, Iron Age, and Bronze Age seem essentially inapplicable and thus irrelevant to American history. These terms apply neatly to Old World civilization because they represent the historical reality of technological evolution in that part of the world. Even though Indians used stone and metal, they lived in a virtually eternal "wooden age." They were the true forest people. Anthropologists apply the descriptive label of "Woodland" to the cultures of most of eastern North America between 1000 B.C. and A.D. 1700. This includes everyone from the Adena people and the builders of the pyramids during the Mississippian phase until the Iroquois and Cherokee who met the arriving settlers.

In still more recent times, the Kwakiutl, Tlingit, Haida, Tsimshian, and other groups of the northern Pacific Coast built large houses and public buildings with planks. The intricate designs of some of these plank houses placed the entry so that a visitor appeared to be walking into the jaws of gigantic animals or human figures. The Navajo built hogans of logs covered with earth, but occasionally built them of stone as well. Eastern tribes made long houses of wood or bark on wooden frames, sometimes chinked with mud or lined with woven mats.

*   *   *

The modern people of North America do not follow the ways of the old Woodland culture, but lumber continues to be a major industry in the United States and Canada. The exploitation of the forest is seen as the tapping of a "natural resource." People chop down trees in much the same way that they might dig copper or silver out of the earth, carve salt from a prehistoric lake bed, or scrape up nitrates from an open pit, but unlike minerals, metals, and naturally occurring deposits in the ground, the forests of America were not simply a natural resource that happened to be here waiting for use by anyone who arrived. The Indians had lived in and around the forests for millennia, and had carefully managed and shaped the forests through these years. They consciously followed practices that maximized the growth of trees and plants that they found useful, and minimized those that obstructed them.

The Europeans found large trees in these forests because native forestry practices produced this particular type of forest. In New England the Indians burned the forest every year to destroy the small brush. This allowed hardy trees such as the pines to grow tall, but destroyed the smaller trees and the less fire-resistant varieties such as the firs.

In addition to keeping the forests open, the controlled fires promoted growth of the large trees that the native people preferred for dugout canoes. Throughout North America, native building styles relied on large trees that the people used as primary supports and roof beams in both domestic and communal architecture.

Indians in different areas of North America burned the forest for various local reasons. In California the smoke killed the parasitic mistletoe that grew on the oak and mesquite. Indians from the Gulf Coast to the interior of Alaska used fire to reduce the number of irritating insects and other pests during the summer. In the Southern states, fire drove out the poisonous snakes such as the rattlesnake. What rattlesnakes remained could be seen more easily and thus avoided by the Indians walking through a forest cleared of underbrush.

In time of hostilities or warfare, a cleared forest offered few places for a potential enemy to hide and thus effect an ambush on a traveling group or a sneak attack on a village. Any land that had not been cleared by fire could easily pose a danger to the people living in it, because not only could their enemies hide in it, but their enemies could set fire to it and thus use it as a weapon against the people living there.

The fire encouraged small new growth that then attracted large animals such as deer, which were unimpeded by small trees and bushes. To maximize their hunting, the Indians wanted large, parklike forests of tall trees but open ground underneath. By keeping the forest free of undergrowth, the Indians kept it from becoming a jungle.

The Indians also burned the tall grasses of the prairies and plains. This created new growth and thus controlled the migrations of the buffalo, but the burning of the plains also controlled the spread of forests. In some parts of the Missouri and Mississippi basins, the Indians used fire as a device for limiting the size of the forest and increasing the grazing area of the buffalo. This type of land management lured the buffalo closer to their villages and made the hunt much easier. The hunters could then devote more time to cultivating their crops in the fertile river valleys, rather than making long hunting treks across the open plains.

The work of the Indians in controlling the forests and prairies gradually extended the range of the buffalo ever eastward toward the Atlantic. The Indians kept the Eastern forests so open and so attractive to larger animals that by A.D. 1000, some of the plains buffalo crossed the Mississippi and took up residence in the large woods. They adapted to the new environment to become forest buffalo rather than plains buffalo, and they provided the Indians of the Eastern forest with new sources of food and raw materials.

In their annual burning of the forests, prairies, and plains, the Indians used fire in a controlled and systematic way that minimized the danger from large, uncontrolled fires set by lightning. By regularly destroying the dead lumber and clearing the undergrowth that died each winter, they lessened the chance of uncontrolled fire that might consume their villages and croplands as well as the animals which they hunted.

The Indians knew how to use fire and to control it in ways that the Europeans did not know. The new settlers did not understand even such a simple process as beating a fire with blankets and buffalo robes as a way to smother it. The Indians also taught the settlers the more delicate and paradoxical practice of using backfires in order to control large fires (Pyne, p. 78).

The annual firings of large segments of the plains kept the forests in check. Through the use of fire, Indians maintained large, grassy corridors through forests such as those of the Shenandoah Valley, which later served as major migration routes for European settlers (Pyne, p. 82). Ironically, with the arrival of the settlers and the decline in Indian population, the amount of forest in many areas increased because the Indians no longer kept the forests under such careful control.

As the settlers pushed back the Indians and stopped them from their annual *light* burning of the forest and the prairies, the land that the new settlers did not use for agriculture became a thick and tangled forest that later posed a great danger as a fire hazard. The changes produced disastrous results for the forests. The scars and the human cost of this new pattern can still be seen today in the town of Cloquet, Minnesota, located about two hundred miles south of Gull Bay and twenty miles south of Duluth on Lake Superior.

Cloquet sits on the edge of the Ojibwa reservation known as Fond du Lac. Like Gull Bay, Fond du Lac has a history closely associated with the lumber industry. The people of Cloquet and Fond du Lac live surrounded by the forest and the timber industry that have always been the economic base of the town. Even the small collection of stores between downtown Cloquet and the interstate highway bear the rather inflated name of Lumberjack Mall, and, as if to underscore the town's association with timber, the weekly newspaper carries the name of *The Pine Knot*. The industries in Cloquet make paper, matchboxes, wood-pulp tiles for insulation, and even disposable chopsticks for the Japanese fast-food industry.

Cloquet has the usual dual brick churches of Minnesota's competing Christian sects of Catholicism and Lutheranism, an old city administration building, a rising community college, and acres of railroad tracks. The town straddles the rows of tracks the way other towns might straddle a river or a central park. Often, hundreds of cars sit silently holding their thousands of logs for processing. The most unusual building in Cloquet is the large gas station at the town's main intersection. The modern design of the cantilevered station seems too new for the old building. It advertises itself as the world's only gas station designed by the architect

Frank Lloyd Wright. Abutting it at the rear is the more recent addition of a self-serve laundry that apparently did not share the same architect.

Although Cloquet is over a century old, it appears to be much newer. This is because of what happened there on Columbus Day, Saturday, October 12, 1918. On that day Cloquet was one of the most important lumber towns in North America. It claimed ten thousand citizens, most of whom worked for one of the five sawmills, or the Northwest Paper Company, which made pulp and paper. The town boasted the ability to mill more than a million board feet of lumber a day (Holbrook, p. 32).

By 1918 the mills had already exhausted most of the lumber around Cloquet itself, and the timber for the mills came from far up the St. Louis River or was shipped in from northern Minnesota and southern Canada by rail. Old logs and discarded timber lay strewn for miles around the town. In the open area left after cutting, weed trees—aspen, jack pine, and balsam—sprang up.

The summer and fall of 1918 had been dry, and as frequently happened in such weather, a spark from one of the trains set off a brushfire that grew into a forest fire. Word of the fire reached Cloquet in the afternoon, when refugees from the town of Brookston arrived on the Great Northern Railway with the terrifying tale that their entire town had been consumed.

By eight o'clock that night, the whistles of the mills screeched a loud wail as a trecherous black cloud darkened the sky and quickly obscured all light from the stars or moon. The fire that followed close behind the thick smoke surpassed the flames of a mere forest fire. The conflagration quickly consumed the scrub forests that had not experienced a fire in decades. Living trees ignited in seemingly spontaneous explosions like Roman candles in the night sky.

As the fire raced across northern Minnesota, it accelerated with a speed and fury that caused a hurricane-force wind to rush before it, ripping up trees, flattening buildings, tossing over cars, and hurling stones. When the fire hit the sawmills of Cloquet, it encountered a hundred million board feet of lumber. The wind hurled the burning boards through the air to make a firestorm of flaming timber. Gases from the fire formed clouds and then exploded in bursts that witnesses described as looking like gigantic burning balloons. These burning balloons catapulted the fire over rivers and cleared areas for a distance up to half a mile.

Refugees fleeing by cart and car from Moose Lake and Kettle River created a traffic jam at Death Curve, where more than a hundred people died as the fire overtook their stalled caravan. Forest animals, cattle, and draft horses trampled people as they too fled the conflagration. Survivors reported that some of the fleeing people and animals burst into flames just like the trees that ignited from the heat of the air rather than from the touch of the flames themselves.

The fire did not spread slowly across Cloquet, but exploded throughout the entire town instantaneously, setting everything in it ablaze. Twenty miles away, in Duluth, on Lake Superior, the weather station recorded the wind from the firestorm at seventy-six miles per hour, one of the strongest in its history.

By the end of the fire, Cloquet and twenty-seven other small communities had been burned to the ground. It will never be known how many other people died in the small communities, Indian villages, and isolated farms of the area. Survivors found suffocated remains at the bottoms of wells, where people had taken a deadly refuge. The documentary evidence places the total number killed at more than five hundred people. Estimates of the size of the burned forest reached a million acres. The land surrounding the town lay covered with up to several feet of ash interspersed with smoldering stumps. The damage in dollars was estimated at $30 million (Holbrook, p. 38).

The Cloquet firestorm does not rank as the worst fire in American history. It was only one of the approximately sixty major fires and one dozen or so firestorms that cut through the Great Lakes area of North America between 1870 and 1918. Firestorms hit Peshtigo, Wisconsin, in 1871, killing 1,500 people, and Hinckley, Minnesota, in 1894, killing 418 and burning 320,000 acres. These fires reached such magnitude that after the first one in 1871, the word *firestorm* was invented to describe it.

The great holocausts stopped with a concerted effort by local and national governments to develop better forest-management procedures and firefighting techniques, including a return to some of the native practices. They cleared more land beside the railroads, cut firebreaks through the forests, used controlled replanting, built rural fire stations and lookout towers, trained professional corps of firefighters, and started massive public education projects.

A major impetus for the involvement of the government came from the successful lawsuit filed by the citizens of Cloquet against the federal government, which was found liable because sparks from the train started the fire. Because the federal government operated the railroads under its wartime powers during World War I, Cloquet won a court award of $12 million against the federal government (Pyne, p. 210).

Similar though less extreme fires plagued other parts of the country, and many different areas invoked some odd innovations. The Southern states imported kudzu from Japan, and quickly saw its land covered with the plant that itself posed a fire hazard when it died after the first frost. California imported hundreds of thousands of Australian eucalyptus, only to find that when cold weather hit them, they died and themselves became fire hazards.

The firestorm that destroyed Cloquet and the other communities resembled the firestorm that engulfed Dresden, Germany, a little more than two decades later. The firestorm of Dresden resulted from saturation bombing by the Allies during World War II, whereas the firestorm of Cloquet seemed to have been a natural catastrophe.

We can classify such firestorms as *natural* catastrophes only in the sense that they started accidentally, but their true causes originated in human usage of the area. The European settlers had harvested the old forest, but they left the land covered in debris that impaired the ability of the land and vegetation to retain moisture. The timber industry had left dried wood scattered throughout the area, and for several generations no one had practiced the Indian tradition of the annual *light* burning of the forests. The entry onto the scene of the woodburning steam locomotive with its trail of cinders literally provided the sparks for this gigantic tinderbox. The firestorm represented the combined force and fury of decades of small fires that never happened.

The Native Americans developed a unique forest-management system. They controlled the forest and lived from it in such a way that both the forest and the humans thrived. Through thousands of years of living in America, their relationship with the forests and prairies reached a symbiotic equilibrium, but this equilibrium collapsed under the assault of new people arriving from Europe with different ways of using and managing the environment. After upsetting this ancient balance, modern Americans are still searching for a new equilibrium in their relationship to the forest as well as to the remainder of the North American environment.

5

THE TREE
IN AMERICAN
HISTORY

Eureka, the largest town along northern California's redwood coast, boastfully displays a love of ornate wood in its multi-colored gingerbread houses. Built during the late Victorian era and the early twentieth century, when the jigsaw first came into prominent use in home decoration, the exteriors drip with carved wood that the builders nailed onto every balustrade, window, door, and porch. Rococo wooden embellishments so completely cover whatever they decorate that an onlooker can scarcely decide just what architectural function it obscures. The same building could just as easily be a home, a funeral parlor, a restaurant, a boutique, an insurance office, a museum, or a boardinghouse, and at some point in its life cycle, it may have been any of those.

The stretch of highway between Eureka and Trinidad, California, runs between a series of large sawmills. Adjacent to them, large stacks of logs await their turn on the saw belts. The stacks of logs reach up to fifty feet, and some of them run along the side of the road for over a mile, a wooden wall of logs stretching as far as a person can see. Much of the timber came from the nearby Hoopa Valley Indian reservation, which contains some of the most beautiful and valuable lumber in the world.

If perfection can be measured in size, longevity, density, and tenacity, then the California redwood is the most nearly perfect form of life on this planet. Humans and cottonwoods live a mere seventy-five years; tortoises and elephants can survive a century; the oak can live three hundred years; but the redwood lives thousands of years. It has a natural resistance to most insects and can withstand most fires. The largest of the giant redwoods surpass eighty-three feet in circumference, tower over three hundred sixty feet into the air, and weigh more than twelve million pounds, about thirty times as much as the largest animal, the blue whale.

In mere statistics, the redwood taxes our ability to imagine, for it is the tallest, the widest, the densest, and one of the oldest living things on earth. In the statistics of modern life, a single redwood supplied enough wood to build twenty-two homes. Another was wide enough to cut a car tunnel through; one was hollowed to make a mobile home. The stump of yet another found use as a stage for forty dancing couples.

Animal life on land reached its greatest size with the dinosaurs, but they seem to have been unable to withstand subsequent environmental changes. The plant kingdom reached its largest size millions of years ago in the redwood, and the redwood has maintained the same size and appearance to the present day. The tree survives as a direct link between modern industrial America and the era of the dinosaurs. This longevity prompted John Steinbeck to write, in *Travels with Charley,* that the redwoods stand as "ambassadors from another time."

A restful silence shrouds the redwood forest as pervasively as the fog. The trees have wrapped themselves in thick layers of fibrous bark, and they have littered the ground with a dense insulating layer of needles that muffle the cries of animals and small children, leaving the forest in an eerie silence even when large families picnic or huge, churning machines belch diesel fumes into the moist air.

The hard trees radiate a mammalian warmth when touched. The massive trunk and branches absorb the sunlight at the top of the forest and convey it throughout the tree like a giant solar conductor, keeping the tree warmer than the air around it in the dark groves.

The redwood forests of the northern Pacific Coast stretched for some 450 miles from Monterey, California, to the Oregon border. Never stretching much more than thirty miles inland, the redwoods hug the foggy coast like a small, delicate ribbon, a ribbon now moth-eaten with little towns, farms, and factories that have nibbled away at it during the last century. At one time the redwoods covered much more of North America, as well as large parts of Europe, China, and even Greenland. The entire genus *Sequoia* has been reduced to the coastal redwoods of northern California and the giant redwoods of the western slope of California's Sierra Nevada mountains. The giant redwoods now survive in one of the smallest habitats of any tree in the world.

Some of the redwoods standing today began growing at the beginning of recorded history. They had already grown large before the Roman Empire emerged on the world scene, before the Aztecs raised up their pyramids or the Incas built Machu Picchu. A seedling planted today will not mature until the year 2400, and it will not reach its climax stage until the year 3000. We will have to wait until the year 4000 and beyond for one of today's seedlings to replace these antique giants of today.

Individual trees reach back several thousand years in time, but each grove and even the forest as a whole is more than a collection of trees; it is an organism in its own right, a macro-organism that comes to life, flourishes, and can die. As such a living creature, the California redwood forest goes back into time for around 20 million years, long before the emergence of the first human. The redwood forest predates humanity itself.

By the time the settlers and pioneers of America reached the West Coast, they had gone through many dramatic landscapes, but nothing quite prepared them for the size of the California redwoods. The giant trees led to many disputes, including the very name that should be applied to them. In 1853, British botanists proposed to name the trees *Wellingtonia gigantea* and called them "Wellingtonias" in honor of the Duke of Wellington, who defeated Napoleon at Waterloo. They justified the name on the grounds that the greatest tree in the world should bear the name of the greatest general in the world.

Fortunately, the Americans resisted this choice and supported instead a native American name. Conservationists felt that so great a tree should not be named for a military general. They proposed instead the name *Sequoia sempervirens,* "evergreen Sequoia," in honor of the man who invented a way of writing the Cherokee language and worked hard to promote literacy among his people. Both the coastal redwoods and the giant redwoods of the Sierra Nevada bear the genus name *Sequoia,* in honor of one of the greatest Indian intellectuals and leaders of the nineteenth century.

The settlers who arrived from Europe learned from the natives how to utilize the food and medicinal resources of the forest. The settlers had some knowledge of forests, but the North American forests offered new plants. The Indians taught the settlers to gather pecans, hickory nuts, pine nuts, acorns, and walnuts, as well as wild fruits such as pawpaw and maypop. The Indians introduced the settlers to the uses of sassafras and cranberries. The European settlers already knew about honey, but they had no experience with maple syrup and its by-products, which quickly became important parts of the colonial economy and cuisine.

The Indians used these resources for subsistence, but the settlers came to America for much more than mere subsistence. They wanted a profit. In addition to living from the forest products, they wanted to turn the forest into a marketable commodity. They wanted to sell the products of the forest, but the settlers had problems finding something to export from America. Despite the vast size and luxuriant condition of American forests, the world did not want to buy more nuts and berries, particularly not unknown ones.

Settlers found two of their first marketable commodities in sassafras and ginseng. The Indians used sassafras as a medicine by applying the leaves directly to wounds. The most important uses came from the root, which they used as a dye, and from the bark of the root, which they used to make tea and as flavoring for bear fat. Because the Indians used the medicine so effectively in some areas, the Europeans thought that sassafras was something of a miracle drug and could cure many other ailments, including the dreaded sexual plague of syphilis. In 1602 and 1603, well before the first British settlement in North America, British ships came to northern Virginia and Massachusetts to trade with the Indians for this new medicine and flavoring, which produced a stiff profit on the London market (Sauer).

Ginseng had already achieved popularity as a medicine in Asia before its discovery in America by the new settlers. It attracted the commercial attention of traders, who found the Indians using it from southern Canada down through the Appalachian Mountains as far as Cherokee territory in the Carolinas. French Jesuits organized the ginseng trade in Canada when they sent the first shipment to China in 1718. The Indian root sold in the markets of Canton for an astronomical five dollars a pound, making it one of the most valuable exports America had to offer in the eighteenth century (Sauer).

Because herbs could be sold in small quantities, they were cheap to transport and highly profitable, but no matter how profitable herbs such as ginseng and sassafras proved to be on the international market, they could not form the basis for a whole economy. To make more profitable use of the forests, the British began tapping them for resources such as resin, tar, and pitch, as well as lumber for building and shingles for roofing. Even though these items could not be considered exotic commodities on the world market, they were so plentiful in America that they could be easily harvested and transported in bulk. European attention quickly turned from harvesting the plants of the forest to finding ways to harvest the forest itself by cutting down and exporting the massive trees growing over most of North America.

The British found a special commercial use for New England's tall trees; they made excellent masts for ships. White pines grew in a wide belt along the coast, as far north as Penobscot Bay in Maine and extending south to just below Massachusetts. The trees reached inland along the Connecticut River valley, which divided Vermont from New Hampshire almost to the modern Canadian border. The largest of the giant white pines soared to an incredible two hundred fifty feet, with a diameter of five feet (Cronon, p. 30).

The British had no such trees in their island nation, but needed them desperately for the masts of their rapidly growing mercantile and naval fleets. To make their masts, the British had to buy special firs at great expense from the Baltic nations. Even these trees had to be spliced together in order to make a single mast, which was then vulnerable to breaking.

After the English discovered the giant white pines of New England, they wanted to harvest the trees, but lacked the technology. They had never transported anything so large across such a large expanse as the north Atlantic. The British navy solved the problem by constructing a new type of cargo ship especially for transport of the giant pines.

Because the white pines of America grew taller than any other trees known to the Europeans at that time, the British navy experimented with ever-larger masts. This made possible the construction of larger commercial ships that could carry more cargo, and of warships that carried larger guns and more men over longer distances. The commercial and military might of the English nation grew according to the growth in size and the increase in the number of its ships. The New England forests supplied Britain with an abundance of raw materials to build as many ships as they could without depending on the Scandinavians, the Dutch, or the Russians for access to the Baltic coast. In addition to freeing the British from foreign dependence, the new masts caused a rapid sequence of major technological changes that produced great economic and political benefits for England and helped it gain international naval superiority.

The white pine masts provoked one of the most dramatic technological changes in British naval history, and the harvesting of the American forests produced a wide variety of products that helped to make new fortunes and propel other technological innovations.

The French proved slower to realize the importance of the American forest, and by then the English had claimed much of the best forestlands. King Louis XVI of France dispatched the father-son botanist team of André and François Michaux to America to assess the value of the American forests in comparison with those of France. After exhaustive study and collection of species in America, they found that while France had nine species of tree suitable for carpentry, America had fifty-one. Their research also indicated that while France had only thirty species of trees that exceeded thirty feet in height, the United States had more than one hundred forty (Perlin, p. 331).

Since the French did not control most of the American lands where these trees grew, they sought to remedy this imbalance by wholesale reforestation of France with American trees. François Michaux sent home enough seeds to start a quarter of a million new trees, from which millions of descendants have since flourished in the estates, parks, and forests of France and throughout Europe. Had the French Revolution not intervened, France might have been able to produce for itself a much larger forest industry, but the forests of France, even when planted with exotic American trees, never rivaled the forests of the British colonies in North America.

The New England settlers conducted a brisk business selling lumber and firewood to European ships. In 1770, shortly before the colonists finally declared independence and took over management of their own forests, the British imported fourteen thousand tons of American timber at a cost of approximately thirty thousand pine, oak, and cedar trees felled to meet this growing trade (Perlin, p. 321).

The Europeans, with their steel and iron tools, hardly needed Indian technology for lumbering; they had already learned the trade well enough to strip their own continent. Frequently they used Indian labor. Even in colonial New England, some Indian communities, deprived of their farming and hunting lands, had to earn money by cutting wooden shingles for the siding and roofs of settlers' homes, and to make staves for the barrels needed by the Spanish to ship Madeira wine (Cronon, p. 112). Still today, many Indians may be found working in lumbering operations throughout the forests of the United States and Canada, but essentially the lumbering industry, quite unlike the fur industry, operated as a European enterprise, with European technology and organization. The labor of the Indians could just as easily have been done by any other group that happened to be there and needed to earn money.

As more settlers arrived from Europe, they needed wood to build their homes and the extensive fences with which they surrounded their farms, and for fuel. In less than two hundred years after the arrival of the Puritans, the settlers of New England consumed an estimated 260 million cords of firewood (Cronon, p. 121).

After the American colonies gained independence from Europe, their economies expanded as the wealth of their trade remained in the coffers of Boston, Philadelphia, Charleston, and New York rather than going into the royal treasury in England or into the pockets of British merchants. Using the rich timber resources of New England, the merchants made their area into an international center for shipbuilding. They could build larger ships more cheaply than anyone else because they had vast resources of cheap, good lumber. They built ships in New England, but they also sent them out to exploit the rich fishing waters of the North Atlantic and to hunt whales. Because they had cheaper ships, the whaling expeditions of New England became some of the most profitable in the world.

New England's ships also supplied massive amounts of fish and firewood for the peculiar needs of the Caribbean market. The New Englanders shipped to the Caribbean the wood from a quarter of a million trees between 1771 and 1773. The sugar mills of the Caribbean boomed in this period, but the Caribbean settlers had already consumed their own forests to feed the high-temperature fires needed to extract sugar from the cane. The West Indians needed massive amounts of firewood to continue making sugar, and to distill their molasses into rum. The West Indians sold sugar to Europe, but they bought timber from New England to operate these industrial plantations.

The New England merchants sold timber and fish in the Caribbean, and in turn received much larger amounts of molasses and rum than they could utilize in the North American Indian trade. They carried the rum to Africa, where they traded it for slaves, then they brought back their human cargo to the Caribbean and then to Charleston, Savannah, New Orleans, and Annapolis, where they sold the slaves for new plantations opening on the mainland.

The Yankee merchants of New England, as well as the Quaker merchants from Philadelphia, grew rich on this trade of timber, rum, and slaves, which they plied across the Atlantic. With this newly acquired wealth, they replaced their timber-frame homes with houses and large colonial buildings built of brick, facing onto streets paved with brick.

In the early history of the United States and its trade with

Europe, wood filled most of the industrial usages that metal, cement, and plastics have come to fill, and wood provided the primary fuel before its eventual replacement by coal, petroleum, and electricity. Wood served as the basis of industries as varied as liquor distilling, brickmaking, and meat drying, and was used in making potash, pitch, tar, turpentine, and charcoal. All of this could be done more cheaply in America than in Europe because of the abundance of inexpensive firewood for use as fuel. This abundance of firewood raised the standard of living of settlers in America, and made it possible for them to undercut the prices of trade goods made elsewhere.

The settlers who arrived from Western Europe came from a stone-oriented society. For Europeans, stone made the building material of highest prestige. They built their palaces, mansions, temples, cathedrals, and universities of stone. Brick, a sort of artificial stone, came next in prestige, followed by wood. Only straw and mud rated lower than wood as a building material in Western Europe, but in Scandinavia, Russia, and other parts of Eastern Europe, wood played a much more important role.

The European settlers in America found that wood was not only plentiful in America, but that it provided a building material that was superior in many regards. It proved easier to use than stone, a characteristic of particular importance to people needing to build in a hurry, without benefit of expert stonecutters or masons. In addition to being easier to use, wood proved to be a much better insulator in America, where winter temperatures dropped far below those common in Europe, and where summer temperatures rose well above those in most of Europe.

Wood furnished the primary building material for the American frontier, as the settlers used wood to build their homes and barns as well as their extensive systems of fences. In the small towns that sprang up, merchants and government officials also used wood to build their stores and offices. The lack of wood on the plains and prairies slowed settlement there, since homes had to be made of sod, and the settlers had to burn buffalo and cow dung for fuel. Settlement of the great American plains did not boom until the introduction of the railroads, which brought large shipments of cheap timber to the plains for use in building and as firewood.

In the early phases of the Industrial Revolution, craftsmen made most machine parts from wood. They used wood to construct waterwheels and mills for grinding grains and sugarcane, as well as for pressing oils. Windmills and even the paddlewheels of ships were made of wood.

As late as 1880, all but a half-dozen of North America's nearly forty thousand boats were wooden. Even the early toll highways relied on wooden plank roads before the development of modern roads based on concrete and asphalt. People riding over these wooden roads traveled in carts or carriages also made of wood. In addition to using river and ocean boats made of wood, the early railway cars were made mostly of wood, rode on rails made of wood, and crossed rivers on wooden bridges (Perlin, 347). In time, iron and steel replaced much of the wood, but the ties connecting the rails continued to be made of wood until concrete replaced them in the twentieth century.

With the invention of steam engines for both trains and ships, wood supplied the primary fuel for several decades before its gradual replacement by coal. Water traffic along the Mississippi River system as well as on the Great Lakes depended exclusively on wood fuel, and the early railroads that passed through large forests also burned wood for fuel. In this way the trains could live off the land as they crossed it, consuming the seemingly limitless forests of America.

Today our civilization has turned to plastics made from petrochemicals, and to metals, but the people who settled America created a civilization based on wood. They were able to do this because the Indians of America had nurtured such large and luxuriant forests that proved to be an easily harvested and exploited resource on national and international markets.

The redwoods evoke varied responses from different people. Some people show a bizarre hatred and envy of the trees. Steinbeck suggested that we resent knowing that the trees will be here thousands of years from now, after we are long gone. Through their seeming immortality they remind us of our mortality.

When writing or talking about the redwoods and other large trees, some people use religious metaphors and almost whispered tones as they compare the groves to outdoor cathedrals. The light streams down among the redwood branches in slanted rays like the light filtering through stained-glass windows in a medieval cathedral, and the pathway between trees looks like an aisle through the pews.

I never quite understood the comparison of trees to cathedrals, since I had never seen a building, no matter how grand, that compared to a forest. I understood the comparison better only after spending time in the treeless Sahara and then visiting the Temple of Karnak just outside Luxor in Egypt. The now roofless temple's massive columns of limestone tower over a mere mortal. The large number of massive pillars resemble a petrified forest, but the builders of that temple would have never seen a forest, since none existed in Egypt. Instead of making the columns look like trees, they tried to make them look alive through the vegetative motifs of papyrus and lotus they used to decorate the pillars.

The ancient Egyptians had no forests. They could see only a mere hint of a forest in their cultivated date groves. Today a few exotic trees such as eucalyptus and other drought-resistant trees have been imported into Egypt, but for all of recorded history Egypt has been one of the most treeless places on earth. Yet we see in Egyptian architecture a strange phenomenon. In the earliest temple rooms around the step pyramid built for King Zoser at Saqqara, near Memphis, during the Third Dynasty, the limestone is carved to resemble wood. The ceiling, of pure stone, appears to be of logs fastened in a line. The columns of stone rising to support the roof also resemble logs twined together.

Humans in ancient Egypt, medieval Europe, and modern America seem to have an instinctual, primitive yearning for the security of the forest in which our protohuman ancestors lived for so long. When they stray too far from this forest or when they destroy it, they try to re-create it, even if they have to make the trees of stone. The first documented case of this occurred in ancient Mesopotamia, in the city of Babylon, where King Nebuchadnezzar II built his famous Hanging Gardens and filled them with exotic trees to remind his Median wife Amytis of her wooded home. The gardens marked one of the first attempts to re-create a forest in the middle of a city. The ancient Greeks and Arabs continued this trend with their small parks and elaborate courtyards. From the ancient Persian word *pairidaeza*, meaning "park," is derived the Greek *paradeisos*, the Latin *paradisus*, and the

English *paradise,* which played a major conceptual role in Western religious and secular thought.

Something of the forest can be seen even in the column clusters of Greek and Roman temples, and in the cathedrals of Europe. After the Europeans destroyed most of their great forests and covered the land with farms, manors, castles, and cities, they built large temples such as the cathedral of Notre Dame at Chartres, which was finished around the year 1300 and bore two large spires that rose over the surrounding community like giant trees. Like the forest of stone in the interior of the Karnak Temple, great columns rise in the middle of the cathedral. The interior of the building reaches toward the sky, and the builders decorated it with multicolored windows that let light stream in as though coming through the trees.

Only after repeated visits to the redwoods as well as to temples in Asia, Africa, and Europe did I realize that the forest does not look like a cathedral or a temple; rather, the temples and cathedrals of the world imitate the primeval forest, the forest of the redwoods. No matter how urban humans have become, something within them still longs for the forest.

6

HUNTING

On the shore of the Arctic ocean near Tuktoyaktuk, two old Inuvialuit hunters gather driftwood to build a fire and heat a kettle of water for making tea. They share a lunch of fresh caribou meat and *muktuk,* the blubber taken from the sides of the beluga whale. They warm the caribou leg in the fire, and then cut off chunks of it, still dripping with blood. They alternate bits of caribou with fatty slices of muktuk, which has a rubbery consistency somewhat resembling that of squid or a chicken gizzard. It tastes distinctly of the ocean and leaves a fatty coating on the inside of the mouth. By contrast the fresh blood of the caribou tastes sweet, and the soft flesh has a flavor milder than beef and without a wild or gamy aroma.

The favorite food of the villagers comes from the white whale, or beluga, which usually reaches from fourteen to sixteen feet in length. The small-headed belugas congregate in the food-rich Arctic waters in the summer, and they supply a nutritious food for the long winter. The beluga concentrates many vitamins and nutrients, including the easily destroyed Vitamin C, in its blubber. The preserved strips of muktuk supply a steady source of Vitamin C throughout the Arctic winter and prevent scurvy and related nutritional diseases even in people who eat no fresh plant food for several months.

This habit of eating uncooked meat led to these people being called Eskimo, which means "eaters of raw meat" in the language of their Algonquian-speaking neighbors to the south. Most of the world adopted this name for these people, and the people around Tuktoyaktuk became known as the Mackenzie Eskimo or Western Eskimo. Most of the native people of the American Arctic prefer to be called Inuit, or, in the language spoken by the people of Tuktoyaktuk, *Inuvialuit,* both of which mean simply "the people."

Tuktoyaktuk sits in the northwest corner of Canada's Northwest Territories near the borders of the Yukon and Alaska. At the northern extremes, most modern maps of the world are somewhat compressed and difficult to comprehend for those of us who usually live in temperate zones, at seemingly wider latitudes. Tuktoyaktuk lies closer to Siberia in the west and to Greenland in the east than to the contiguous forty-eight United States to the south.

At this northern latitude, the meridians of longitude become squashed together as they move closer to their merger at the North Pole. A hunter moving either east or west out of Tuktoyaktuk would cross a meridian every 23.72 miles, as compared to a hunter at the Equator who would have to travel nearly 70 miles between meridians. Even though it is at 133 degrees west longitude, Tuktoyaktuk occupies approximately the same longitude as Pitcairn Island and the Marquesas in the South Pacific, and could just as easily be said to be due north of Seattle. Tuktoyaktuk lies more than 3,000 miles northwest of Chicago. Washington, D.C., is as close to the Equator as it is to Tuktoyaktuk. Even a city such as Minneapolis, one of the most northern in the United States, lies as close to Havana, Cuba, as to Tuktoyaktuk.

Time becomes even more warped than geography for the southerner at this latitude of 70 degrees north. The sun disappears completely for six weeks in the winter, and for months it makes only a token appearance each day on the tip of the horizon. In summer, the sun refuses to set; instead, it whirls overhead in a clockwise circle, twenty-four hours a day. The time zones of the earth become virtually arbitrary at this latitude. The sun reaches its zenith in the summer sky between two and three o'clock in the afternoon, and the high temperature for the day frequently occurs at midnight.

Despite the high summer sun, temperatures in the summer usually fail to rise above the fifties (Fahrenheit), and a windy blast from the nearby polar ice cap easily sends the thermometer plunging back down to freezing. In January, the average daily temperature hovers around minus thirty degrees Fahrenheit, but cold fronts and winds in January can send it crashing down to nearly minus one hundred degrees.

The people of the Arctic coast of Canada, together with the tribal people of Siberia, endure the harshest climate in the inhabited world. Unlike Alaska, where the warm Pacific waters ameliorate the cold of the Arctic Ocean, and unlike northern Scandinavia, which benefits from the last drops of heat left in the Gulf Stream, the Canadian Arctic faces the full fury of winds circling the North Pole and its frozen ice cap. No mountains protect them; no tropical waters flow north to help them. Behind them lies the cold interior of the Canadian tundra; in front of them lies a thousand miles of solid ice.

Even in the summer, when the coastal edge of the ocean melts, the dark gray waters that lap the Tuktoyaktuk shore retain a bone-chilling cold that can kill a swimmer within thirty minutes. Occasionally a stiff wind sends the tide flooding into the village, but normally the water rises and falls on a rugged but placid shoreline covered with rocks ranging from sesame-seed-sized pebbles to stones as large as a bowling ball. Despite the variation in size and color, almost all of the stones have rounded edges, smoothed by eons of pounding by the Arctic seas and the scraping and pulling of advancing and receding winter ice.

The Inuit culture stretches along a thin coastal ribbon and adjacent rocky islands for five thousand miles from the eastern Pacific and Arctic shores of Siberia and the coasts of Alaska to the eastern shore of Greenland in the northern Atlantic. Over this whole area, the Inuit area share a mutually intelligible language. Living in small pockets and villages scattered over such a large portion of the Arctic, they created one of the most dispersed cultures on earth. Prior to the creation of modern Canada and the United States, the Inuit represent the only cultural group in the world ever known to live on the shores of three of the earth's major oceans—the Pacific, the Atlantic, and the Arctic.

In some ways, Tuktoyaktuk seems to be a place suspended in time. Three large oil companies already have drilled off its coast in the Beaufort Sea and found huge reservoirs of oil—perhaps the largest petroleum deposits in all the Americas. The oil is there, the companies are in place, and they are waiting until the right technological developments allow them to tap the oil and transport it south to the urban areas of the continent.

Some investigators have proposed that the oil companies build an overland pipeline like the North Shore pipeline across Alaska. A variation of this scheme would run the pipes underwater to make them invisible and thus less threatening to visitors. Other proposals include massive icebreaking oil barges that can plow through six feet of solid January ice and keep the oil flowing throughout the year. Yet another proposal advocates development of submarine barges that could float beneath the ice. In due time, one or another of these scenarios will be enacted to open up the Beaufort Sea reserves. When the international price of oil rises high enough, when another war in the Middle East threatens to cut off North American supplies, or when some of the other reserves begin to run dry, someone will come forward with the new technology to open the wells off Tuktoyaktuk.

Even though the approximately nine hundred Inuvialuit have left their traditional sod houses to live in uniform, government-supplied houses painted in institutional monochromes of brown or gray, the traditional skills of hunting and fishing play a major role in their sustenance. The evidence for the older way of life still lies scattered throughout the village. Caribou antlers cover the village roofs, where the hunters throw them to dry and bleach in the summer sun, beyond the reach of mischievous children and hungry dogs. Inside the homes, many of the Inuvialuit have decorated their walls with modern photographs of polar bear and caribou interspersed with family portraits and wall hangings of the Last Supper or Jesus and the Virgin Mary.

On the edge of Tuktoyaktuk, by the bay, rises an inconspicuous wooden shed painted white and ringed with ventilation slats punctuating the top of its walls. The small building proves to be much larger on the inside than it appears from the outside, because it leads to a passageway dug down into the permafrost, where the access tunnel divides into three tunnels, each lined with rooms about the size of a small van. This serves as the village freezer. Any hunter can bring his kill into the tunnel and store it in one of the large lockers. The meat in the lockers remains frozen throughout the year because it lies in the permafrost, never thawing, even on the warmest summer day.

Anyone digging only twelve to eighteen inches in the soil at the warmest time of the year will still hit the rock-hard layer of permafrost. Graves for the dead must be dug with jackhammers, and then only in the summer. The village cannot install water, sewage, or gas pipes through the ground because of the permafrost. Water and gas must be delivered to holding tanks in each home, and similarly sewage and other waste must be picked up and hauled away. Because of the permafrost, the houses must be built several feet above the ground, on pilings sunk fifteen feet into the ground. If the houses rested directly on the ground, their heat would create a slow but persistent melting of the top layer of permafrost and cause the house to sway and sink gradually into the thawing muck.

Traditional sledges and modern gasoline cans lean against the houses throughout Tuktoyaktuk. Although hunters frequently pull their sledges by snowmobile rather than by dog, many of the hunters use both. The dogs surround the village; they live outside even in the coldest weather, each one staked to a separate post in the ground. Their owners have trained the silent dogs not to fight and not to growl at one another. Like their wolf ancestors, huskies do not bark, but they sometimes howl.

Staked around the periphery of the village, the dogs serve as an early-warning system against predators. A few years ago a hungry male polar bear about seven years old wandered in from the ice cap. The polar bear is the world's largest land carnivore, and it needs large quantities of meat. This particular bear had not reached full maturity; the polar bears in this area can grow to eleven feet in length. When a bear of that height rears up on its haunches, it can tower over a human from a height of fourteen feet.

Because of the age of the stray polar bear that wandered into Tuktoyaktuk, he had great strength, but he lacked experience in hunting; otherwise he would have avoided the tempting prey offered by the village of humans and their dogs. He first attacked a dog, and in the manner of the polar bear on the hunt, he killed three dogs in quick succession. The polar bear normally goes into a killing frenzy when it hunts, killing as many prey as it can before stopping to eat one of them. The dogs had been staked just beyond the path on which the children walk to school. If the dogs had not been staked there, the bear might easily have attacked the column of children making their way through the dark. The commotion made by the bear slaughtering the dogs roused the people of the village, and the hunters came out and killed the bear before it attacked a human.

In recent years, hunters have bestowed renewed respect on their dogs as the limits of the snowmobile became better understood. As one musher explained to me, "A Ski-doo doesn't know the way home in a whiteout." Among the Inuvialuit, men and dogs hunt as a team. A trained team of huskies knows how to surround musk oxen in the autumn and to drive them into their defensive formation, in which the larger animals form a circle with their horns facing outward. The dogs help to track caribou, but more dangerous game, such as the polar bear, requires all the cunning and strength of both the hunter and the dog team.

In the winter, the value of the dogs increases markedly. The Inuvialuit hunters rely on their dogs to sniff out the breathing holes of seals in the ice. Because the seal is a mammal, it must come up for air regularly. To accomplish this feat even while swimming under several feet of polar ice, the seal maintains a sequence of small breathing holes scattered throughout its territory. When covered by a thin layer of snow, the breathing hole becomes virtually invisible to the eye, but the husky's keen sense of smell leads the hunter straight to the holes.

The polar bear hunters still occupy the top rung in the social hierarchy of respect among the Inuvialuit hunters. The hunt for *nanook*, as they call the polar bear, requires a lifetime of careful training and strict personal discipline, but the Inuvialuit, with their palates well-developed for variations in meat flavors, still prize the strong flavor of polar bear meat. The hunters of Tuktoyaktuk always take special parts of the kill to the row of small apartments that house the village elderly.

Our word *Arctic* derives from Greek, and means "bear." It seems a fitting tribute to the polar bear, but in fact the ancient Greeks knew nothing of this large animal. They called the area to the far north *arktikos* because that was the region beneath the seven-star constellation of the Great Bear, also known to us by its Latin name, Ursa Major. We call the constellation the Big Dipper, but we kept the Greek name *arktikos* for the whole northern land below it.

Western science has had trouble categorizing the bear. For a while they called its genus *Thalarctos,* but the polar bear was the only animal so classified. Unlike the koala "bear," which is not a true bear, the common name *polar bear* proved more appropriate than the scientific name because the polar bear really *is* a bear, clearly related to the black, brown, and grizzly bears farther south. Scientists have put the polar bear back into the genus *Ursus* with the other bears, and we now call it *Ursus maritimus,* "sea bear."

The Inuvialuit eat or use virtually all of the animal, except its toxic liver which can kill a dog or a human. The native people either use or sell the polar bear pelt, but as with silver fox, seal, badger, and many of the other pelts taken by Inuvialuit hunters, the international prices have fallen as more fashion designers use synthetic materials, and as new restrictions in various countries limit their importation.

Southerners who have moved into Inuit territory in recent centuries have been forced to learn from the Inuit. The nineteenth-century whalers came annually and brought their own food supplies with them, but, unable to survive the Arctic winter with their own technology, they left before the winter freeze-up. More recently, as the United States and Canadian governments built their system of Distant Early Warning bases across the Arctic coast, oil and mineral prospectors entered and scientific researchers of various types have set up stations in the north. They all depended on long, fragile supply lines that connected them with their own societies to the south.

Because of the harshness of their land, their remoteness from the sources of manufactured goods, and the general slowness of whites to settle in their area, the Arctic natives experienced little outside interference in their traditional life prior to the twentieth century. They still practice many of the hunting skills that native people once shared throughout North America.

The natives of North America were some of the best hunters ever known anywhere in the world; their skill and accuracy frequently astounded the early European explorers. When the Arctic explorer Martin Frobisher made his voyage to Baffin Island, the skill of the Inuit so impressed him that he kidnapped a hunter to take back to England as a prize. The hunter's skill with a harpoon thrilled Queen Elizabeth I so much that she invited him to harpoon her royal swans for the amusement of her court.

Despite the speed and accuracy of Native American hunters, their genius lay in their intimate knowledge of animal habits and in their sophisticated approach to hunting, which stressed tactics over technology. Rather than simply overwhelming their quarry with ammunition and firepower, the hunters cajoled and tricked it.

One method they used was to imitate the calls of birds and animals. The hunters made most of these whistles and calls by using only their voices, amplified or modified by cupping their hands over their mouths in various configurations. The Assiniboin hunters attracted the curiosity of buffalo cows by bleating like a buffalo calf. A young Inuit coming of age as a hunter was expected to imitate the calls of ducks, geese, gulls, and auks, as well as the less common guillemots, kittiwakes, puffins, and razorbills.

To reproduce sounds that the human voice could not make, the hunters manufactured whistles of wood, clay, antler, and bone to summon prey by imitating a courtship or distress call. The smallest and simplest of these calls consisted of nothing more than a blade of grass held between two fingers and blown to imitate the sound of a fawn in distress, a sound that could summon a doe. The Shoshoni banged rocks together to imitate the crash of male mountain sheep fighting, a commotion that usually attracted the curiosity of other mountain sheep. Similarly, hunters attracted deer during rutting season by clashing antlers together. The natives of the Canadian boreal forest summoned the attention of amorous male moose by pouring buckets of water into a stream or lake in imitation of a female moose urinating (Driver, p. 86).

The natives of the Great Lakes crafted the largest animal calls. Ojibwa and Cree hunters rolled sheets of birchbark to fashion a megaphone that they used to amplify their moose calls, while the Dene, farther to the north, used a similar but smaller device to call the caribou.

In addition to calls and whistles, the Indian hunters manufactured decoys to lure animals or birds. Archaeologists have found ancient wooden and straw bird decoys throughout North America. The hunters placed the wooden ducks and geese out to float on ponds in order to attract real birds migrating overhead to land on the water.

Many hunters wore the skins of the animals they hunted as a means of disguising themselves and sneaking into the midst of the quarry. A sixteenth-century drawing by the Flemish engraver Theodore De Bry depicts three Timucua hunters stalking a herd of deer in Florida. De Bry's drawings were first published in 1591 to illustrate the account of Jacques Le Moyne, who described in detail the Timucuas' method of hunting, after his visit to America in 1564–65 (Swanton, pp. 312–21). This technique required of the hunter not only a convincing animal costume but also an intimate knowledge of the movements and behavior of the deer in order not to startle or frighten them.

Early French chroniclers described the Natchez hunters along the lower Mississippi River as always carrying on their belts the treated antlers and head of a deer, which they could slip on and use for hunting at any moment the prey might be spotted. An item of such practical use as the decoy mask easily lent itself to ceremonial use, and we know from historical records that such use of masks in dances and ceremonies was very common.

Using similar tactics, Indian hunters on the plains dressed in bison skins, which could be heavy and awkward, so they often preferred to use a wolfskin instead. Since bison in large herds showed little fear of wolves, which usually stalked only the sick or elderly strays, the hunters dressed as wolves and crept within easy bow range of the herd.

During the summer, when seals frolicked on the rocky shores of islands around the Arctic, Inuit hunters would dress in seal-skins, and in some instances put on a special helmet carved to look like a seal head. With this disguise the men crawled onto shore, carefully imitating the movements and barks of the seals, and thereby infiltrating their gatherings. Inuit hunters made snow blinds that they pushed ahead of themselves as they slowly encroached upon an unsuspecting seal sunning on the ice. The hunters also made shields from polar bear skins and used them as white blinds that blended in with the snow, and from behind which they could sneak up on the seals. Seal hunters today still use the same technique, but they often substitute a frame of white linen for the polar bear skin or snow shield. They even carried a scratcher to imitate the sound of seal flippers scraping on the rocks.

Throughout the Americas, hunters used similar techniques of camouflage and imitation with the skins, horns, or antlers of virtually any large animal. When the hunters did not have a deerskin, sealskin, or buffalo hide at hand, they camouflaged themselves with plants that they tied onto their bodies, or with irregular patterns of paint that they wore on their faces and torsos, similar to warpaint but in darker camouflage colors rather than the bright reds and yellows of war.

Hunters all over the Americas still use many of these techniques. Men and women go out to hunt wearing camouflage clothes and sometimes camouflage greasepaint, and they carry with them bird decoys and assorted whistles and callers, without realizing that all of these devices came directly from ancient Indian hunters.

Native hunters also used a variety of traps. On the plains, where the eagle feather had such a high value, hunters devised a way to trap the animals without harming or marring the quality of the feathers. They dug a pit covered with branches and secured a small animal or bird on top of the branches as bait. A hunter waited silently in the covered pit beneath the bait. When the eagle seized the tied bait and could not pull it aloft, the hunter rose quickly up from the pit, grabbed the eagle, and strangled it. Considering the large beaks and vicious claws of the eagle, this hand-to-hand combat with the eagle seems more a proof of bravery and strength than of mere cunning.

Indian hunters devised ways to manipulate entire herds. On the Great Plains, hunters knew how to stampede the herds to run them to exhaustion and often to send part of the herd over an embankment. The hunters then harvested the carcasses that collected at the bottom. Paleo-Indians apparently used this technique thousands of years ago, but later generations of hunters refined it into a less wasteful type of herd management.

In central Canada, the practice of animal hunting and trapping reached a sophisticated complexity among the Chipewyans.
Prior to the annual migration of the caribou, the Chipewyans
erected a series of brush-and-pole figures that looked like scare-
crows spread over many miles of the plains and tundra. The
human-looking figures frightened the caribou, which steered
their herds away from them. By carefully situating the scare-
crows into a funnel formation, the Chipewyans could direct a
small herd of caribou into a corral called a surround (Kopper,
p. 117). Made like a wooden stockade with timber and brush,
the larger surrounds exceeded a mile in diameter and stood as
permanent parts of the landscape. The neighboring Assiniboin
to the south made a structure called a pound in a similar way,
with logs and dirt.

Inuit living west of Hudson Bay erected similar traps for caribou, but in their central Arctic homeland they had no brush or
pole from which to construct the large manikins. The Eskimo
substituted large stone cairns called *inukshuk* (or *inukshuik* in the
plural) on which they piled large, flat rock slabs on top of two
upright slabs that resembled legs. The resulting *inukshuk,* which
means "something like a person," looked enough like a human to
repel the caribou and thus push them toward a spot where the
Eskimo hunters waited in ambush. In the timeless Arctic, one can
still see the *inukshuik* standing, holding eternal vigil like the colos-
sal statues of Ramses II that litter the Egyptian desert.

While the Inuit men waited in hiding to attack the caribou once
driven to them, the women spread out at a distance from the
ambush site, and howled in imitation of the wolf. As a reverse
strategy of the summoning call, the howl of the wolf frightened
the caribou and made them run faster in the direction of the
waiting hunters in the ambush.

The Indians of New England, who specialized in hunting deer,
used hunting techniques that paralleled those of the Inuit and
Chipewyan hunters of caribou. In order to control the deer on the
run, the Indians planted and maintained hedges up to a mile in
length. These hedges subtly channeled the unsuspecting deer
toward the waiting hunters at the vortex of the funnel (Cronon,
p. 47). In other parts of North America, Indians commonly used
fire as a way to drive toward waiting hunters animals such as deer

·and buffalo, and also to flush out animals as varied as rabbits and alligators, depending on the region.

Even though the natives of America relied heavily on tactics, they crafted a variety of weapons. Hunters throughout North America used the bow and arrow as well as an older weapon, the spear. These formed the universal tool kit for the whole of the continent. In addition, the natives of various areas used special weapons suited to the particular natural resources and appropriate to the prey of that area.

The natives in roughly half of North America used slings for hunting small animals and birds. The Cree of Canada's subarctic region hunted small animals with a bolo made from stones tied together with leather thongs. The hunter twirled the bolo overhead, and upon its release the rocks spun through the air and entwined the legs of the prey.

Hunters made an *atlatl,* or spear thrower, from a short piece of hardwood that could be carved with a handle at one end and a notch at the other. By holding the atlatl by the handle and inserting the butt of the spear into the notch, the hunter essentially was able to lengthen his throwing arm, thereby achieving much greater force behind his throw. With the atlatl, the spear traveled farther and hit harder. Even though the atlatl consisted of only a single stick with no moving parts, it constituted the first known tool made by humans to operate another tool. In this regard it was something of a mega-tool or a machine.

In the southeastern United States, among the Creeks, Cherokees, Choctaws, and others, hunters used blowguns made from hollow canes three or more feet in length and much like the ones still used in the Amazon forests of Peru, Ecuador, and Brazil. The hunters used these blowguns to shoot poison darts. The technology for this also predates the development of the bow and probably diffused into North America from Central America or the Yucatán across the Gulf of Mexico.

The hunters of Tuktoyaktuk often guide affluent hunters and fishermen from the south. These men trek northward during the constant daylight of the summer, and they enjoy hunting or fishing for prey larger and more exotic than they can get down home. A hunting license for the larger prey can run several thousand dollars and requires the assistance of a licensed outfitter and guide. Still, the experience attracts hunters and fishermen willing to pay for the unique Arctic experience, even if it results in shooting only a rabbit.

Game hunting and fishing have become such an important part of the economy that the community college in Inuvik offers special courses on these subjects for Inuvialuit and Dene who want to become licensed guides. Regional planners and economic developers expect that as transportation into the area improves in the twenty-first century, ecological tourism and nature tourism as well as traditional hunting and fishing may become a major part of the economic base of the Arctic and subarctic regions.

The men of Tuktoyaktuk working as guides for hunters represent an ancient pattern in native-white relations stretching back to the first colonists who arrived in America from Europe. The colonists came with virtually no hunting experience in Europe. Even though the ancient European tribes had great hunters several thousand years ago, the overgrazing, overfarming, and overcrowding of Europe in subsequent centuries destroyed most of the hunting grounds. Many of the small forests that remained fell under the exclusive purview of the aristocratic landowners. They limited the hunting of stags, foxes, swans, ducks, boars, and even rabbits to themselves and their cadres of specially trained dogs, horses, and falcons.

A peasant or commoner caught hunting in medieval Europe faced severe punishment. The crime, which was called poaching, occupied many pages in the law books and was the subject of repeated royal edicts and decrees leading to some rather dramatic court cases. Lords used guards and special game wardens to protect their hunting grounds from poaching by peasants and other common people.

For the Europeans arriving to settle in America, hunting had virtually nothing to do with subsistence; it was a sport. Its practitioners dressed conspicuously and used elaborate equipment; large hunting estates were used as settings on which to stage grand ceremonial and theatrical hunts followed by sumptuous feasts. In England the hunt, particularly the fox hunt, eventually became an elaborate ritual of the landed gentry and their imitators, but it had nothing to do with providing food for anyone.

Not only were the new colonists ignorant of hunting, but as common people and usually city dwellers, they appeared haunted by a general fear and mistrust of hunting and of forests. They even considered it remarkably uppity of the Indians to spend so much time at what William Byrd II of Virginia called the "Gentlemanly Diversions of Hunting and Fishing" rather than in working. Even William Penn, who usually showed such great respect for the Indians, referred to their "Hunting, Fishing and Fowling" as "their pleasure." (Axtell 1981, p. 52). For the class-conscious colonists, the Indians' audacity in hunting grossly violated the English notions of proper behavior. To the colonists the Indians were inferiors, and yet they claimed rights to hunt and perform other acts practiced only by aristocrats in Europe.

In America the colonists needed food. The early settlers could scarcely rely on shipments from England, and their crops often proved unsuited to American soil. Yet all around them in the forest and along the waterways flourished an abundance of deer, bear, elk, rabbit, squirrel, duck, goose, beaver, pigeon, and some formerly unknown but tasty regional game such as opossum, turkey, armadillo, alligator, bison, moose, caribou, musk ox, and antelope.

From the first colonization efforts in Virginia and Massachusetts, the newcomers depended on the natives for food. The Indians supplied large amounts of meat and fish as gifts to the colonists, who traded trinkets and other goods for a steady supply of protein.

In time, this supplying of meat by the Indians developed into a large-scale and well-organized Indian business. Indians supplied fresh and smoked meat as well as dried jerky and pemmican all along the frontier of America, but it was in the French and British holdings in Canada that this trade in game foods became most highly organized and institutionalized.

Particularly in the interior of Canada, or Rupert's Land, where colonization came much more slowly and agriculture proved more difficult for the colonists, the Hudson's Bay Company continued its traditional reliance on Indian hunters not only for furs but also for food to feed its army of employees. In time the hunting became the special domain of the Métis (pronounced *MAY-tea*), the French-Indian mixed-bloods who organized large annual buffalo

hunts on the plains. Operating out of St. Boniface at the confluence of the Assiniboin and Red rivers at what is now Winnipeg,
the Métis hunting parties frequently grew to several thousand
hunters and had a highly organized and disciplined command
chain. They traveled across the Great Plains of Manitoba, Saskatchewan, and Alberta and into Montana and the Dakotas with
large wooden carts pulled by oxen and horses. Made entirely of
wood and rawhide with neither nails nor axle grease, the carts
creaked with a piercing screech as the wooden wheels scraped
ceaselessly against the wooden axles.

After the hunts, the Métis women skinned and butchered the
animals on the spot where they fell. They cut the meat in long
strips, dried it in the sun, or smoked it over fires to purge the
moisture and thus preserve the meat. The Métis women dried the
meat to make jerky, pounded it to make a powdery meal, and
mixed it with dried berries and fat to make pemmican, the staple
food that the Hudson's Bay Company used to feed its employees
through the long winter. Only after the women completely processed
the entire slaughter did the Métis load the meat supply on their
carts and then distribute it by cart and canoe throughout central
and northern Canada (McMillan, p. 278).

As the colonists of North America pushed the Indians back, and
as European diseases decimated the Indian villagers, the colonists
learned to hunt for themselves. They did not, however, learn the
dramatic pageantry of European hunting on horseback; they
learned the simple, direct methods of the Indians creeping silently
through the forest in search of prey. Under the tutelage of the
Indians, the colonists became frontiersmen. They substituted some
pieces of their own European technology, such as the musket and
later the rifle, in place of the Indian bow, spear, and blowgun,
but in most respects the frontiersman followed Indian custom even
to the point of wearing buckskin clothes, moccasins, and buffalo
robes and coonskin hats in the colder weather. They also adopted
the Indian equipment of canoe, kayak, snowshoes, waterproof
ponchos, and snow goggles.

The Indians and colonists together synthesized a frontier culture
from their two markedly different traditions, and the core of this
frontier culture centered on hunting for subsistence. In this way,
the Indians Americanized the settlers.

7

How the Fur Trade Shaped the American Economy

New York City has defined the twentieth century. Sometimes a place so dominates an epoch that the time becomes forever associated with that place, as New York has been with the twentieth century. Seemingly every major event of the century began in New York, ended in New York, passed through New York, or was financed in New York.

In an era when the world focused on the North Atlantic, New York City ruled the transatlantic world. Europe had several major ports, but they all traded with New York, which served as the shipping, communications, and air link between Europe and America. Radio and television grew up in New York during the twentieth century, and the city controlled the international arts and publishing world.

New York served as gateway for the greatest migration known in human history when the poor millions left Europe looking for a better life in America. The Great Depression that rocked the world began with the collapse of New York's Wall Street in 1929. New York became the port of embarkation as two generations of

American soldiers sailed away to fight in two world wars. For many of those young soldiers, the Manhattan skyline became the last glimpse they ever had of their homeland. But for those who survived the second of those wars, that skyline became their welcome home at its end, when New York hosted what was probably the most jubilant celebration of the century.

Broadway dominated theater, Wall Street became the focal point of world finance, and Madison Avenue invented modern advertising and the entire field of public relations. New York captured the crown of international finance much as London had in the nineteenth century; at the same time, New York dominated fashion and the arts much as Paris had during the eighteenth century. With the multiple crowns of finance, art, communications, and advertising, it seemed inevitable that world diplomats would select New York City as the seat of the United Nations, the world's largest political organization.

New York so encapsulates the modern era that it almost seems to be a city without a history prior to the twentieth century. It seems to be *sui generis* a creation of the electronic world. Even the Statue of Liberty, the Brooklyn Bridge, and the subway system all seem to belong more to the twentieth century than to the nineteenth century, when they originated. Knowing that New York City started as a small Dutch trading post on Manhattan Island seems as irrelevant to what it became as knowing that Paleo-Indians rubbed sticks together to make fire on Manhattan Island ten thousand years ago.

Yet even New York had a beginning and a reason that made it appear and flourish as such an important commercial center; it did not arise by mere accident or at random. New York became the twentieth century. That century did not belong to the warmer city of Charleston, South Carolina, the older city of Boston, or the more historic city of Philadelphia, all of which once outranked New York in both size and wealth. New York took the honors because of its location and its early trade patterns. That trade focused mostly on Indian furs.

As much as any man, John Jacob Astor shaped the early financial history of New York and built the fur industry of the United States. Astor came to America from Germany, where he was born in 1763 to a butcher's family in Waldorf, near Heidelberg. By the time of his death, in 1848, as a feeble, sickly man unable to chew and forced to take nourishment by nursing at the breast of a young nursemaid, Astor had become the richest man in North America and one of the world's first men to accumulate over a million dollars, fashioning an estate valued at between sixteen and eighteen million dollars. Astor did not accumulate his massive hoard of money by being an industrialist, a railroad tycoon, or a plantation owner; he made it buying and selling furs through the American Fur Company, which he created in 1808.

Through his American Fur Company and its subsidiaries, Astor operated the first monopoly in United States history, but he had trouble competing with the Hudson's Bay monopoly in Canada. Because Canada still belonged to England, Canadian furs dominated the London fur market. Astor had to search elsewhere to sell his furs; he had to move outside of Europe and the closed markets of Europe's colonies.

He found the market he needed in China. For centuries the Chinese had sold their silks and porcelains to the world, but they bought little on the international market, and thus accumulated great reserves of silver and gold. Astor arrived with something they wanted. Furs provided warmth in the frigid Chinese winter, and American furs became more important as the Chinese hunted their own animals to near extinction and chopped down their great forests for fuel. Astor's ships crisscrossed the Pacific to supply his newly discovered market.

Astor also carried cochineal, the bright red dye produced by the Indians of Mexico, ginseng grown in North America, and sandalwood grown in Hawaii and used as incense in Chinese temples. His ships brought back tea and silks from China, as well as opium, which was still legal on the North American market. Astor expanded his fur business into an international trading empire that presaged what New York City would become on a much larger scale in the century to follow.

The North American fur trade with Indians began with the first explorers and continued as one of the major economic forces until the middle of the nineteenth century, when it declined rapidly in the face of a growing American agriculture and the newly emerging industrial sector. From its start to its decline, the American fur industry depended on Indian hunters and trappers. They knew the land, understood the behavior of the animals, and possessed the skills and technology to capture them. White frontiersmen served mostly as traders who collected the furs and skins in exchange for ammunition, metal goods, whiskey, tobacco, and a few imported foods such as sugar.

The fur trade operated in a similar manner throughout North America. Small groups of Indian men trapped the animals and transported them back to a base camp, where Indian women processed them into marketable skins. Both parts of the enterprise depended primarily on Indian knowledge, skills, and technology.

The animals grew their thickest and finest furs in the coldest part of winter, and thus winter became the primary season for trapping. European transport and technology, which depended largely on horses or other draft animals pulling wheeled vehicles, proved useless in such an environment. Even on the Great Plains, the pioneers had to travel with their covered wagons during the warm months to avoid getting snowed in, and for much of the year their horses proved a useless luxury.

The Indians had already developed the technology for winter travel. For centuries the natives of Canada and the Great Lakes area made and used snowshoes that distributed the weight of the wearer over the top of the snow, preventing him from sinking into it. With the native knowledge of animal habits and their careful application of such knowledge, perhaps they invented these snowshoes after watching Arctic mammals cross the snow so easily with their large, padded feet. One of the most common methods employed wooden frames of spruce laced with rawhide thongs called *babiche*, but native groups developed different kinds of snowshoes depending on the weather and the natural resources of their particular home areas.

Snow glare presented special difficulties for winter hunting. Winter cold fronts that sweep across North America carry very little moisture after crossing the frozen, dry regions of the Arctic or Siberia, where the air picks up little moisture, dirt, or dust. What moisture the air contains quickly falls in the form of snow, leaving the air crisp and clear. The clear air allows pure sunlight to shine down at just the time of year when the sun stays at an oblique, low angle in the south. This creates the notorious snow glare that blinds travelers for the few hours of the day when the sun shines. To protect their eyes while hunting in such areas during the winter, the northern Indians and Inuit used goggles usually made of bone, antler, or ivory, with slits cut in them to admit enough light for vision.

To transport large loads of cargo over the snow, the Indians used toboggans, which were sleds with a curled front end and without runners. They also used the *cariole*, which resembled the toboggan but had bison-hide sides that made it look more like a large, moving bathtub. Humans or dogs pulled the toboggans and the carioles; only in areas with relatively light snows and wide roads could horses or oxen be used. Not until the twentieth-century invention of the snowmobile did anyone find a quicker way to travel freely across the cold northern plains and forests, but the financial and ecological costs of the snowmobile proved particularly high compared to the slower toboggans and carioles.

Weight was as important a consideration for trappers in the seventeenth and eighteenth centuries as it would become for air transport in the twentieth. Because the trappers or their dogs had to transport almost everything used, the trappers preferred to make simple wooden traps whenever possible, rather than carry heavy European metal traps with them or rely on weighty guns and ammunition. The heavier a trapper's load, the more his snowshoes sank into the snow. An Indian trapper might be able to make several hundred traps in a year and then leave them where they were used, rather than carry with him several hundred pounds of heavy metal.

Indians used a variety of traps depending on the quarry, the terrain, and even the time of year. The most common types consisted of snares and deadfalls. The deadfall attracted mink, ermine, otters, wolves, or martens with a small piece of meat; when the animal tugged on the meat, it pulled a wooden peg that triggered the fall of a large log, which killed it.

Snare traps contained rawhide loops placed along animal paths in such a way that a rabbit, fox, or lynx might pass through it or inadvertently stick its head through the loop, which then snapped and choked the animal to death, in some cases literally hanging it from a suspended tree branch or sapling. If the initial shock of the trap did not instantly kill the animal, it could chew through the cord or rawhide and free itself. This changed in the late 1700s with the introduction of European snare wire, which could not be chewed by the animals.

The Indians used their weapons to hunt the larger animals such as deer, moose, caribou, bison, and bear, which were generally too large to trap. For muskrat and beaver, they often combined hunting and trapping.

To the Indians' surprise, the traders preferred to buy old beaver pelts. The Europeans liked the soft undercoat of beaver fur, but disliked the coarse outer coat. If the Indians wore the beaver pelts for a year, the large hairs fell out or rubbed away, leaving a somewhat ragged-looking fur. The European trader paid more for these old furs than for new ones.

Europeans wanted the furs primarily for clothing. In drafty manor houses, wool offered scant protection from the damp European cold. Rich people wore clothes lined with fur, and carried large fur muffs to warm their hands.

Hatters used the soft undercoat of the beaver to make the tricornered hats of the eighteenth century and the top hats of the early nineteenth century. The notion of a fur hat might conjure images of a Russian's furry head covering, but the hats made from beaver pelts did not resemble a fur pelt. Hatters pressed together the shaved fine hairs of the beaver to make what should more precisely be called felt rather than fur, since it was not cut from the whole pelt. Because the hatters pressed the individual hairs together into a type of fur cloth, the hat could be molded into almost any shape and then brushed to give it a high luster that made the final hat look more like lacquered cardboard than fur.

Rather than pluck the long hairs out one at a time, hatters usually used mercury to facilitate removal of the coarse hairs. This heavy use of chemicals led to the occupational hazard of mercury poisoning and the ensuing mental debilitation that gave rise to the phrase "mad as a hatter."

When Jacques Cartier sailed up the St. Lawrence River for the first time in 1534, he did not find the Northwest Passage to Asia which he sought, but he did find a land with an abundance of animal life far beyond his European experience. With some irritation, he found evidence that European fishermen had been trading with the Indians of the St. Lawrence River even before he officially "discovered" the area. Not only did he surprise one fishing boat in the river just after he had claimed the river for France, but all along the river the natives, probably Micmacs, paddled out in their canoes and held up furs on the ends of sticks, clear evidence of prior trading experience with European boats. The Indians even knew to hold up their old beaver pelts rather than the fresh ones.

The French made episodic trading trips back to the area, but not until 1603 did the French government send Samuel de Champlain to New France, now Quebec, to establish a permanent trade system between the French and the Indians. From 1627 until 1663 the Company of One Hundred Associates or the Company of New France controlled the French fur trade, but in 1663 the crown assumed direct control of the trade under the king.

The first shipment of American goods sent by the Pilgrims in 1621 back to England to pay the Plymouth Company included two barrels of furs, but most of the cargo in the aptly named *Fortune* consisted of lumber (Cronon, p. 109). During the first half of the eighteenth century, furs accounted for only 0.5 percent of all British imports from their colonies. Tobacco, sugar, and rum from the warmer colonies had already surpassed furs in importance. Even though fur accounted for a small percentage of total British imports, it constituted a major portion of North American exports. Fur exports varied from one-third to one-half of all exports from the colonies of New York and Pennsylvania between 1700 and 1750 (Axtell 1988, p. 55).

While the Pilgrims settled in New England and the French took control of the St. Lawrence River, the Dutch consolidated a claim on the Hudson River. After the St. Lawrence, the Hudson offered the best access into the American continent from the Atlantic Ocean. For the Dutch, the Hudson River seemed like a new Rhine, and just as the Netherlands had profited for centuries by being at the mouth of Europe's greatest river, they hoped to create, almost literally, a new American Netherlands at the mouth of the Hudson. They bought Manhattan Island in 1598, and by 1614 Dutch traders had ascended the Hudson River as far as Albany, where they erected Fort Orange.

The Dutch named the new settlement on Manhattan Island New Amsterdam. The first known illustration of the settlement that eventually became New York occurs in a Dutch book published in 1651. Under the title *Fort nieuw Amsterdam op de Manhatans,* the artist shows a small fort surrounded by windmills and farms on the tip of Manhattan. Several Indian canoes appear in the water, with Indians paddling their stock of furs toward the small settlement for trade (Brandon, p. 167).

The fur trade attracted English and Scottish traders all along the Atlantic Coast, including the Carolinas and Georgia, where the mild winters did not produce the rich fur pelts of Canada. The southern Atlantic Coast, however, teemed with white-tailed deer, whose skins proved as lucrative in trade as the northern furs. In an era before plastic- and rubber-coated coverings, leather made from deer or cattle hides served myriad uses in Europe. Deerskins could be used in making a softer leather that was particularly good for clothing and accessories.

Charleston, South Carolina, became the primary trading center for the trade in Southern furs and deerskins. The English and the French Huguenots operated trading houses in the city, while Scotsmen went out and lived among the Indians to do the actual trading. The Indians, of course, did the actual hunting and processing of the skins.

The Dutch entered the United States at the Hudson River, the British created the Hudson's Bay Company and entered through the north of Canada, the Swedish entered south of the Dutch in what is now Delaware, on the mistaken belief that the Delaware River might prove as large and easily navigable as the Hudson. The French came up the Mississippi River from the south and down the St. Lawrence River from the north. The Russians, the last to enter the race for North American furs, crossed over from Siberia into Alaska, and came as far south as northern California, where they met the Spaniards moving northward.

The Spaniards still claimed North America, but the monarchy largely ignored the northern parts of the continent because explorations by Coronado, De Soto, and others had shown little indication of gold or silver. Compared to the wealth buried in the earth in central Mexico and high in the Andes, North America rated poorly, hardly worth the military effort it would have required to keep it out of the hands of the English, French, Swedes, Dutch, and Russians, who sent in traders and claimed various strips and pieces of the continent.

Of the colonial powers, only the Portuguese made no claim in North America, choosing to ignore the fur trade and concentrate on spices instead. They already had enough empire and trade to occupy them in Africa, Asia, and Brazil.

Rivalries over the fur trade underlay most of the European competition and fighting in North America for nearly three centuries. The Dutch and French each had good vantage points from which to pursue their trade, but the British had only Hudson Bay. The British built York Factory as a trading post on Hudson Bay, but despite its high profits, the long Arctic winter froze the bay, leaving it inaccessible by ship for most of the year.

The British moved early to take over the Dutch and Swedish possessions. In 1668, England acquired New York after seizing it in 1664, and then began the century-long rivalry between the two superpowers of the eighteenth century, Britain and France. Britain steadily pushed back the French and, in the long French and Indian Wars, finally routed them from Canada entirely.

In the eighteenth century the Russians moved onto the Pacific Coast of North America and started a fur trade similar to that of the Dutch and French on the Atlantic Coast in the previous century. The Russian fur trade slowly crossed Siberia from Russia to the Pacific Ocean, depleting the native stock of Asian animals as it progressed. In 1741, Vitus Bering discovered the rich fur country of the Aleutian Islands.

Russian *promyshlenniki*—fur traders—descended on the peaceful Aleuts, who proved to be some of the best hunters and trappers in all the Americas. Unlike southern tribes, who could depend at least in part on agriculture or on the gathering of abundant forest products, the Aleuts depended almost exclusively on hunting and fishing to feed and clothe themselves.

The Russians made no attempt to hunt for themselves; instead they seized villages of Aleuts and demanded that the men bring furs, or the traders would kill the Aleut women and children. Until the Aleut men returned with the furs, the *promyshlenniki* kept the hostage women as slaves and concubines.

The Russian government exercised little control or interest over the activities of its traders halfway around the world from the new European capital at St. Petersburg. So long as the traders paid the *yasak,* the royal 10-percent tax on furs, the czars ignored them, leaving them to steal, enslave, and even kill Native Americans at will. As the animal population decreased, the usually peaceful Aleuts began to fight against the *promyshlenniki,* who then waged a war of extinction in 1766 to thin the numbers of Aleuts and leave only enough to serve the sexual and financial needs of the *promyshlenniki.*

In order to exercise better control over the natives, and to resist the intrusion of fur traders from the East Coast, the Russians created forts, settlements, and a few Russian Orthodox missions, beginning in 1784 with Three Saints on Kodiak Island. In 1799, administration for the entire area went to a newly created Russian American Company, and by 1812 the Russians had built Fort Ross in northern California.

Even though they entered the fur race later than others, the *promyshlenniki* moved steadily from island to island across the northern Pacific Ocean and down the Alaskan coastline to California. To deny the Spanish claim to discovery and conquest of the Pacific Coast, the Russians called the area Nova Albion, the early name bestowed on it by Sir Francis Drake, rather than using the Spanish name California.

By 1825 the Russians were working the coast of southern California in the vicinity of Santa Barbara. In a typical Russian fur enterprise, a group of twenty-five Russians and Kodiaks were dispatched to build a base on San Nicolas Island. The Russians exterminated all the men on the island and captured all the women, while they put the Kodiaks to work hunting sea otters. For some reason the supply ship did not return the following year to pick up the pelts, and the native women seized the opportunity to rebel and kill their Russian captors (Farris).

Until the Russian sale of Alaska to the United States in 1867, the Russian American Company, the Hudson's Bay Company, and John Jacob Astor's American Fur Company dominated the international fur trade.

By the middle of the nineteenth century, the fur trade had started to collapse. The European fashion of the rainproof men's beaver hat declined as men adopted smaller felt hats and discovered the Asian umbrella, and as the military began to use rubberlined ponchos.

During these three centuries, the fur trade underlay much of the economic development of Europe and North America. The whole concept of the trading post conjures images of cheap beads, European trinkets, rum, and whiskey. Those items certainly carried great importance in the European side of the trade, but that view also demeans the Indian contribution. The Indians traded millions of beaver pelts, deerskins, bison hides, sealskins, moose hides, bearskins, and otter pelts.

These skins and furs formed the early capital of North America and financed the expansion of Atlantic Coast settlements, and a few on the Pacific Coast, into cities. Montreal, New York, Detroit, and Charleston, as well as Sitka, Alaska, owe their early existence to this supply of Indian goods. Traders in these settlements forwarded the Indian merchandise to Europe for sale at high prices. With the revenues generated by these sales, they bought more cheap goods for the Indians. The traders imported luxury goods for themselves and thus filled their homes with English silver service, Chinese porcelains, French furniture, Italian glassware, and Dutch crockery. More significant than the importation of European luxury goods, however, was the accumulation of vast new capital reserves. Through investment in other companies, land, and entrepreneurial schemes, the fur fortunes financed much of the subsequent development and industrialization of the United States and Canada.

The level of profit earned by the fur traders appears clearly in an account given by the partners of the Pacific Fur Company in 1813. Writing from Astoria, Oregon, a partner explained that the Indians gave him twenty beaverskins for a gun. He in turn sold the twenty skins for about twenty-five pounds, with which he could buy another gun for a little over one pound seven shillings. Similarly, he bought cloth at six shillings a yard and sold it for three or four beaverskins worth four to five pounds (O'Connor, p. 27). The traders received roughly ten times as much money as they paid the Indians for the furs, a high rate of return for any business, in any era.

Profits from the fur trade financed much of the development of the early settlements into national and international cities. Indian furs paid for the building of wharves and docks, and for the expansion of warehouses. The most important source of revenues for the colonial government came from tariffs and taxes on trade, most of which was supported by the Indian fur trade. The Indian trade helped to underwrite the cost of building roads into the wilderness, and later financed construction of canals and dredging of rivers.

The profit and new investments generated by the fur trade did not stay on the frontier; the money moved to the Eastern cities, of which New York benefited more than any other. John Jacob Astor sold his American Fur Company in 1834, when fur sales in Europe began to slide, and when he realized that North America had been nearly depleted. Astor had already accumulated a fortune of several millions from the fur trade, and he invested this money in New York. He invested in virtually every enterprise associated with New York, but, most important, he invested it in land. He bought many of the farms on Manhattan Island. He and his descendants sold and leased parts of this land and also constructed new buildings and houses, making the Astors the landlords of the city.

John Jacob Astor used his fur profits to build the Astor House, a modern six-story building that offered a washbowl and pitcher in every room along with free soap. Astor wisely leased operation of the hotel to others while he continued to own the building and the site. A similar arrangement underlay his ownership of the Park Theatre and the City Hotel. By the time Astor died in 1848, he owned 470 such leases throughout New York, producing over $200,000 in annual rents (O'Connor, p. 52). The majority of his New York lands, however, sat idle, waiting for development by future generations.

Astor concentrated on simple investment strategies for his lands. He leased the land for twenty-one years, with the leaseholder bearing responsibility for paying the taxes and for making any necessary improvements on the land. Most people who leased the land then erected buildings on it, in expectation that after the contract expired in twenty-one years, the lease might be renewed at the same rent. When the lease expired, Astor increased the rents greatly or reclaimed his land. He then gave the owner of the building ten days to remove it, or the building too passed into Astor ownership. In this way, Astor's capital grew with only minimal effort on his part. Astor's descendants continued the tradition of investing in New York through extensive holdings in real estate and through creation of hotels such as the Astor and the Waldorf Astoria.

Astor financed some of the earliest efforts to build railroads in the United States. He helped to found the Mohawk & Hudson railway, which eventually became part of the New York Central. He invested a million dollars in the construction of canals through New York, Ohio, and New Jersey. As a merchant who needed to move large amounts of cargo over long distances easily and cheaply, Astor understood the value of good modes of transportation such as canals and railroads. As a landlord, he also understood the value that these new canals and railroads had for his properties in and around New York City. His descendants inherited that understanding, and when the city grew beyond the limits of even their real-estate holdings, they fought hard against the development of the New York subway, because it would alleviate the crowding in the city and thus lower demand for their urban tenements (O'Connor p. 166).

Astor decendants played key roles in many of the railroad lines of the East, in coal-development projects, in the Westchester Gas Light Company, in the developing telegraph industry that became Western Union, in Niagara Falls Power, in American Telephone and Telegraph, and in other basic services for industry.

The Astor blood and monies commingled with the elite of New York and eventually with European aristocracy as part of the family moved abroad to assume control of such institutions as *The Times* of London. They served in the House of Lords, and Major John Jacob Astor ironically became the mayor of Plymouth, England, the city from which the Pilgrim settlers of Massachusetts sailed.

John Jacob Astor created the Astor Library, the finest research facility in North America, and one of the few public gifts ever made by Astor from his immense fur fortune. He left $400,000 for the library and a set of John James Audubon's *Birds of America*. The library opened on Lafayette Place in 1854 with 100,000 books, making it easily the largest library in North America, since the Library of Congress had only half that number, Harvard had 72,000, and the Philadelphia public library 60,000 (O'Connor, p. 89). The Astor heirs continued to maintain the library, and only five years after it opened, William B. Astor added another wing to it. Under Astor patronage, the library acquired an unprecedented 235,000 volumes by 1875. It became the basis for the New York Public Library in 1895, when the Astor Library combined with the Tilden and Lenox libraries to make a larger system that catered both to scholarly research interests and to the general public.

Astor invested very little in industry, aside from a single cotton mill, but he left his heirs investments in the Bank of America, the Manhattan Company, the Merchants Bank, The Mechanics Bank, and the New York Life Insurance and Trust Company, as well as in government and transportation bonds. His investments in banks and insurance companies helped to create the financial underpinnings necessary for the industrialization that sprang up in the northeastern United States in the second half of the nineteenth century. Just as the vast earnings from the fur trade helped to make the communications and transportation structure for America, the same monies built the infrastructure that sustained New York at the center of American financial life during the nineteenth century, and at the center of international financing through the twentieth century.

Modern New York, like the rest of America, has changed markedly since the fur trade. The ensuing Industrial Revolution restructured the economic base of the nation and altered the face and function of urban areas. Modern America is a product of the Industrial Revolution, but it is a product financed in large part by the fur trade, and therefore by the technology of the native men and women who trapped and processed the furs that made America rich and created the financial base for subsequent industrial development.

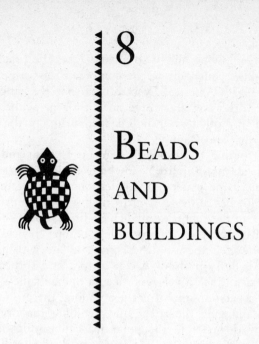

8

BEADS
AND
BUILDINGS

On a bright summer evening, a small boat leaves Yellowknife harbor to take a group out for a picnic on the Great Slave Lake, in the heart of the Canadian north. Yellowknife, with a population of only 13,500, serves as the capital of the Northwest Territories, a jurisdiction as large as India and five times the size of Texas. The Dene and Inuit constitute a majority of the territory's people, but the small total of only fifty thousand gives the territories fewer residents than some universities.

The Great Slave Lake is 298 miles in length and covers an area of 10,980 square miles, making it the fourth-largest lake in North America after Lakes Superior, Huron, and Michigan. The lake roughly equals the size of Belgium, and is larger than nine states of the United States. The Great Slave Lake receives the waters of the Hay, Peace, and Slave rivers, as well as many smaller tributaries including the Cameron, which tumbles over a roaring waterfall before quietly drifting into the placid lake. The outlet of the Great Slave Lake is the 2,640-mile-long Mackenzie River, which carries the waters of the lake north to the Arctic.

As befits a river flowing out of so great a lake, the Mackenzie drains a total area second only to the combined Mississippi-Missouri system in North America. Even though sparsely settled, the Mackenzie River drains an area three times as large as the Rhine and larger than any other river in Europe, including the much better known Volga and Danube.

On a summer outing I sailed with a group of Inuit and Dene to a small peninsula jutting into Yellowknife Bay. The large gray rocks jut up out of the water like whales, covered in green and bright orange splotches of the slow-growing but ubiquitous lichens of the tundra. Over the centuries the lichens break down the rock and cause small patches of soil to collect in the crevices. Like planted window boxes, these patches spring to life with mosses, brilliant fireweed, fluffy puffs of Arctic cotton, and spruces that grow as slowly as an inch a year and need a human's life span to grow as tall as a person. Small trees grow along the ground like evergreen vines, hugging the rocks and avoiding the dry, cold winds that blow down from the polar ice cap throughout the winter. The bleached white roots and trunks of dead trees line the shore like beached whale bones at the water's edge.

Along the coast, one can see an occasional small *inukshuk,* the stones piled to look like a human figure and used by the Inuit in hunting and as landmarks. These *inukshuik,* however, rise only three or four feet from the ground, and the relatively haphazard arrangement of the rocks shows that Inuit did not make them; foreign tourists and visitors like ourselves probably made them for fun on other outings on the lake.

In the clear night light of the Great Slave Lake, the tall, blue tower of the gold-mining shaft rises distinctly just outside Yellowknife. This tower, the tallest structure in the Northwest Territories, reaches twenty-five stories into the air in order to house the equipment, machinery, and cables that have cut a shaft a mile and a half into the earth. That shaft leads into eighty-five miles of underground tunnels that snake throughout the surrounding areas and even under the lake itself. Some fishermen claim that in the clear Arctic light of summer, they can see the tower from up to seventy-five miles out into the lake.

Swarms of midges buzz around harmlessly although irritatingly. The least breeze casts them to the ground or pins them to clothing, until a white jacket quickly becomes a mottled gray from all the midges stuck to it. More annoying swarms of mosquitoes also venture out into the dusk of a summer evening. They come in great swarms that some people say resemble tornadoes up to one hundred feet high. Dene tales relate the sufferings of people who traveled across the tundra and mistook a massive mosquito swarm for the inviting smoke of a distant campfire and headed right into them.

The insects of the tundra can drive humans and animals insane. Because of them, explorers found horses useless on the open, flat landscape that seems so appropriate for travel on horseback. The explorers who arrived on horseback soon found that the tormenting bites of blowflies and mosquitoes crazed the horses, causing them to bolt away. The horses ran, kicked, jumped, and bit at the air and the swarms of bugs until they died of exhaustion. Even the native caribou and musk oxen, as well as imported reindeer, suffer from the relentless insects, but the thick coats that help them survive the long winter also help them survive in an environment that rejects cattle and less-hairy creatures of the temperate zones.

Because of the lack of soil in the tundra, the air maintains a dust-free, crystalline appearance that makes distant objects appear many times closer than they are. The acoustics of the area also deceive a southern ear. Sounds carry for miles in the air without pollution and competing sounds to muffle them. In that atmosphere the clicking of a single dragonfly's wings sounds more like the noise of a rattlesnake than a small insect, and the clicking of a thousand of them sounds like the crisp popping of automatic weapons. The crunch of a foot on the dry lichens reverberates like the amplified sound of someone tromping on popcorn.

Far out on the Great Slave Lake, we seem to have left behind the noise of the miniature city, but my traveling companions for the night claim still to hear the roar of motorboats and trucks in Yellowknife. Most of them live in far quieter places scattered across the tundra, and with their acute hearing they can still perceive the sounds of the town and even of the gold mine long after my ears have ceased to hear anything but a light wind, the lapping of gentle waves, and the rattle of dragonfly wings.

Thirty people have assembled for this picnic from small villages above the sixtieth parallel, which divides the northern Yukon and the Northwest Territories from the southern Canadian provinces. They came from Edzo, Rae, Dettah, and Snowdrift, around the Great Slave Lake and from Hay River, as well as from Inuvik, Arctic Red River, and Aklavik, even farther north.

The women wore parkas that they had made themselves and trimmed with the warm fur of the ferocious wolverine. Lorna Storr from Aklavik carried a baby on a traditional sling about three inches wide and covered with thousands of multicolored beads. The beads spelled out the name of the child, Wills Storr, and his date of birth, November 27, 1988. She had made seven of these slings in her lifetime, one for each of her children.

We sailed on the *Naocha* (which means "big boat"), a touring boat owned by the Yellowknife Dogrib Dene band of Dettah, a lake village of 151 inhabitants, located three miles across the water from Yellowknife. The group on the lake that evening consisted almost exclusively of Inuit and Dene women with a handful of children. We headed out for a picnic feast of grilled whitefish, fresh salad, fruit juice, and tea, served with piles of bannock, the traditional biscuitlike bread of the north.

These women were all skilled artisans who specialized in their native traditions of working furs and skins, and sewing and embroidery with porcupine quills as well as beads. They had gathered in Yellowknife for three days of meetings on native crafts, and now they celebrated the meeting's conclusion with a traditional feast out on the water, away from the town. The women gathered with representatives of the territorial and federal governments to discuss better ways of producing and marketing their traditional crafts of worked skins, leather, and beads for a larger national and perhaps international market.

With the decline in world prices for fur pelts brought in by men, the role of the women in their traditional crafts has assumed a greater share of northern economic development. The traditional men's activity of hunting still produces large amounts of food, but their families need cash as well as food. In their symposium, the women sought to learn more about financial markets for their creations and the use of cooperative marketing efforts to increase their profits, and they shared information with one another about techniques and new ideas. They hoped to combine their traditional crafts with the modern market, without losing complete control of what they were doing.

The women with whom I shared a lakeside picnic on a bright July night in the northern tundra are continuing a tradition of thousands of years of native technology in the working of furs. Men hunted and trapped while women did the manufacturing.

Throughout the great era of the fur trade, the Indian hunters returned with their pelts to camp, and immediately turned them over to the women. These pelts varied in size from the small muskrats of under a foot, through the timber wolves, whose pelts stretched to over six feet, to an occasional grizzly or polar bear skin of twice that size. Beavers and martens usually made a medium pelt, just under three feet in length.

Because the pelts faced a long journey from the Indian camp in North America to the furrier in London, Paris, or Canton, they needed very careful preparation and curing before shipping. After thoroughly washing the fur, the women painstakingly removed every bit of meat or fat that still adhered to the pelt. If left on the pelt, the meat would attract mold and maggots, which could destroy the value of the fur long before it reached the first trading post. To scrape the pelt clean of adherent flesh, women used a flesher, a tool made from a large leg bone, with one end fashioned into the shape of a curved chisel.

After removing the flesh, the women stretched the hide on a frame. Large skins such as deer or bear needed to be stretched on a large frame sunk into the ground and often taller than the women processing the skin. Smaller animals, such as beaver, could be stretched on willow hoops with a diameter of about two feet, which looked like large embroidery hoops.

The women made soft buckskin and leather from the hides of deer, caribou, and elk. Even though these animals lacked thick fur, they did have hair that had to be removed to make the final cloth wearable. The women used scrapers to depilate the skin on one side in much the same way that they used the flesher to deflesh it on the other side. These skins also required more work during stretching; in order to cure them properly, the women had to oil them, rub them with urine or brains, and smoke them.

In addition to preparing skins and furs for sale, the women manufactured the clothing for the hunters and voyageurs who transported the furs. Inuit and Aleut women made fur-lined jackets with an attached hood, giving the world the parka. They called the special high boot of sealskin a *mukluk*. The parkas and jackets made by Inuit women had a sophistication of design that surpasses our concept of a mere jacket or coat.

The women who made these specialized clothes understood the requirements of the human body in the Arctic weather. They used the warm down of the king eider duck for extra insulation on the sides, where a person moves very little and thus requires extra warmth. Less-insulating cormorant feathers could be used on the back and chest so that these areas might "breathe" and prevent the wearer from overheating. The clothing crafted by the Inuit women had to serve many purposes: it not only kept the wearer warm, but it had to minimize perspiration, which would wet the clothing and then freeze, possibly endangering the life of the wearer in the Arctic cold. To make one piece of clothing, the women might use feathers with different insulating properties from a half dozen species of birds.

A series of drawstrings secured in various places allowed for quick and simple opening and closing of the clothing to adjust it for changing temperatures, winds, and moisture. By adjusting the strings, the person wearing the garment could make it cooler or warmer without removing the attached mittens.

A woman often added strips of fur to the collar of a jacket, the cuffs of sleeves, the ankles of moccasins, and to the rim around the face of a hood or the waist of a jacket or pants. In addition to blocking the cold air from entering these places on the clothes, the strips of fur minimized wear at points where the clothing might begin to ravel and fray. Even more important, these strategically placed strips prevented chafing from the rubbing of the clothing against the wrist, waist, neck, face, or other points where the clothing might irritate the skin. Because heavy winter clothes had to be worn for so much of the year, even a minor irritation arising from them could cause severe problems after a few months.

As a substitute for fur along such edges, the women often used strips of caribou hide or, in the south, strips of deerskin. The women also used the fringes for decoration. These dangling strips of rawhide on native clothing became emblematic of Indian or western-style clothing.

In temperate zones, cultures usually strive to control a large section of the environment through architecture. Roofs block the sun and protect people from rain, snow, blowing sand, or harsh winds. Windows and air shafts minimize cool air in hot periods or prevent the loss of warm air in cooler seasons. In English, we call people who design these large indoor environments architects, and consider them professionals of great learning. The word *architect* derives from the Greek, and means "primary doer."

By contrast, women who make clothing are merely seamstresses, a word derived from an Old English verb meaning simply "to sew." Theirs is presumably a craft that requires great training and some skill, but little knowledge or understanding. The making of clothing in temperate zones is rarely considered a matter of life or death; the clothing is for comfort and protection only so long as the wearer has to be outside during inclement weather.

In the Arctic, where the control of such large spaces through architecture has proven difficult, the Inuit culture adapted to the harsh climate through carefully constructed clothing. In performing their craft, these women act as architects of the microenvironment encasing the body. In the Arctic, where clothing represents a life-or-death protection almost every day of an individual's life, their work makes life possible.

The art and craft traditions of the Native Americans underwent a profound change when they encountered the European mercantile tradition. Their work in fur, leather, and beads had to be standardized into items that could be sold on the world market. The beadwork found few buyers, but the sophisticated techniques used by native women in processing furs found an important role in those markets.

The Indian women scattered across the forests and plains of the North American interior from the seventeenth through the nineteenth centuries worked as piece workers in the preindustrial phase of textile and cloth manufacturing that depended on dispersed labor operating out of women's homes. The Ojibwa, Cree, and other native women of the north played as important a part in the international manufacturing system as did contemporary women weaving wool in rural Britain, or peasant girls in Chinese filatures drawing silk threads from cocoons.

In addition to processing the furs, Indian women sewed the

canoes and kayaks needed to transport them. The light but sturdy bark canoe was usually the best type of boat for the small streams and rivers of North America, because the paddlers could easily portage it overland from one body of water to the next, a distance that could vary from a few feet to several miles.

From making wooden baskets and bark containers, the women possessed the knowledge and skill to work bark. They sewed the canoes together and coated them with pitch in much the same way that they sewed together their skins or pieces of bark to make smaller containers. Dugouts, by contrast, often required more manual labor, particularly upper-body strength, to dig out the wood, and thus men usually made this form of canoe.

Traders who employed Indian men to transport furs often employed the women of their families to work in gangs making canoes at the fort. The women made them in several standardized sizes, from the one-person canoe, about fifteen feet long, to the large Montreal canoe, which surpassed thirty-five feet in length and was five feet wide amidships, with a carrying capacity of four tons and up to twelve adults. The larger canoes were more than double the size of the modern, mass-produced canoes used for recreation.

Inuit women sewed kayaks from sealskin in much the way that southern women sewed bark canoes, but the Inuit women faced the added necessity of making their seams watertight without the use of pitch or resin, since no trees grew in their Arctic homeland. They developed an intricate series of minute stitches and folds that made the sealskins waterproof without adding measurably to the weight of the kayak. They named this specially sewn seam *silalik,* meaning "takes the weather." After sewing, they coated the entire vessel with seal oil to protect the kayaker even further from the seawater laced with piercing ice. The women used the same techniques to make thin sealskin raincoats that kept the wearer dry in the summer, when the air was too warm for a person to wear fur, but the seawater was cold enough to cause death through hypothermia.

In Inuktituk, the language of the Inuit, a man does not *ride in* a kayak; he *wears* it, much the way he wears a parka on land. The kayak is actually a piece of sewn sealskin clothing much like the other pieces made by his wife, except that she makes the kayak to be buoyant. These special qualities allowed the Inuit hunters to roll over in a 360-degree turn with their kayaks and then right themselves without wetting their inner clothing or the contents of the kayak.

Because of the mobile life-style of the hunting peoples of North America, they had little incentive to acquire heavy objects. Their creative work went into very small objects rather than into large constructions such as temples, pyramids, statues, or furniture. Art existed in the decoration of utilitarian objects. The women who made clothing decorated it with designs made with moosehair, dyed threads, or colored porcupine quills. Later they used small glass beads brought in by white traders.

From earliest times in North America, we see evidence of the creation of beautiful objects with great care, and we see consistent themes and cultural patterns. Some of the earliest archaeological sites in eastern North America date from the Hopewell culture (named for the farm on which the first relics were discovered), which radiated from southern Ohio and flourished for about half a millennium until around A.D. 400. In that ancient culture we see some of the same creative emphasis that we see in Native American craft work to the present day.

This appeared clearly in one of the earliest burial mounds found on the Hopewell farm. There, archaeologists found a young man and a young woman buried side by side. As Stuart J. Fiedel describes the burial in *Prehistory of the Americas,* "She was bedecked with, and surrounded by, thousands of pearl beads and buttons made of copper-covered wood and stone; she also wore copper bracelets. Both individuals wore copper earspools, copper breastplates, and necklaces of grizzly bear canines" (Fiedel, p. 238). The skulls had even been buried with artificial noses made of copper. Their bodies were then surrounded by a line of copper earspools. Archaeologists found more than 100,000 pearls in the Hopewell mounds (Prufer).

Other graves revealed individuals buried with hundreds of spearpoints, effigy figures made of sparkling mica, effigy pipes, pearls, quartz crystals, copper panpipes, clay figures, and bear teeth inlaid with pearl, as well as worked and unworked pieces of obsidian, green chlorite, gold, silver, meteoric iron, and flint.

In the absence of other forms of ivory, the Hopewell people carved the fossilized tusks of the giant mammoths that had become extinct thousands of years earlier. Some of the graves even included decorated, engraved human bones, and perforated jaw-bones of humans and animals.

The Hopewell people delighted in diverse and exotic material objects. They collected alligator teeth from the southern swamps, barracuda jaws, turtle shell, and conch shell from the Atlantic and Gulf coasts. They imported copper from Lake Superior, blue flint from Indiana, chalcedony from North Dakota, mica from North Carolina, galena from Illinois, obsidian from Wyoming, and the teeth of grizzly bears from the Rocky Mountains (Fiedel, p. 239).

In a direct precursor of Cahokia and other Mississippian towns that followed the Hopewell culture, we see trade networks that spanned about two-thirds of what is now the United States. The obsidian from near the modern border of Wyoming and Idaho traveled the farthest of the items traded by the Hopewell people. To reach the central Hopewell sites in southeastern Ohio, it traveled roughly two thousand miles. Even today the trip from Yellowstone Park in Wyoming to Chillicothe, Ohio, by car requires approximately four days of ten hours' driving each day over modern freeways. In Hopewell times, the obsidian and bears' teeth possibly took years to reach Ohio as they were slowly passed from one trader to another and transported that long distance by foot. From Ohio the materials passed on to even more remote parts of the Hopewell world, until they finally came to rest in a burial mound.

Animal effigies reached their most artistic form in the Hopewell "platform pipe." On these objects, a carved animal usually stands on a small platform about twice as long as the animal. The back of the animal has a bowl carved into it, and one end of the platform on which it stands has a small opening. One shows an erect beaver carved in pipestone and sitting on his tail. The eyes were inlaid with pearls, and the buck teeth of the beaver were carved from bone. Another pipe features a falcon with a cocked head looking up toward the sky with pearl eyes with the pupils clearly carved into them.

The artists did not create mere abstract versions of animals; in almost every case one can readily identify exactly what kind of bird or mammal is depicted. Apparently the artists observed these animals with great care and then depicted them in natural poses that most clearly characterize the particular animals. Platform pipes show a coyote howling, a raven picking at the ground, a falcon springing into flight, an eagle soaring, a snarling panther bearing its teeth and about to pounce, a duck diving into the water, a turtle swimming.

A similar realism appears in their terra-cotta statues of humans. Because the material is relatively perishable, fewer of these survive. One sees clear images of a mother nursing her child, a man kneeling or sitting as though in a public meeting, athletes playing ball. The peaceful pursuits and the simplicity of these pieces perhaps accounts for their lack of renown. We have no sculptures of gladiators or warriors in the heat of battle, no heroic struggles of humans against lions, no erotic sex goddesses. We have simple people performing the tasks of daily life and merely living their unheroic lives.

Adena and Hopewell art can be almost surrealistic in its attention to the mundane. One of the most magnificent pieces ever created in America, prehistoric or contemporary, depicts a human hand. About two thousand years ago, some unknown artists cut a sheet of mica into the shape of a human hand with long, elegant fingers and a naturally crooked thumb. This simple piece of art, without gender or generation, portrays the most human part of the human being, the part of the anatomy that separates the human from all the other animals. Other pieces of mica depict the claw of bird, the whimsical profile of a human with a comically large mouth and pointed nose, a coiled snake, a swastika, a human torso.

The tradition of skillful work seen in Hopewell artifacts continues today in the elaborate beadwork applied by Native Americans to the most mundane articles—a button or a snap, a belt or a buckle, a hair clasp or a barrette. At virtually any powwow or other large gathering of Indians today, one can see an array of modern daily items covered with beads and small plastic decoration. Beadworkers spend hours carefully making a case to cover a keychain, a coin purse, a disposable cigarette lighter, the cover for a tissue box, or a small, beaded picture frame.

One of my own cherished objects is a fountain pen case covered in beads and presented to me by Twila Martin Kekahbah, the first woman elected tribal chair of the Chippewa Band of Turtle Mountain on the North Dakota–Saskatchewan border. I value that pen both because it reflects not only the friendship behind the gift but also the meticulous work that created it. The person who made the case tied each knot separately to create a geometric zigzag pattern interspersed with small floral motifs. The art and care that went into the case will outlast the manufactured pen inside, but I can remove the case and put it around another pen.

A large display of Indian beadwork may look at first glance like the craft exhibit from the local prison or from a summer camp for youngsters. Displayed in large amounts, it looks cheap and rarely impresses the observer with its artistic delicacy. Beadwork was not made to be looked at en masse, as on a store shelf or in a museum case; it was made to be appreciated through the use of one small piece at a time. It was made to show its beauty through use.

The same attention to appearance that we see in the beadwork of the north and the plains area also appears in the baskets woven over a large part of the southern and western United States. Basket weaving was concentrated in a wide belt area from South Carolina to California and up the Pacific coast to British Columbia; it was done primarily in those parts of North America that lacked birch trees, which had loose, pliable bark that could be removed easily in large sheets. Wherever such birch trees grew, women usually found that they could work its pliable bark into an array of excellent containers much faster and easier than by weaving them.

In the southern and western quadrants of North America, which usually lacked birch trees, the natives developed weaving techniques for hundreds of types of plants. Basket weavers learned to work with roots, reeds, the bark of trees, plant stems, palm fronds, and whatever other plant could be sliced into long, narrow strips of a flexible yet durable material.

Pima women of southern Arizona wove baskets by coiling strips of willow around cattails. The Hopi of northern Arizona wove patterns of kachina images in varied shades of green, blue, and red into their serving trays woven with the stems of hilaria grass and yucca leaves. The Salish of the interior plateau in Idaho and western Montana wove baskets from cedar and spruce root in a design that made them appear to be shingles. The Chitimaca of the Gulf states created square baskets with lids and decorated in a distinctive red-and-black geometric design made from cane strips.

Basketry reached its most elaborate expression in ancient California. The mild climate minimized the need for elaborate shelters, and the abundance of seafood, land animals, and plants eliminated the need for agriculture. California natives used baskets for gathering acorns, trapping fish, and storing food, and because they knew how to make baskets waterproof, they cooked in them by dropping heated stones into a basket of water. They also used the same weaving techniques to make hats, serving trays, and mats for sitting or for protection against sun and wind.

Some of the best baskets in museums around the world today come from the California Pomo, who lived north of San Francisco, around the Russian River. The Pomo lived in simple conical tepees and collected food with a heavy reliance on acorns, from which the women leached the bitter tannin through a long process that resulted in a healthy and nutritious flour.

Among most native groups, women did most, if not all, of the basket weaving. Among the Pomo, however, men did the basic items—the large mats, the baby carriers, the fishing traps. This left the women free to experiment with different materials and designs in their much more finely crafted baskets.

The baskets woven by the Pomo women were diverse and magnificent, varying in size from that of a thimble not able to hold any more than a teaspoon of liquid to baskets as large as three feet in diameter. They used willow for the warp, sedge root for the weft, and a variety of bulrushes and barks that they dyed to give them contrasting red, black, and brown shades. The Pomo wove these wooden materials into designs as elaborate and varied as those found in the finest textile designs of wool.

In addition to weaving designs into the baskets, the Pomo women decorated their finished baskets with multicolored feathers, particularly those of the yellowhammer, and with shells, strings of handmade beads, and abalone pendants. The women could produce a rich, velvety texture with the feathers that sometimes made the baskets appear to be woven from fur.

Because of the perishable materials used to make baskets, they do not survive as long as do items made of stone or pottery. Only in areas such as the Southwest, with its especially dry climate, do we find the remains of baskets much over a hundred years in age. In the cultural hierarchy of crafts and arts, baskets lack the prestige of more durable goods, and thus have found less museum space than ceramics and carved artifacts.

Basketry requires a tremendous amount of work to produce an object that may easily be burned or rot. Thus, as we find in ancient American civilizations, settled populations usually replace baskets with pottery whenever practical. This transition occurred most clearly in the Southwest, when the civilizations based around basketmaking turned to ceramics. Mesa Verde in Colorado, Chaco Canyon in New Mexico, and Canyon de Chelly in the Navajo Nation of Arizona show the high level of the general Anasazi culture and of their ceramics in particular.

Native American pottery reached its highest expression in the southwestern United States. This highly evolved ceramic tradition arose very early among both the Anasazi people of the Four Corners area and the Hohokam of New Mexico. During their Golden Age, from A.D. 1100 to 1300, the Anasazi created a complex design of distinctive black-on-white pottery made with a dye from the woodland aster. They decorated mugs, pitchers, vases, ladles, bowls, and animal effigies with constant variation within a very narrow range of motifs and figures such as the mysterious figure of Kokopelli, the hunchbacked flute player.

The ceramic traditions of the Anasazi people traveled southeast to the Mogollon people of New Mexico, where the tradition reached a distinctive expression among the people along the Mimbres River, which runs for a mere sixty miles before it is defeated by the desert and the scorching sun. The people along this river created exquisite pots, which they buried with the dead. Often, one of these pots had a hole punched in it as a way of ritually killing the object before burying it.

The Mimbres pottery has a characteristic black-on-white or red-on-white design that includes stylized drawings of insects, animals, birds, and humans. Some of the designs appear similar to those used by the central Mexican civilizations. Other works show abstract geometric designs of great complexity. The unique quality of Mimbres pottery shows in the imaginative combination of naturalistic and geometric figures, such as two swirling and interlocking sets of rams' horns. Some of these abstractions become visual puns in which the black foreground may form the figure of a human face while the white background forms a bird. They seem to be distant precursors of the twentieth-century drawings of M. C. Escher, in which fish become birds and birds become fish.

Together with the Anasazi people, the Mogollon probably merged into the people that we now call Pueblo, living in eastern New Mexico and along the Rio Grande River, south of Taos. They have kept their traditional emphasis on ceramics, and today some of the world's greatest potters live in the New Mexican pueblos such as Acoma and Zuni, as well as in the Hopi pueblos of Arizona.

Throughout the Southwestern tradition, we find a great emphasis on ceramics—bowls, jars, cups, beakers, and large storage pots commonly called *ollas,* as well as various forms for which we have no name. Even though the creators of these objects put tremendous effort into creating diverse forms and into decorating them, these objects usually were made for daily use by common people. These egalitarian societies did not craft precious porcelains for an elite class; instead, they created beautiful utensils for themselves and their families. The people of the Southwest tradition lacked the Old World distinction between higher-class ceramics and common pottery.

The contrast between the egalitarian nature of native American *crafts* (beadwork, basketry, weaving, and pottery) and the elite nature of the grander Old World *art* (sculpture, painting, and architecture) appeared to me most vividly during a visit to the Anasazi ruins at Mesa Verde.

The best view of the Cliff Palace site at Mesa Verde comes from across the canyon on the western side, facing the ruins. The first time I saw it, the whole area had been dusted with a heavy coat of spring snow. Snow hung in the juniper trees in large clumps molded into odd shapes by the wind and the sun at midday. The snow gathered on ledges and crevices along the red and black walls of the canyon, forming alternate stripes of white, red, and black that appeared almost to have been laid out by a careful gardener. Protected by the overhanging cliff, the courtyards of Cliff Palace looked almost as though they had just been cleaned and all the snow swept neatly over the lower side of the canyon wall.

Seen from the western side of the canyon, Mesa Verde looks almost like a city suspended in midair, hovering above the earth. The afternoon sun, shining through the thin air of the high plateau, gave the buildings a crisp, clean appearance, as though they were newly made. Given the Anasazi penchant for selecting dramatic sites and making such dramatic structures, it is little wonder that so much mysterious and mystical nonsense has been written about them and their creations.

Cliff Palace is the largest of the ruins at Mesa Verde. It consists of a series of multistoried sandstone buildings that abut one another to form a single large edifice. Rectangular and round towers rise up from among the rooms with their precision-made square corners. Interspersed amid these 217 rooms are twenty-three large, circular rooms, the sacred kivas where the ancient ones enacted the ritual life of their pueblo. Even from the far side of the canyon, one can still see the airshafts built next to the kivas for ventilation in the underground chamber.

Under any circumstances, this castlelike structure would provoke the interest of a visitor, but its location frames it in a surreal setting. The whole city rests in the three-hundred-foot-wide mouth of a cave in the middle of the canyon wall. The steep walls of the cliff above the city and below it seem to offer no means of approach. The brown color of the buildings blends with that of the surrounding rock, creating the illusion that the entire structure was carved from the living rock, rather than having been pieced together stone by stone.

To reach the ruins themselves from the western side of the canyon, one must drive all the way around the canyon and approach Cliff Palace from the rear, where the mesa hides the community from sight until one is right on it. Without making the short trip down the side of the cliff to the opening, a person unfamiliar with the area could literally stand on top of the entire community and never know it existed.

Moving from the west side of the canyon to the east on a cold day, one moves from the shadow into the sunshine and quickly appreciates the comfortable practicality underlying the plan of this city. In the colder months, the ruins of Cliff Palace radiate heat absorbed from the sun that shines directly into it all during the day. The sunshine streams into the sheltered niche and reaches far back to the rear of the cave, and the sandstone walls absorb its warmth. The setting—inside a cave located in a canyon—protected the community from cold winds, especially from the north.

In the summer, when the sun shone relentlessly from almost straight overhead in this part of the world, and the atmosphere at such high elevations offered little escape from the penetrating rays, the overhanging cliff shielded the entire community. Thus the city was protected except for the front row of walls, which were usually shaded by overhanging roofs.

Such skilled use of passive solar energy minimized the amount of fuel that the Anasazi people needed to gather, transport, and burn. In the semiarid conditions of the mesa, this helped to preserve the fragile ecology by not overusing the trees for firewood, and prevented the use of potentially good cropland for housing.

We do not know the name of the people who lived there; we call them simply the Anasazi, a Navajo name meaning "ancient ones." The Anasazi lived for thousands of years in this area of the southern Colorado plateau; they started building their major cliff dwellings about A.D, 900, and reached a climax in the thirteenth century. Even though Cliff Palace is the largest of the dwellings, dozens more dot the surrounding cliffs. Square Tower House rose to eighty-six feet, with eighty rooms and seven kivas. Balcony House had two kivas and forty-five rooms, and Spruce Tree House had 114 rooms and eight kivas, while Long House had 150 rooms and twenty-one kivas. The Anasazi built between five hundred and one thousand such cliff settlements in the Mesa Verde area. Other canyons in neighboring Utah, Arizona, and New Mexico contain thousands more such ruins built in the cliffs and on the flat land at the top of the mesa or, in the case of Chaco, on the canyon bottom.

If we look around the world at other buildings erected between the tenth and thirteenth centuries, we find that the unique setting of the Mesa Verde cliff houses places them in a separate architectural category. At first glance, the cliff dwellings seem to lack the great sophistication of contemporary buildings of other cultures.

During the same time that the people of Mesa Verde built their cliff houses, the Maya built pyramids in the Yucatán and Guatemala, the Italians built the Doge's palace in Venice, the Arabs built the Fatimid mosques of Cairo, the English built Westminster Abbey, and the Moors built the Alhambra in Granada, Spain.

Each of these structures tells us something important about the people who built it. The ruins that they left show us what values they wanted to express in their architecture. The power of a ruling aristocracy appears clearly in their castles, built as giant military machines, or in their palaces, built as theme parks of amusement and entertainment. The power of an organized religious group and the state behind it show clearly in the cathedrals, monasteries, mosques, and temples built for the lavish display of religious rituals.

At Mesa Verde we see none of this. Compared to St. Paul's Cathedral, a kiva is a stone-lined hole in the ground. Compared with the palace of the Venetian Doge, the unadorned rooms of Cliff Palace seem small and quite plain. The towers of Mesa Verde show no signs of military use, and appear puny and weak against the power implied in the massive towers and gates of the castle of Nuremberg or the Kremlin of Moscow. The courtyards where Anasazi women ground corn at Cliff Palace lack the grandeur of the courtyard in the Alhambra, where the women of the harem recited poetry beside flowing fountains and pools of cool water. The Anasazi dance and ceremonial areas offer the visitor none of the opulence of the palaces of Europe.

Mesa Verde did not serve as home to kings, popes, caliphs, khans, harems, monks, or knights. The common Anasazi people built their buildings for themselves and their children. The rooms of Mesa Verde housed their builders and their builders' children and grandchildren for centuries. The ruins are the remnants of homes built by and for the common people, built by a people without a rigid class structure. Nowhere else in the world of that time do we find such spectacular and well-built homes for the common people

For every castle and palace in the world, tens of thousands of laborers, slaves, prisoners, serfs, and common people lived in hovels that have long since disappeared, leaving very little archaeological trace. Millions labored in the fields to feed the thousands who served the civic, martial, and religious edifices of the powerful elite. Most of the great architectural wonders of the world, from the pyramids of ancient Egypt to the Great Wall of China, were built at the expense of poor people who had to live in huts and eat gruel in order that some great prince, emperor, shah, pope, or pharaoh might be protected or exalted by massive structures of monumental design.

When the early European explorers and settlers saw the ruins of the Anasazi and the other Indians of the area, they gave them names such as Cliff *Palace* at Mesa Verde, Montezuma's *Castle* in Arizona, Cutthroat *Castle* in Utah, or *Casas Grandes* in northern Mexico. The whites saw the ruins through European eyes, attuned to the culture of a highly stratified society; therefore they assumed that anything so grand must have belonged to some type of aristocracy. It was inconceivable to the class-ridden Spaniards, and later to the Anglos, that common people could have built such residences for themselves.

I saw in the work of the women picnicking on the Great Slave Lake the same values, the same attitude toward creativity, that I had seen at Mesa Verde. A thousand years and three thousand miles of space separate the ancient Anasazi people of the warm, sunny south from the native Dogrib and Yellowknife people about the Great Slave Lake in the subarctic. Despite this spatial and temporal distance, tremendous cultural continuity persists in the Native American perspective toward social life and toward the objects of social life.

In weaving a baby sling for her son, Lorna Storr made an object that would endure for his entire lifetime and could be passed on to his descendants through the twenty-first century. Her art went into her family, into the immediate life around her. That same attitude toward creativity and daily life would have been understood by the ancient workers who skillfully placed one rock on another to build the great buildings of Mesa Verde.

9

CORN,
COTTON,
AND
TOBACCO

The most common way to see Pueblo Grande is from the air, not because it lies in a remote and inaccessible place, but because it lies near the end of a runway of Sky Harbor International Airport in the middle of Phoenix, Arizona. Thousands of passengers fly directly over it each day without noticing it. The ruins appear directly beneath the airplane almost as soon as the wheels lift off from the pavement at the east end of the runway.

It is easy for a passenger to miss the ruins, since they lack the colorful motion and visual interest of the district surrounding the airport. Due north of Pueblo Grande, the affluent suburb of Scottsdale spreads out beneath the imposing mass of reddish brown Camelback Mountain. To the west the scattered high-rises of downtown Phoenix dot the skyline, and in the south rises the dramatic architecture of Arizona State University at Tempe. The relatively empty and sparse Salt River Indian Reservation fills the airplane window in the northeastern quadrant beside the scar of the dry bed of the Salt River.

All towns seen from the air seem to resemble quilts with their patchwork of blocks, but Phoenix must have the oddest pattern of all, for each patch seems to have been designed and sewn without any knowledge of the others. The squares do not connect with one another; they do not look outward. Each square faces inward on itself as each housing development focuses on its own lake, pool complex, golf course, community center, or shopping area while erecting walls and other barricades to cut it off from the surrounding quadrants. Only the interlocking ribbons of canals sew together this crazy quilt.

The canals, fountains, pools, and ponds make Phoenix into a virtual water city. Nowhere outside of the Netherlands has an urban people built so many canals, and nowhere outside of the Arabian world can one see such a passion for water fountains. If one ignores the desert surrounding this oasis, Phoenix could easily be in the Florida Everglades.

Amid so much theatrical display of water and tropical lushness, one must look hard to see the earth-colored ruins of Pueblo Grande. The eye tends to divert toward the bright green golf courses, the sparkling blue pools of water, the rushing cascades of artificial waterfalls, the soft pastels of the new architecture, the jets of water from fountains so high that they seem to threaten the aircraft. The mud walls of Pueblo Grande are barely visible in the wide, dusty zone where they crouch between the airport and a largely deserted industrial area. Next to the platform mound, the ruins of an ancient ball court look more like a sunken oil or water tank than an ancient sports facility of the Hohokam.

The contrast between modern Phoenix and the ancient, almost hidden ruins of Pueblo Grande seems immense. The ruins seem to have no more connection with the modern city than if the archaeologists had found the fossilized skeleton of some ancient whale or mastodon on this site.

As the airplane rises over the ruins, one notices a curious pattern of dried canals and waterways radiating out from Pueblo Grande. Crisscrossing these ancient canals and sometimes following them are the modern canals that feed the incredible thirst of this desert city. Seen from the air, the Hohokam settlement of Pueblo Grande sits at the hub of Phoenix today because it was the prototype for the modern city. The network of ancient canals also made Pueblo Grande into a water city that otherwise would not have survived long in the incredibly hot and dry area now called the Valley of the Sun.

For more than two thousand years before the first European ever came to America, the Hohokam people around the Salt River irrigated their crops of maize, squash, cotton, chilis, and beans. The land of the Sonoran Desert of Arizona was not a desert because of poor soil but merely because of a lack of water. Sand deserts such as the Sahara do not produce crops even when water is added, because sand, not soil, covers the land. To grow crops in the Sahara, the farmer needs, in addition to water, all the chemicals that good soil provides. But the land around the Salt and Gila rivers of southern Arizona needed only water to make plants thrive in the rich soil.

Scientists still debate the exact date of the arrival of maize in the area. Some evidence indicates that farmers grew maize there as early as 3500 B.C.; other evidence indicates that true domestication began two thousand years later.

No matter when maize arrived, by 300 B.C. we find the first results of this revolutionary food and the novel technology it engendered. The community called Snaketown arose near the Gila River, south of modern Phoenix. This marked the beginning of civilization in the North American Southwest, and we call the people and their culture Hohokam. As with most ancient Americans, we do not know what they called themselves. We call them Hohokam based on the Pima words for "ancient ones," although the name might be more accurately translated as "all used up." The Hohokam occupied most of the territory along and between the Salt and Gila rivers in southern Arizona.

Occupation of the Pueblo Grande site began about A.D. 300 and lasted until about 1450. During this time the community may have reached about one thousand inhabitants, but much of the evidence for its true size and history has now been lost beneath the urban growth of the modern city. The community possibly stretched out as far as two miles, but today only this center part remains.

The Hohokam built the most extensive system of canals in North America. A canal is much more than just a ditch. The

Hohokam had to build the canals to take advantage of the natural slope of the land and the course of the river. To minimize loss of water into the dry earth of the desert, the Hohokam occasionally lined some sections of their canals with a protective layer of clay, thereby making them watertight.

The Hohokam irrigation system became the magnet that attracted Anglo settlers after they had consumed most of the good farmlands of North America. In 1868 the Swilling Irrigation Canal Company took over the ancient Hohokam irrigation system, cleared the sand-filled canals, and filled them with water again. Colonists fleeing the civil strife of the East and the debilitating Civil War eagerly staked land claims in the newly opened lands of the Arizona desert. Freed slaves and displaced whites from the South found that cotton grew better in Arizona than in the over-farmed and exhausted soils of Georgia, Alabama, Mississippi, and Louisiana.

These colonists created a new city near the confluence of the Salt and Gila rivers, but even in building their new city, they recognized that they were reviving something far older. The desert settlement was but one more in a long line of civlizations in this place. In recognition of the debt the new settlement owed to the old Hohokam one that came before it, the settlers named their new place Phoenix. Like the mythological bird that was reborn from the ashes of its own burning every five centuries, this settlement rose from the ruins of the ancient Hohokam settlement and canals after five centuries of abandonment.

Like the Mississippian civilization at Cahokia, the southwestern United States produced a civilization based on maize. Starting before the Hohokam and continuing to the present, corn constituted the staple food of the daily diet in the Southwest, as is evident in the corn tortillas, corn tamales, corn soups, corn stews, and in a dozen varieties of baked or grilled cornbreads. The agriculture of modern Arizona grew from Hohokam irrigation systems and Hohokam crops, and today the diet of the people depends heavily on the same staple foods.

This legacy of the Indians in Arizona is shown clearly in places such as Pueblo Grande in the heart of modern Phoenix, but the agricultural debt to the ancient Indians is no greater in Arizona than in other parts of the United States. The difference is that the debt goes unrecognized in most parts of the country, but it remains markedly visible in Arizona, which still uses the same canals to water the same crops.

The Pilgrims of Plymouth survived the winter of 1620–21 in America thanks to the generous help of the Wampanoag, Massachuset, and neighboring Indians who supplied most of the food for the first Thanksgiving feast as well as for subsequent ones. One Wampanoag, who has become known to us as Squanto, taught the Pilgrims so effectively because he spoke fluent English and had already traveled to several European countries after escaping from an English slaver. The Pilgrims arrived not knowing how to speak any of the Indian languages or how to grow European crops, much less American ones. Because the Pilgrims emigrated to America from cities and towns in Europe and not from the countryside, they knew nothing of living in the forest, or of farming. Squanto and other Indians patiently taught them to plant and cultivate Indian corn, pumpkins, beans, and squash.

After helping the Pilgrims start their farms, Squanto died in 1622, as did thousands of his fellow Indians who fell victim to the many fevers and epidemic diseases introduced by the Europeans. When the Indians died from disease or warfare, the Pilgrims took over their neatly prepared fields and storehouses. Even the settlement that we know as Plymouth began as the Wampanoag village of Patuxet before the Pilgrims appropriated it for themselves, taking over the Wampanoag houses, cleared fields, corn bins, and even tools.

After only seven years in America, the Puritans had accumulated enough money to create the Massachusetts Bay Company and buy out the stock of the Plymouth Company, which had financed and owned the Massachusetts settlement. Within another six years the Pilgrim settlers managed to pay off the entire debt of this company through trade with the Indians and their own production of American Indian crops.

Despite hideous crimes against them, the Indians continued to help the newcomers to America. As new waves of settlers washed up on American shores in the decades after the arrival of the Pilgrims, new generations of Indians introduced them to the flora and fauna of America, and taught them how to farm. The American colonial economy, like our modern one, depended on a solid base of American Indian crops. The early settlers exported tobacco, cotton, and corn supplemented by the Indian trade of fur pelts in the northern colonies and deerskins in the southern colonies. Throughout all of this, Indian corn served as the new staff of life for the colonists.

If humans ever invented a miracle food, it must have been corn. All types of corn belong to a single species, *Zea mays,* but a world of variation exists within that species. Over the last few millennia before the European arrival, the American Indian farmers developed a type of corn for virtually every ecological niche from southern Canada to northern Chile and Argentina. Farmers grew corn in the deserts of the southwestern United States and northern Mexico, in the swamps of the southeastern United States and Central America. They grew it high on the slopes of the Andes as well as along the coasts of the Caribbean islands.

Corn was the only staple grown in both the northern and southern hemispheres, and even today it grows in virtually every part of the world where humans can grow crops. Unlike rice, which grows best in tropical climates and is ill-suited to most of North America, and unlike wheat, which grows well in the northern and central parts of the continent but not in the southern and far western parts, corn grows everywhere.

Corn proved higher in nutrition than most other grain crops, and it gave higher yields. Corn syrup is the closest to human glucose of any plant derivative. The uniqueness of corn becomes more apparent when we realize that at the time the Europeans arrived in America, their grain crops usually produced six measures of seed for each measure planted. By contrast, from one kernel of corn, a whole corn plant grew with several ears of corn. This yielded a crop of one hundred fifty measures for each measure planted, making corn thirty times more productive than the traditional grains (Warman). In the best of years, some corn yields reached as high as eight hundred new kernels produced for each kernel planted.

The settlers ate corn chowder, cornbread, corn tortillas, corn tamales, hominy, and grits as well as fresh corn and popped corn. Just as important, they fed corn to chickens, turkeys, and pigs to give American settlers more meat in their diets than their European counterparts enjoyed back in the home country.

Corn became so important as a crop for the early settlers that it substituted for money in the Massachusetts Bay Colony during the 1630s, when the colony suffered a shortage of silver coins. John Winthrop ordered that Indian corn should "pass in payment of new debts" at a rate of four shillings to the bushel (Hosmer, p. 6).

The colonists who lived along rivers and coastal areas also exported corn to the Caribbean, where it fed the millions of slaves working in the sugarcane plantations. As long as the European demand for sugar remained high, the Caribbean plantation owners found it more lucrative to devote all their lands to sugarcane cultivation while feeding the slaves on cheaper food imported from the American mainland.

Dependence on corn as a staple food became so great among slaves and poor settlers in the southern United States and the Caribbean that a new disease began to stalk them. The method by which the colonists processed the corn leached out the niacin—vitamin B—and this resulted in the nutritional ailment pellagra, which caused the skin to erupt in hideous sores. If not treated, it also affected the nervous system and led to eventual dementia and death. Even though pellagra became common, especially in the rural South, and lasted until the twentieth century, it occurred only among people of European and African descent, but not among the natives. The native cooking methods, which included adding wood ashes to the food, enhanced niacin in the corn, but the Indians also showed less physiological susceptibility to the disease.

In Europe, people showed little interest in importing American corn, but they developed a voracious appetite for American livestock fattened on that corn. American hams and dried beef, from animals fed on the cheaper produce of America, supplemented the large catches of codfish to help feed an overcrowded and protein-deficient European population.

During the twentieth century, colonial Williamsburg in Virginia was remade into the grand eighteenth-century capital of Virginia through the financial backing of the Rockefeller family and their foundation. The renovators stripped away the modernized additions of nineteenth-century builders and exposed the natural brick stateliness of the United States' first elegant city. The renovated area of Williamsburg includes the symmetrically perfect buildings of William and Mary College, the old courthouse, the public gaol, several stately offices, the ammunition storehouse, taverns, stores, homes, and the governor's palace.

The modern tourist attraction of colonial Williamsburg exemplifies the basic, traditional American values of balance, orderliness, simplicity, and ingenuity. The buildings lack fancy decorations, but each one shows precise mathematical symmetry. On the William and Mary campus, the Wren Building, the oldest surviving academic building in the United States, demonstrates this precision in the way it radiates from a large central doorway on the ground floor. A balcony sits directly above the door, on the second floor, and a small cupola with a clock rises directly above the balcony on the roof. To the left and right of this central axis, each floor has six identical windows on each wing. The six windows of the first floor are placed directly beneath those of the third floor, and those of the roof are directly above the six of the basement. The chimneys stand like precise and even-numbered sentinels jutting from the roof of both wings.

On the Wren Building, only the weathervane rotates, of necessity, in an asymmetrical manner, with one side protruding more than the other. Perched atop the cupola, the moving weathervane only emphasizes the otherwise exact symmetry of the building.

The modern renovators of Williamsburg shaped the land outside the buildings to emphasize the precision that made Williamsburg the first "planned community" in America. Picket fences, brick walls, and split-rail fences neatly cordon off the various strips of property from one another, according to function and ownership. The barriers carefully separate each domestic complex with its concomitant outbuildings for kitchens, dairies, springs, smokehouses, and toilets from each other one.

Walking through Williamsburg, one half expects at any moment to round a corner and trip over the string of Benjamin Franklin's kite, or maybe even the fallen cherry tree of George Washington. This is America as we all remember it from some mythic images we learned even as we grew up in a world filled with automobiles, urban blight, suburban sprawl, drug addiction, vacant lots, and television chatter. No matter how we live today, this is the way life is supposed to be, and the way it supposedly once operated in America.

The simple symmetry of Williamsburg is matched by the cleverness of it all. Each of the small gates in the picket fences has a metal chain from which hangs an iron ball that weighs down the chain and thus automatically pulls the gate shut each time it is opened. Visiting parents stand around the gates and marvel while pointing and gesturing to impress on their bored children the finer points of such sound, all-American engineering. Any modern American can easily see in the gate the cultural predecessor of the automatically opening and closing garage door or the electronic doors in the suburban supermarket, but the achievement of the colonials is all the more remarkable because they did it without electricity.

Proof of the mechanical cleverness of our ancestors abounds in Williamsburg. The clocks and weathervanes stand out dramatically on public buildings, and large locks with gigantic keys seem to be the aesthetic and technological focus of each home. Large chimneys dominate each building. Behind the scenes, one can see glassmaking, leatherworking, printing, dairying, metalworking, the smoking of foods, and the weaving of Christmas wreaths from local flora. It's a busy little place. Even Santa's elves could not be expected to work any harder than the colonists of Williamsburg or the college kids who portray them today for visitors.

Colonial Williamsburg contrasts starkly with the reconstructed settlement of Jamestown, only a short drive away on the banks of the James River. At first glance, Jamestown resembles the Indian villages depicted in early etchings and engraved prints made by travelers in the sixteenth and seventeenth centuries. It looks like a summer camp for scouts. The rustic buildings, made of wood, bark, and thatch, appear to be simple, almost playful, adaptations of Indian designs and the natural resources of the Virginia coast. Walking among the small buildings in the fortress today, one almost expects a camp counselor to step out, blow a whistle, and have hundreds of screaming kids pour out of the rustic but cute buildings.

Whereas Jamestown is small, jumbled, and built of wood, Williamsburg is large, expansive, and made of brick. The reconstructed Jamestown and the reconstructed Williamsburg belong to totally different worlds, but the grandeur of Williamsburg arose within a mere century of the founding of Jamestown.

Viewing Williamsburg today, it is easy to imagine how the colonists turned a simple, almost Indian-style camp into a grand city. It must have been through the clever industriousness of the people in making their clocks, weathervanes, automatically closing gates, printing presses, butter molds, cookie presses, and tin lanterns. This is a view of American history that suits us very well: our European ancestors arrived in nothingness and, through diligence and their natural cleverness, made a beautiful city.

The cleverness and the stately buildings of Williamsburg *resulted* from American prosperity, but they did not *create* that prosperity. The reason that Williamsburg rose within a century of the founding of simple Jamestown has nothing to do with closing gates, weathervanes, brickmaking, and all the other clever technology displayed there. All of this prosperity came from the highly profitable sales of one single Indian crop—tobacco. Because of tobacco, Jamestown turned into Williamsburg and made Virginia into an aristocratic state that some Virginia patriots pretentiously called the "fifth crown" of the British monarchy, following the other kingdoms of England, Wales, Scotland, and Ireland. Without tobacco or some comparable crop, Virginia would have fared little better than the other American colonies of Great Britain in Guyana, Jamaica, and Belize.

Tobacco grows in almost as many diverse environments as does corn. Indians cultivated it throughout North and South America, but it seems to grow best around the Caribbean and adjacent mainland areas, including the fields of southeastern North America. Virginia, Maryland, and the Carolinas became virtual "tobacco colonies" devoted to this monoculture.

After experimenting with several potential cash crops, the Virginia colonists eventually concentrated on Indian tobacco as the source of the highest profits from their fields. Throughout the seventeenth century, tobacco in Europe graduated from the status of an occasional fumigant and medicinal drug (used, among other things, as a treatment for pellagra) to become a common and habitual social vice.

Tradition maintains that John Rolfe played the crucial role in turning tobacco cultivation into a mercantile endeavor by Englishmen in America. Rolfe arrived in Jamestown in May of 1610, after nine months shipwrecked in Bermuda. While trapped in Bermuda, his wife, whose name we do not know, gave birth to a daughter whom they named Bermuda, but who soon died. The ordeal of Rolfe and the other emigrants on the ship, aptly named the *Sea Adventure*, became the kernel around which Shakespeare wrote his play *The Tempest*.

Safely rescued from Bermuda, Rolfe settled in Jamestown, in a home much like those primitive structures still visible there for modern tourists. In Virginia, Rolfe returned to his habit of pipe-smoking, something he had not been able to do while stranded in Bermuda. Rolfe tried the tobacco grown by the Indians of the area, but did not like the native Virginia tobacco. The Indians grew a very strong tobacco, *Nicotiana rustica*, which they used primarily for ceremonial occasions. It had much too powerful a bite for the Englishmen, who wanted to smoke it frequently after a good meal, while playing cards, with a pint of ale, or at other relaxing times in the daily routine. The milder *Nicotiana tabacum* grown by the Caribbean Indians and sold by the Spaniards suited the tastes of Englishmen much better than the native Virginia varieties.

Rolfe acquired some of the seeds of the tobacco grown by the Caribbean Indians, probably from Trinidad, and planted them in Jamestown by the year 1612. Soon thereafter he exported the first small shipment of the leaf to England. During the time when Rolfe was experimenting with the new tobacco crop, his English wife died. In April 1614, Rolfe married Chief Powhatan's daughter, Pocahontas, whose name became much more famous than his own.

In the long process of turning tobacco into a large-scale commercial crop, Rolfe and the other tobacco colonists adopted agricultural and technological procedures from the Indians. Eventually the colonists standardized a procedure of planting the seeds in beds where they could be carefully nursed and tended until the plants became large enough for transplanting into fields. As the plants matured, the farmers learned to remove the buds and break off the smaller suckers that grew on the stem, in order to produce larger, more flavorful leaves.

The farmers found the picking of the large, moist tobacco leaves a messy procedure because the thick, gummy sap of the plant stuck to everything it touched, including human skin. After only a few minutes working in the fields, sap usually covered the pickers' arms and heads, matting down the hair and trapping small insects attracted to the smell of the plant. After this difficult process of picking the leaves, they must be dried either in the sun or with fire.

The Indians traditionally pulled the whole tobacco plant out of the ground and dried the stalk and leaves together in order to avoid the stickier process of picking individual leaves. Initially the colonists followed the traditional Indian way of hanging entire plants up to dry, or of stacking them into piles in the sun, but Rolfe and the Englishmen found that with their large fields of tobacco, the drying of whole plants required too much space. Despite the mess involved, the colonists had to pick the leaves from the stalk and dry only the part that they would ultimately be able to sell.

Each of these stages in the procedure of growing and preparing tobacco for shipment required many trials and much experimentation with Indian cultivation and technology before the colonists found the right procedure for mass production. The final tobacco culture combined traditional aspects of both native American and European knowledge with some innovations developed in Virginia and neighboring tobacco colonies.

The Indians used tobacco in many ways other than smoking it, such as drinking it mixed into an herbal tea, or snorting its fumes. The Europeans tried all of these methods, but showed a marked preference for smoking the tobacco in pipes of the same type as those used by the natives. The natives of Virginia produced a variety of clay, bone, wooden, and stone pipes over many centuries before the colonists arrived. They manufactured them with straight and curved stems, and stems angled from the bowl. After the great success of the tobacco crop in Virginia, craftsmen did not want to waste time making pipes. They either bought them from the Indians or imported the lighter, polished pipes made in England.

By 1616, within a decade of their arrival in America, the Virginians exported over a ton of tobacco to Britain. Within seventy-five years, by 1689, this increased to more than seven thousand tons (Hamilton). By the time of the American Revolution, tobacco accounted for approximately a sixth of the combined exports of all thirteen colonies (Hobhouse, p. 181).

Tobacco cultivation spread from Virginia south into the Carolinas and north around the Chesapeake Bay into what became Maryland and Delaware. The Chesapeake soon became famous throughout Europe as the source of the world's best tobacco. Farmers of the area specialized in two mild types of *Nicotiana tabacum,* known as Orinoco (named for the South American river where it originated) and Sweet-Scented.

With the development of the slavery-based plantation system to cultivate tobacco, a new social form was created and imposed on North America. Modeled after the Caribbean sugarcane plantations, which themselves derived from the ancient Roman *latifundia,* the newly created tobacco plantations of North America relied heavily on forced labor. This slavery system spread precisely to those places where tobacco grew best. The northern edge of the tobacco country ran roughly along the northern boundary of modern Maryland, and that became the Mason-Dixon Line, the traditional division between the slave states and the free states.

Farmers managed to grow commercial tobacco crops in only a few places outside of the South. Farmers in the Connecticut River valley planted tobacco, but their short growing season confined the practice to an area circumscribed by the river valley stretching in a small band from Connecticut through Massachusetts to the Vermont and New Hampshire border. This area produced a small amount of high-quality tobacco important in the manufacture of snuff and later of wrapping leaves for cigars. Because of the limited scale of production in this area, small farmers could handle the requisite work without resorting to slaves.

The French planted tobacco along the lower Mississippi River in their colony of Louisiana. Despite the changing ownership of this land among Spain, France, and Britain, it produced a half-million pounds of tobacco a year by the 1780s. The American colonists on the Atlantic pushed westward toward the Mississippi River, and planted tobacco throughout the intervening states of Kentucky and Tennessee, then crossed the Mississippi into Arkansas and Missouri.

Unfortunately for the North American colonists, tobacco grows easily in many different climates; so the colonists could not maintain a monopoly on it. Tobacco cultivation followed fairly closely behind the introduction of tobacco use across the Old World. Soon the farmers of Turkey, of the Ottoman holdings in southern Europe, and of Italy all had tobacco farms. African and Asian farmers quickly followed, producing enough tobacco to meet their local demand and to export some of their crop to Europe in competition with the American farmers. As the European powers colonized more of Africa and Asia, they imported their tobacco from their own colonies and not from the newly independent United States.

Throughout most of the nineteenth century, revenues from tobacco declined in the United States, but late in the century, the invention of the automatic cigarette-making machine temporarily revitalized tobacco cultivation in the United States and created a whole new industrial sector for the tobacco belt. North America has continued to be a major exporter of tobacco, but during the twentieth century, China became the world's largest producer and consumer of tobacco.

Natchez, Mississippi, is an odd little town that flourished for one brief moment of intense excitement just before the American Civil War, and since then nothing else has happened beyond the level of local gossip and an occasional murder. Natchez squats comfortably beside the Mississippi River in the land of catfish and beauty queens, a land of strong flavors and exaggerated gestures, where iced tea comes sweetened, sauces come peppered, and English or French words have extra vowels and missing consonants.

With such a large expanse of flat, rich land beside a gigantic river, this has always been the scene for dramas larger than life. In the nineteenth century, gangs of hundreds of brightly clothed slaves with cotton bags slung over their shoulders worked the fields in unison and retreated at the end of the day to plantation towns of thousands. The magnificent wealth of the planters in their grandiose houses contrasted dramatically with the shacks and unrivaled poverty of the blacks, the poorest people in America, even after they ceased being slaves. Such scenes of incredible excess and massive buildings amid unspeakable horror and suffering have long elicited the creativity of painters, film-makers, and writers of novels in which the characters never quite measure up to the scale of the bizarre social system and historical circumstances in which they thrived.

The rich black soils that washed downriver for millennia from the Dakotas, Iowa, and Minnesota had been deposited along the lower Mississippi River, and this land proved the best in America for the cultivation of cotton. In the late eighteenth century, when the industrial mills of England began to gobble up all the cotton British merchants could find, they developed a special appreciation for the soft, long strands of Mississippi delta cotton. Natchez served as the port connecting the delta cotton planters with the British textile manufacturers.

This brief boom ended with the Civil War. When the United States Navy successfully blockaded Southern ports, the Khedive Ismail of Egypt cleverly seized the opportunity to plant the rich Nile delta with the best American cottons. The Nile delta, covered with the rich earth washed down from Ethiopia and Uganda, proved just as fertile and hospitable to cotton as the Mississippi delta. The British manufacturers eagerly switched to this new supplier located closer to their ports and offering cheaper agricultural labor in a more politically tranquil country.

The American South languished as a backwater for the next century. While other parts of the South eventually found new crops and new ways to make money, Natchez clung tenaciously to the few trappings of a former boomtown. The rich merchants moved away, thus deserting their ostentatious houses built in those few short decades when money flowed so bountifully.

Every boomtown I have visited throughout the world displayed the same set of houses, no matter whether the place happened to be a rubber town in the Amazon jungle, an oil town in the Arabian desert, a henequen-fiber town in the Yucatán, a spice town in Zanzibar, or a cocaine town in the Andean mountains. The newly enriched merchants built homes that mimicked the palaces of Europe, and each newly rich planter or merchant tried to outdo the last one with an even more ostentatious building. They constructed Italian villas with imported marble, Tudor country homes with paneling ripped from real homes in England, French chateaux with crests carved into the stone archways, Moorish palaces with ornate fountains, and German castles copied directly from the drawings in Grimm's fairy tales. A few merchants have even sought to imitate some famous building and have erected a miniature Versailles, an oversized Mount Vernon, or a replica of the Taj Mahal. The buildings stand not as mere homes but as loud proclamations of wealth.

Once the architects of the boomtown have exhausted the stereotyped set of European building clichés, they reach for fantasy designs, often called "Oriental villas," which throw together motifs from ancient Constantinople, India, China, and the Arabian tales. One of Natchez's most unusual structures from the antebellum period, Longwood House, is an octagonal pagoda topped with a Muslim dome and trimmed in Victorian Italianate porches. The unfinished house now admits the public, and its tourist brochures proclaim it a "monument to the heart-rending break [sic] of the War of Southern Rebellion."

Dozens of such homes line the banks of the Mississippi around Natchez. Just as, a century and a half ago, each house screamed for attention to the dollars that went into building it, so today each house screams out through the advertisements around town, on billboards and in the local newspaper, for the tourist dollar to maintain it and to validate it as a building worthy of attention, even though nothing of historical importance ever happened there.

To support the cast of historical characters, the whole town devotes itself to an antebellum charade of affluence and refinement, a veritable amusement-park luxury. The town survives by entertaining factory workers from the North and by admitting the descendants of slaves and sharecroppers into its fancy rooms to eat and sleep and savor a life that existed more in Hollywood films than in historical reality. Natchez offers Americans that forbidden pleasure of pretending to be aristocratic, nonegalitarian, and gloriously rich. It survives as a place that elicits both derisive scorn and tremendous lust. It is a place of aristocratic paste and pretense.

Natchez illustrates how quickly and permanently the demand for native American crops such as cotton can transform a landscape. The demand for American products—tobacco and cotton from North America, henequen from Mexico, rubber from the Amazon, and coca from the Andes—traditionally arose in tidal waves that brought fast but temporary riches before crashing just as quickly as they arose. They left behind boomtowns, but they also created substantial wealth that helped to finance other commercial enterprises. The modern town of Natchez may be a moribund monument, but the entire economy of the modern South survives as a living and prospering descendent of the wealth that cotton produced.

Cotton failed to surpass tobacco cultivation in the United States until sometime in the 1820s. Prior to that time, cotton came mostly from the small holdings of white families who owned and worked their own subsistence farms, with cotton supplying a modest amount of cash. Not a single cotton plantation existed as late as the year 1800, but following the mechanization of the ginning process, cotton changed from a small-farm product into a plantation crop produced by slaves.

The plantation owners of the southern fringe of the tobacco belt found that in addition to growing good tobacco, their land could produce the best cotton in the world. South Carolina, Tennessee, and Mississippi quickly abandoned tobacco for cotton, which also grew in areas such as Georgia and Alabama, where tobacco had never been very successfully grown.

In 1820 the United States produced about 400,000 bales of cotton, or about 200 million pounds. By 1861, on the eve of the Civil War, this had increased to 4 million bales or about 2 billion pounds of cotton, with a value of nearly $200 million. During this time of expansion, African slaves brought approximately 10 million acres of the American South into cultivation for their plantation owners. Cotton exceeded the combined total of all other American exports, including agricultural, manufactured, and natural resources (Hobhouse, p. 154).

At the beginning of the Civil War, nearly a thousand mills in the Northern states produced $55 million in cotton products, a massive sum in the mid-nineteenth century. Yet these Northern mills could only consume a quarter of the Southern cotton crop. Another 11 percent of the crop went to French mills, and the remaining 60 percent went to English mills. Cotton ranked as the most valuable export on the world market, and approximately 80 percent of the world's cotton exports grew in the United States (Hobhouse, p. 176).

From South Carolina straight across the lands of the Creek,

Seminole, Cherokee, Choctaw, and Chickasaw to Texas, the plantations took over the Indian farms and made them into a single, almost uninterrupted cotton field. Because the planters took the lands from the Indians by trickery when possible and by force when necessary, the land remained cheap. The planters then used it like a disposable resource rather than a renewable one.

As soon as the land wore out, usually within a decade or so, the planters moved their slaves and equipment farther west, into new Indian lands. The planters quickly depleted the soils of South Carolina and Georgia, forcing their children to move on to new plantations in Alabama and Mississippi. In the southeastern United States, only the coastal plantations of the exceptionally fertile Sea Islands of Georgia and South Carolina continued to produce high profits from cotton.

The planters acquired land more easily than they acquired slaves, who could no longer be legally imported into America after 1808, in accordance with the United States Constitution. With the shortage of field hands, South Carolina and Georgia became breeding grounds for slaves to supply the insatiable labor appetites of the new plantations farther west (Hobhouse, p. 161). The number of slaves in the United States grew from less than a million at the time of American independence from Britain to 4 million at the time of the Civil War, less than a century later. The Southern states probably had more money invested in slaves than in all their land combined.

The United States supplied seven-eighths of Britain's cotton before the Civil War (Hamilton). The cotton from Natchez was shipped down to New Orleans and across the ocean to the textile mills of Britain. Britain became the world's greatest producer of textiles, and had such close ties to the Southern states that the Southerners hoped for British intervention in the Civil War. Had the Confederate States of America become truly independent of the Washington government, it would most certainly have become an economic if not a political colony of Great Britain.

Rather than becoming an economic colony of Britain, the Southern states of the United States became an economic colony of the Northern states, which could monopolize Southern cotton for their own burgeoning textile industry. By 1872 the Southern states were producing as much cotton as they had before the Civil War.

The new cotton came from a reorganized agricultural system of sharecropping, which replaced the slave labor of the plantations. The sharecroppers included poor laborers, many of whom were freed slaves, but the majority of whom were poor and landless whites.

In the post–Civil War era, the revenues for cotton came not merely from the fiber itself but from newly developed uses for the by-products, which exceeded the value of the raw fiber in some years. Each bale of cotton weighed about five hundred pounds, but the ginning also produced massive quantities of seed and other by-products. The oil from the seed went into industrial processing for making soap, lamp oil, and edible oil. The cotton meal or "cake" remaining after the extraction of oil could be used as fuel, as fertilizer to restore nitrogen to the soil, or as animal feed (Hobhouse, p. 184).

Today, dinosaurs of farm machinery menacingly prowl the fields and backroads across the Mississippi delta. Mile-long mobile irrigation pipes look like serpents slithering across the fields on wheels, slowly watering the sun-blistered land. Cotton pickers, like green monsters as tall as telephone poles and wider than the length of a bus, stalk the cotton fields, whose length must be measured in miles. The great machines swallow rows of cotton faster than the largest slave gang with the fiercest slave drivers. After devouring the white cotton bolls, the behemoths disgorge them into large containers so that another long-armed machine can push and pack them like the arms of a gigantic spider wrapping its prey in silk. These gigantic cotton bales hold tons of cotton and can accommodate the equivalent of dozens of the old cotton bales that used to be taken down to the levy for shipment.

Today these gigantic bales travel in sixteen-wheel trucks that have replaced the farm pickup. The trucks prowl the backcountry roads that were not made for vehicles so large or heavy. When it rains, the trucks stick in the mud of the soft shoulders along the road, and bog down in the muddy fields and slide into the ditches that drain them. Their engines groan and their wheels squeal uselessly as they spray mud all around and strain to free themselves from the great bogs like dinosaurs trapped in a tar pit.

Dotted across the landscape, large cotton gins rise up like tin mountains. Laid out in neat rows in front of them, beneath plastic sheets to protect them from the rains, the gigantic cotton bales wait to be ginned. Like huge larvae individually wrapped and lined up, they sometimes stretch for miles and will one day make thousands of miles of cloth.

In the late summer and early autumn, the plains of the delta seem as white as the plains of Manitoba in January. Anyone who has seen the delta during cotton time understands the constant allusion of the Confederate poet laureate William Gilmore Simms to "the southern snows of summer"—an almost frightening whiteness. The white cotton covers the fields and litters the sides of the highway, obscuring even the grass. Road signs and the limbs of trees snag tufts of cotton from the air, creating the illusion of an ice storm. The only relief from the whiteness comes in an occasional line of laundry hung out to flap in the wind like Tibetan prayer flags strung over a glacial pass.

Natchez no longer enjoys the great wealth it once did, and the plantation system has gone with the wind, but cotton remains. It continues as one of the most important of the United States' agricultural crops, although not nearly as lucrative a crop as it once was.

Nowhere does North America's abiding agricultural debt to the Indians appear more clearly than at the state fair. This celebration starts in August in the far northern states and drifts south until the start of Christmas season. Farmers and politicians nudge their way through machinery exhibits and civic displays to see the best of the nation's agriculture, machinery, and youth. Housewives bring out their best blueberry pies, pickled tomatoes, and dahlia arrangements. A visitor can see things at the fair that never seem to appear anywhere else in America: a pumpkin the size of a Japanese car; the crop-art portraits of John Kennedy and Martin Luther King made of sunflower and cotton seeds; thumbnail-sized doughnuts and lifesize sculptures of the Dairy Princesses cut from hundred-pound blocks of yellow butter.

On display at the fair are some of the crops the settlers brought to America from Africa, Asia, and Europe. These include wheat, oats, cabbage, turnips, rice, citrus fruits, apples, and almost all of the farm animals.

The great majority of crops exhibited and eaten at the fair came originally from American Indian agriculture. The native crops include tomatoes and potatoes; all the squashes and pump-kins; almost all the kinds of beans; peanuts, pecans, hickory nuts, black walnuts, sunflower seeds, cranberries, blueberries, strawber-ries, maple syrup, and Jerusalem artichokes; all the peppers, prickly pears, chocolate, vanilla, allspice, sassafras, avocados, wild rice, and sweet potatoes. In the four hundred years since the Euro-pean settlers began coming to North America, they have not found a single America plant suitable for domestication that the Indians had not already cultivated.

By the last decade of the twentieth century, crops of Indian origin constituted approximately one-third of the annual harvest of the United States. Corn alone accounted for nearly 15 percent of the cash receipts from all crops. According to USDA figures published in 1989, in addition to corn, cotton, and tobacco, the American Indian crops of potatoes, tomatoes, and peanuts each had cash sales in excess of a billion dollars, with sunflower seeds closely trailing them. American Indian crops formed the basis on which the powerful agricultural economies of the United States and Canada developed and matured.

In contrast to the important role played by American Indian crops, animals domesticated by the Indians had a less impressive role in either the international or local markets. The greatest impact came from the turkey, which is still growing in importance within the United States. Following the decline in tobacco cultiva-tion, North Carolina, which once led the nation in tobacco acre-age, became the leading producer of turkeys in the United States in 1990, followed closely by Minnesota. Turkey sales grew to a little more than 2 percent of total U.S. livestock and poultry sales in the early 1990s.

Even today, when the United States suffers under an astronomi-cal trade imbalance, crops of Indian origin still supply some of our most desired exports. While we consume a seemingly endless flow of European and Asian automobiles, textiles, and electronic geegaws, the world is not buying our industrial products in return. Foreign markets want our farm produce and its by-products: corn, corn oil, corn syrup, cotton, cotton oil, cottonseed, sunflower seeds and oil, tobacco, potatoes, peanuts, and dozens of other crops given to us by the American Indians.

10

THE TRADE IN INDIAN SLAVES

At the Santa Barbara Mission, before the sun rises and before the noisy traffic begins the daily commute down the mountain to work in the town below, a visitor can almost hear the whispered groans of the thousands of Chumash who lie buried in unmarked graves in the mission graveyard. The mission exudes an eerie quiet in the early-morning stillness. The night fog recedes back toward the ocean after providing the meager moisture for the imported trees and plants that suck droplets of mist from the damp night air. The lingering fog obscures the rising sun, making it hard to tell exactly when day begins, but gradually light descends and the rays mop up the air to reveal a spectacular view of the town and ocean below.

The Mission of Santa Barbara sits a few miles inland and upward from the ocean, in the mouth of a canyon lined with stately coastal live oaks and sturdy sycamores with bark so pale that at night they look almost like birches. The classical white but somewhat squat façade of the mission reflects an Italian influence that gives it the most European and least rustic appearance of all the California missions. The nearly pink trim gives the building a sugary appearance, like a gingerbread house trimmed in pink icing. This polished and classically worked face earned the building the sobriquet of "Queen of the Missions."

The mission overlooks the red tile roofs and earth-toned walls of one of the most beautiful towns in the world, a place where even the Mormon, Unitarian, and Christian Scientist churches show the graceful architecture of colonial Spanish chapels. Tall, elegant palms and spindly eucalyptus line the roads, where the luxuriant vegetation gives a natural elegance to even the most modest home. The higher up the hills one climbs around the mission, the more expensive the homes become as they acquire a better view of the ocean, more extensive landscaping, larger swimming pools, longer driveways, higher gates, and better-illuminated tennis courts.

Inside the simple mission, a flickering candle burns before the altar. According to tradition, a candle has been burning at that altar without interruption for over two centuries. An expansive wrought-iron chandelier dominates the dank, cavernous interior. The gift shop in the mission plays religious music, Gregorian chants or the thin tunes of the "folk mass" in English.

The Chumash who once lived here have virtually disappeared, but their memory permeates the hillside. Four thousand Indian graves, mostly of Chumash, now surround the mission as a reminder of the great price paid for this place and this building by the natives who lived here for thousands of years. But the mission does not house the memory of these people. That memory and a few physical artifacts of the Chumash now find refuge in the nearby Santa Barbara Natural History Museum.

The missions of California symbolize the Spanish colonial era, but the missions originated as Spanish settlements built in Indian communities as places where the Indians could learn about Christianity and in the process learn about the European way of life. During most of the time when Spain controlled this area, Spanish colonists evidenced little interest in living in California, because Mexico offered much better lands and easier fortunes. Several halfhearted attempts to colonize California failed because the area proved simply too far from Mexico and the center of commerce, power, and social life. For a Mexican colonist, living in California was living in distant exile.

The Spanish authorities took serious notice of California only after the Russians colonized Alaska in the eighteenth century and threatened to move down the Pacific Coast to California. Suddenly faced with the possibility of losing the whole northern Pacific Coast to the Russians much the way they had already lost the northern Atlantic Coast to the British, the Spanish powers in Mexico City finally decided to settle and defend the California coast.

Before the Russians could extend their power south to California, the Spaniards sought to erect a series of forts, but they needed a regular supply of food, cloth, leather, and skilled workers. California lay too far from Mexico to depend on regular shipments of such materials. To supply its forts without having to send in reluctant Mexican colonists, the government devised a plan centered on the Franciscan monks. The friars would convert the Indians, who would then serve the needs of the forts. In this way the financially constrained monarchy of Spain defended what remained of its land claim on the Pacific, and the church forced the Indians to bear the economic burden of this military force.

The Franciscan missionary Miguel José Serra, better known as Junípero Serra, who was already working in Baja California, gladly accepted the challenge to build missions near the forts in Alta California. Between 1769 and his death in 1784, he established nine California missions starting at San Diego and Monterey, and then filling in with more missions, each about one hard day's walk from another. Eventually, twenty-one missions stretched from San Diego in the south to Sonoma, north of San Francisco. The forts and the supporting missions gave the government of New Spain its first visible presence in California.

Before the Spaniards could build a mission at Santa Barbara, they built the Presidio, a military fort, which Father Serra dedicated and blessed on April 21, 1782. The Presidio was erected to subdue the Indians who interfered with mail transmissions along El Camino Real, the "royal road" connecting northern and southern California. Another four and a half years passed before the military controlled the area firmly enough to allow work to begin on the mission in December 1786.

The friars and the soldiers worked together to capture the coastal Chumash and settle them into a life of mission servitude.

Once the Indians consented to baptism, they were irrevocably tied to the mission and to the authority of the friars. The missionaries forced the Indians to clear the land, to farm it, to build mission buildings, to dress in cloth, and to worship the Christian God, the Virgin, and the saints.

The mission offered no school, but its friars taught the Chumash to work. Women wove blankets all day in workshops set up beside the mission. They also ground corn in rows of stone metates, and they cooked the mission's food. The assembly-line nature of their work shows clearly in the laundry pit still standing in front of the mission but now made much more attractive with flowers floating in the pond and turtles swimming amid the pigeons that use it as a large birdbath. Chumash women once lined the sides of the long trough in their ceaseless pounding and scrubbing of piles of laundry.

Men who did not work in the fields built an elaborate system of stone-lined aqueducts, canals, dams, and drainage ditches, some of which still function today to bring water to the modern residents of Santa Barbara. Other men made tiles, tanned leather, dipped candles, and performed the other tasks that transformed their environment from an Indian world to a miniaturized model of a Spanish colonial community. The mission has none of the stateliness or mechanical wizardry of the contemporary settlement Old Williamsburg in Virginia. By comparison, the austere and rustic qualities of the mission settlement show that it was built for work and worship, but not for the daily enjoyments of domestic or urban life.

Junípero Serra and his Franciscan successors concentrated their missions along the coast, which gave them easier access by sea back to Mexico. In this way the Spanish authorities occupied the most fertile strip of California. Prior to the Spanish arrival, the combination of wild foods growing near the shore, the seafood available from the ocean, and the animals living in this thin fertile strip had provided a luxurious living for the Indians for thousands of years.

At the Santa Barbara Mission, which operated as one of the most lenient and enlightened of all the missions, the Indians had time off to gather traditional wild foods in the fall and to visit relatives throughout the year. Nevertheless, the friars whipped the

Chumash for violations of the strict and seemingly arbitrary rules of monastic life. They also imprisoned the Indians in stocks, shackles, and chains.

At night the friars locked unmarried Chumash women in a large room (Forbes 1964, p. 76). This sleeping arrangement kept the Chumash men apart from the Chumash women, but did not keep the Spanish soldiers away from the women. According to a denunciation of the harsh conditions written by Santa Barbara friars Esteban Tapis and Juan Cortés in 1800, the soldiers used the women as prostitutes and paid the malnourished women with simple food (Forbes 1964, p. 79). Such treatment of women seems to have been common throughout southern California and to have caused a high rate of venereal infection among Indian women as well as creating a new generation of mixed Spanish-Indian offspring (John R. Johnson, 1989).

In return for their labor, the Indians received no pay other than the food and clothing necessary to keep them fit for more work; the profits accrued to the missions. The Indians lived in a series of barracks lined up in military fashion next to the mission. The individual family units measured twelve by eighteen feet. Visitors to the modern mission can no longer see the shoddy Indian residences, which disintegrated long ago, but surviving blueprints seem to presage a modern military or work camp lined with identical barracks.

The Chumash inmates wore uniform blue clothing made at the mission. Those men appointed by the friars as leaders separated themselves from the people under them by wearing some items of leather and clothing of Spanish design. While the friars ate baked bread and meat, the daily ration for the Indians consisted of *atole,* a corn mush, for breakfast and supper, supplemented by some vegetables and meat flavoring at noon. The friars imposed a strict regimen with rules to control every aspect of the Indians' family life, work, sexual relations, celebrations, and clothing.

The only escape for the Indians who wished to avoid mission slavery came through a dangerous flight into the interior of California, into the waste areas, the dry hills and canyons, or into the desert, where the shortage of food and water and the oppressive heat made life difficult. Many Indians fled there, and many of them died, but today virtually the only Indian groups left in California are descended from those who lived in the interior. All the tribes who lived where Father Serra built his missions have effectively disappeared.

At the time the missions began in California, approximately seventy thousand Indians inhabited the coast from San Francisco to San Diego. By the time the Mexican government secularized the missions in 1833–35, the friars had reduced the native population to a mere fifteen thousand (Forbes 1964, p. 76).

The leatherbound book of baptisms at Santa Barbara carefully records in neat handwriting the names of all the Indians brought under Spanish authority. The book contains 373 leaves, each listing some of the Christian names of the 4,771 Indian adults and infants baptized between 1786 and 1858.

An equally large burial registry lists the deaths. Only a few months after the first baptism, a Chumash man named Ysaga (but changed to Agustin) of the community of Saspili (changed to Goleta) died and became the first name in the burial registry. By 1841 the friars had filled the Indian burial registry with 3,997 entries, and they had to begin recording deaths in the back pages of the burial book for whites. Fertility among Chumash women declined, child mortality increased steadily, and most of these entries represented children and infants killed by European diseases (John R. Johnson, 1989). By 1872, when registration ceased, the Indian death list had reached 4,645 entries. At each of the Franciscan monasteries established in California, the number of deaths exceeded the number of births as the Spaniards captured and brought in Indians who failed to thrive or even to reproduce.

Of those who died at the Santa Barbara Mission, about four thousand found burial in large pits next to the church. Whenever one of the troughlike pits filled up, the friars had the Indians dig out the layers of bones and deposit them in a charnel house to make room in the pits for new bodies. In a macabre twist of someone's sense of decoration, two of the skulls from the graveyard were mounted on the wall of the church with crossed thighbones beneath them to create a skull-and-crossbones motif above the doorway.

Today a simple wooden sign with white lettering on a black background commemorates the Chumash who lie buried in the courtyard. The large stone vaults and headstones of the cemetery, however, do not belong to the Chumash. They mark the resting places of families with illustrious Spanish surnames, as well as the graves of Irish settlers and New England Yankees who immigrated into the area after it fell to American control.

As the Indians cleared the land and brought it into cultivation for crops or cattle, Mexican colonists moved north to take over the land. Indians continued to die from European diseases aggravated by the hard work and the disruption of their tribal culture. Those who survived did so by surrendering their native language to Spanish, giving up their religion for Catholicism, and casting off nearly every vestige of Indian culture to become hispanicized even to the point of disclaiming Indian descent in favor of Spanish.

An exhibit in the Santa Barbara Mission dryly and naïvely explains the disappearance of the Chumash. "Conflicts arose between the missionaries and soldiers, and between soldiers and Indians. Health-related problems and opposing ethnic practices proved a detriment to the Chumash. . . . The remaining Chumash have been integrated into the American way of life." Some unknown hand corrected the sign by penciling in the prefix "dis"- before the word "integrated."

Of all the Indians who disappeared into the mission system, mystery still surrounds the cryptic Spanish entry number 1183 in the Santa Barbara Mission death registry dated October 19, 1853. "I gave ecclesiastical burial in this cemetery to the mortal remains of Juana Maria, an Indian brought from San Nicolas Island, and since there was no one who understood her language she was baptized conditionally by Father Sanchez." Those few lines serve as a memorial to a whole people whose entire language and even their very name disappeared with only this small entry in a book of deaths.

The subject of the entry was not Chumash; she was a Channel Island woman who had been abandoned on her native island by an 1835 expedition to capture Indians and settle them around the missions. She may well have been a survivor or daughter of the women who massacred the Russian men a generation earlier. For nearly two decades the woman had lived alone on San Nicolas, the traditional home of the Gabrielino, who spoke a Uto-Aztecan language unrelated to Chumash. She supported herself by hunting small animals, gathering food along the shore, and making baskets, clothes, knives, fishhooks, needles, ropes, and fur capes. In 1853 some American adventurers led by Captain George Nidever found her and brought her to the mission.

She had managed to survive alone, in the worst of circumstances, on a deserted island, but in the intervening years since the mission raiders had taken away the other people of San Nicolas Island, none of the Indians brought to the mission had lived. Within seven weeks after her transfer to the mission, she too lay dead without having found anyone with whom she could talk, to whom she could tell her story of how she lived. No one ever found out her name—so they called her Juana Maria.

According to the oral tradition at the mission, the friars gathered all of Juana Maria's interesting tools and creations and sent them to the Vatican in Rome, but no written record remains of what happened to these unique cultural items. They have disappeared along with all other physical remains of the mysterious woman.

The friars buried Juana Maria, like all the other Indians, in one of their Indian pits, so that today we have no idea where in the cemetery her bones might be. In 1928 the Santa Barbara Daughters of the American Revolution installed a small bronze plaque on the mission wall to commemorate the Indian woman of unknown name.

The true name of Juana Maria has been lost, as have the names of many of the settlements along the southern California coast. A few Chumash place names, such as *Malibu* Beach, Point *Magu*, Port *Hueneme,* and *Saticoy,* survive in southern California, but most have yielded to Spanish or English names.

The labor of Indians opened up California to Mexican colonists, who further improved it and then yielded it to Anglo colonists, who may in their turn have to surrender it to yet others. These Indians were not legally slaves, but for moral and practical purposes, there is little distinction between a slave and someone forced to work for an occupying invader.

The importance of Indian slaves in the opening of the land was not a phenomenon unique to California; it was only better organized there. The same process of Indian slavery underlay the development of the English colonies along the Atlantic, and the French colonies along the St. Lawrence and Mississippi rivers.

Indian slavery prepared most parts of North America for coloni-zation. Christopher Columbus started this practice by kidnapping twenty-five Indians whom he took back to Spain with him as slaves. A few years later, when he was pressed to make a profit from his voyages, and had found little gold or spices with which to do so, he began shipping Caribbean Indians back to Spain to be sold in the Portuguese Azores, the Spanish Canaries, and the markets of Seville and other mainland cities.

Miguel de Cuneo, a member of Columbus's second expedition, described one of their slave raids in 1495, writing that of 1,600 Indian slaves, only 550 fit into the ships. The men staying on the island divided up most of those who remained. Of the 550 slaves shipped out on February 17, 1495, 200 died at sea and were thrown into the ocean (Forbes 1988, p. 24). De Cuneo also men-tions that Columbus gave him an attractive Carib woman whom he managed to rape only after a long fight and a thorough beating.

Columbus pursued a deliberate policy of using Indian slavery and Indian labor to finance the conquest of the new lands (Forbes 1988, p. 22). Within the first decade of Columbus's arrival, the Spaniards had shipped out at least three thousand Indian slaves, and possibly as many as six thousand, to Seville (Forbes 1988, p. 24). In addition to the thousands sold in Europe, Columbus enslaved many times that number for use in the early mines and plantations of the Caribbean.

Columbus set a precedent that virtually every other explorer followed in the succeeding years: he financed his explorations by trading in the flesh of captured Indian slaves. When John Cabot made his official discovery of North America for the English crown in 1497, he too seized a few Indians to take back with him to Europe. Cabot arrived on the North American coast 123 years before the first successful English colony, and throughout this time explorers, traders, and fishermen raided the American shoreline for slaves, whom they picked up seemingly as a way to earn a little pocket money in between their major activities. A few Indian slaves could be sold in the Caribbean for food or supplies for one's ship, or a few slaves taken back to Europe could help defray some of the costs of the expedition. Slaves collected on one expedi-tion and sold in Europe helped to finance the next expedition.

Columbus and the other Spanish slave traders incurred quick opposition from the monarchy, particularly Queen Isabella, who insisted that the Indians of the New World belonged to the monarchy and thus could not be sold in Spain. This only encouraged the traders to sell the slaves in other places, notably the islands including the Canaries, Azores, and Cape Verdes. Increasingly the new planters in the Caribbean wanted to keep the slaves in America for use on their plantations, and the exporting of slaves declined quickly.

By 1519 the Spaniards had nearly exhausted the supply of Indian slaves in the Caribbean. A letter from that year can still be seen today in the Gilcrease Museum in Tulsa, Oklahoma. The paper still looks fresh, and the ink has faded to the brown hue of rich Moroccan leather. In a curly and elegant handwriting that must have been that of a scribe, Diego Columbus, the son of Christopher, beseeched King Charles V of Spain for permission to import African slaves to replace the depleted supply of Indians. This letter reveals the earliest known official request to import Africans to the Americas, and with the elegant strokes on that page began three centuries of the cruel commerce across the mid-Atlantic.

The Portuguese, English, Dutch, and French followed quickly behind the Spaniards in the effort to enslave native Americans. In 1500, Gaspar Côrte-Real, a Portuguese explorer from Terceira, in the Azores, sailed up the northern Atlantic Coast to what is now Labrador, where he encountered the Nasquapee or Naskapi people, sixty of whom he immediately captured and took back to Lisbon for sale as slaves. According to some accounts, King Manoel called this land *Terra del Laboratore*, "the land of the workers," or, more freely translated, "the slave coast," and from this inauspicious remark arose the modern name of Labrador. Equally plausible stories offer other etymologies of the name (Grenfell 1909, p. 10). Regardless of the true etymology, the story illustrates how common the practice of enslavement became in America.

Côrte-Real made his third trip to America in 1502, but disappeared while at sea. His brother set out in search of him, and he too disappeared without a trace. Perhaps they died trying to enslave another group of natives in Labrador or somewhere else on the American coast. Perhaps the explorers of a rival European monarch killed them. Or perhaps nature herself destroyed them, but until now no trace of either of them, or their boats and crews, has been found.

In 1524, Juan (or Giovanni) Verrazano explored the North American mainland for the French crown, and captured slaves on his voyages; Jacques Cartier continued the explorations and the Indian enslavement in 1535. In the seventeenth century the French, who made an alliance with the Hurons but failed to do so with the Iroquois, captured Iroquois and sold them to work as galley slaves for the king (Forbes 1988, p. 53).

One of the first of the North American Indian slaves to have his name passed on to posterity was Squanto, the Wampanoag who helped the Pilgrim settlers of Massachusetts. In 1614 or 1615, before the Pilgrims arrived in New England, the English slave trader Thomas Hunt raided the Wampanoag village of Patuxet and seized Squanto. Hunt carried Squanto and twenty-seven other Indians across the Atlantic and sold him in the Spanish port of Málaga on the Mediterranean, about sixty miles northeast of Gibraltar.

Squanto subsequently escaped from slavery and gradually worked his way back to Massachusetts via England and Newfoundland, only to find his village of Patuxet deserted from the combined devastation of slave raids and the epidemic that Hunt's sailors left behind among the survivors of the raid (Forbes 1988, p. 55).

Despite the great services rendered them by Squanto and a few of the other surviving Indians from the coast, the Pilgrims not only continued but expanded the Indian slave trade in the area. War, slave raids, and disease already had eradicated most of the natives along the Massachusetts coast, and the Pilgrims made war on those who survived. In the winter of 1636 they attacked the Pequots of what is now Connecticut, and by the spring of 1637 they had thoroughly defeated them. The colonists of Massachusetts and Connecticut divided the Indian prisoners. The Massachusetts victors sold their slaves for cash, while the Connecticut colonists kept theirs for domestic service.

The Pilgrim settlers enslaved the remnants of the tribe and shipped them out for sale. The Pilgrims could not, however, send them to England. As early as 1596 and again in 1601, Queen

Elizabeth had exiled all dark-skinned people from her realm. This expulsion order included "negars and blackamoores" as well as Indians. Most of the slaves in Britain at that time had to be removed to the British possessions in the Americas (Forbes 1988, p. 55). Since the Pilgrims could not sell their Pequot slaves in England, they sent them to market in Bermuda.

The New England colonists sold some of the Indian slaves across the Atlantic in Europe and even in Africa. In 1683 a shipment of Indians was abandoned in the Algiers slave market after the Muslims refused to buy them (Lauber, p. 127). Other reports list Indian slaves sold in Morocco, along the west coast of Africa, and in the Canaries, the Azores, and the Cape Verde Islands.

As the colonists grew stronger, they engaged in larger wars and attacked larger Indian tribes. In the winter of 1675, the New England Confederation of Massachusetts, Plymouth, Rhode Island, and Connecticut made war on the Wampanoag, who were then led by Metacom, a leader whom the English named King Philip. After a series of brutal victories by the English at Narragansett in December 1675, at Deerfield in May 1676, and near Bridgewater Swamp in August 1676, the colonists assassinated Metacom. With the defeat of the Indian armies and the killing of their leader, the English began their slave raids on the survivors.

The colonists cleaned out large new areas of land for themselves by enslaving the Indians and selling them in Spain and the Caribbean. They executed older males, selling only the younger Indians of both sexes into slavery. By colonial law the English allowed themselves not only to enslave soldiers caught in battle, but to enslave the wives and children of any hostile Indians as well. After a brief biblical debate as to whether a son should be called to account for his father's acts, the colonial officials even seized the widow and son of Metacom and sold them for thirty shillings apiece in the West Indies (Waldman, p. 92).

Massachusetts law allowed owners to brand Indian slaves to prevent their escape. The owners often pricked a letter or symbol onto the cheek or forehead of a slave and then filled the figure with gunpowder and Indian ink to leave a combination of a brand and a tattoo (Lauber, p. 261).

By selling the survivors and the land of the Indians, the Pilgrims financed another phase in their colonization of New England. The

Indians could literally finance their own destruction as the colonists sold the Indian victims and land of one campaign to finance the next campaign, which always penetrated a little deeper into America.

Just as Boston became the major slave market for the northern Indians, Charleston, South Carolina, became the major market in the south. Even before the founding of the Charleston colony, slave raiders such as William Hilton seized slaves for the Caribbean plantations from along the Carolina coast in 1663. With the founding of Charleston in 1670, the port became the primary exit point for Southern slaves, particularly the Cherokee, Creek, and Choctaw.

The Charleston merchants soon had long trade lines that stretched across the Southern states to the Mississippi River. Initially they relied heavily on warfare and kidnapping as the means to capture Indian slaves. In time they encouraged their Indian allies to do the difficult work and then to sell the captives to the whites in exchange for cheap trade goods. As Gary Nash described the situation in the 1760s, "Slave coffles were marching through the Carolina backcountry to the coast as much as they were filing through the African interior to the trading posts on the African coast" (Nash, p. 113).

The Carolina settlers continued the well-established economic pattern initiated by Columbus by using Indian slavery to finance new wars of conquest. They used Indians to fight Indians, then enslaved the losers to finance the next campaign. This strategy found frank expression in a letter of April 9, 1754, from Indian trader Matthew Toole to South Carolina's governor, James Glen. In asking for permission to use one group of Indians to fight another, Toole writes that "[w]e want no Pay, only what we can take and plunder, what Slaves we take to be our own of Indians" (Washburn, p. 245).

In New England, where agriculture played a less important role in the economy, and where the economy suffered chronic labor shortages of many types, the settlers used the Indians in manual trades. Eighteenth-century newspapers in New England carried advertisements announcing the availability for hire or sale of Indian as well as African craftsmen including carpenters, coopers, wheelwrights, and butchers (Lauber, p. 244).

Indian women sold or reared in slavery learned domestic tasks that usually kept them working in a single household for years. The type of work they performed appears readily in an advertisement in the *Boston News Letter* of January 5, 1719. It offered for sale an Indian woman "fit for all manner of household work either in town or country, can sew, wash, brew, bake, spin and milk cows." An advertisement from the *American Weekly Mercury* of April 10, 1729, offered a woman and her child for sale. The advertisement boasted that the woman "washes, irons, and starches very well, and is a good cook."

Indian slaves also found themselves impressed into work as sailors and soldiers by virtually every European nation with whom they came into contact. Law required slaveholders to furnish their slaves for combat in times of emergency. Owners who lost slaves in battle received compensation from public coffers or received newly captured slaves to replace the dead ones.

As late as 1778, during the American Revolution, Washington requested slaves for his battalions. The Rhode Island assembly responded by mustering all Indian, mulatto, and Negro slaves with the promise of eventual freedom for them, if the Americans won the war against the British (Lauber, p. 248).

Along the Canadian coast, the French followed a practice different from that of the English. Even though the first African slave went up for sale in Quebec in 1629, Canadian slavery centered primarily on the Pawnee people. In contrast to British settlers, who preferred African slaves, French settlers in Canada preferred Native American ones. As late as 1760, the Treaty of Montreal recognized African and Pawnee slavery in Canada, and thus the Pawnee became known as the "Negroes of America" (Davis, p. 179). Most of the African slaves brought into Canada came after 1783 with British loyalists fleeing the American Revolution. Even though the English outlawed the slave trade in England in 1772, they did not extend the ban on slavery to Canada until August 1, 1834.

At first, Indian slavery provided a lucrative, albeit episodic, source of income to colonists, who harvested and sold villages of people much the way they did stands of pine or colonies of beaver. The Indians formed part of the natural resources of the rich North American continent. As the colonists became more settled, and as their small colonial villages grew into seaports and they found agricultural crops that they could sell, they began to value the Indians less as a source of income from a one-time sale, and to see them as a source of labor that would produce an income for years and even decades.

In the early years of Indian slavery, the colonists frequently wanted to dispose of their newly captured slaves as quickly as possible by shipping them far away. This reduced the danger of the Indians escaping back to their home villages or being rescued by their kinsmen. As the colonists grew stronger and the Indian nations weaker, the colonists often simply exchanged slaves with another colony. The distance often sufficed to keep the Indian slaves from escaping, and many slaves feared escape because of the presence of Indians hostile to the tribes from which they had been seized.

Americans imported Africans almost from the founding of the earliest settlements, but African slaves had to be transported over thousands of miles of ocean to the Caribbean, and then up the Atlantic Coast. In the early eighteenth century an African cost twice the price of a Native American, and the cost of a healthy African male stayed perpetually high compared to that of a Native American (Forbes 1964, p. 91). North American settlers lacked the rich resources of the Caribbean sugar planters, whose demand for African labor was as inexhaustible as their income from their lucrative sugar trade.

Unable to buy the large numbers of African slaves that they wanted, the early colonists started their plantations with a heavy reliance on the much cheaper and easier-to-obtain Indian slaves. Africans remained the slaves of choice primarily because they had immunity or resistance to many of the diseases that killed Indians—particularly malaria, which the Europeans brought with them very early to the swamps of the American south. Unlike the Indians, who still lived on their home continent, the Africans could virtually never return home to their native people.

As late as 1709, Indians made up one-quarter of all slaves in South Carolina (Lauber, p. 106). In 1708, Captain Thomas Nairne, explaining the importance of Indian slavery in the Carolinas, wrote that the colonists enslaved the Indians because they feared that the French to the west might arm the Indians if the English colonists did not enslave them (Forbes 1964, p. 90). By the middle of the eighteenth century, the Southern colonies focused on a few lucrative plantation crops such as tobacco, indigo, rice, and eventually cotton; from these the planters acquired the financial resources to compete with the sugar planters of the Caribbean and to buy increasingly large numbers of Africans.

By the time of the American Revolution, African slavery had largely replaced Indian slavery in the thirteen colonies. Many Indians had been absorbed into the slave population, and relatively few free natives still lived in the colonies. Planters found it easier and cheaper to buy freshly imported Africans at American docks than to finance lengthy and dangerous expeditions into the continental interior to capture Indians.

Indian slavery continued to flourish, however, in the western part of North America, still under Spanish domination. The slave trade in Mexico started with the conquest of the Aztec empire by Cortez, and quickly spread north. As early as the 1560s, Spanish slave-raiding expeditions reached Texas. In 1581, Gaspar de Luxan led a slave raid into La Junta, along the Texas border, and in the following year Espejo-Beltran took an expedition into New Mexico (Forbes 1964, p. 89). Most of these Indian slaves ended as laborers in the silver mines and ranches of Mexico or in the plantations of the Yucatán, where the slaves grew henequen, the thick-leafed tropical plants used to make a coarse, reddish fiber for ropes and twine.

Throughout the seventeenth century, the Pueblo Indians of the upper Rio Grande valley fell victim to repeated slave raids and to enslavement meted out to them as punishment by secular authorities. The Spaniards usually marched the captive Pueblos downstream to El Paso for sale to rancher colonists, or for work deeper in the Mexican interior.

Slavery as practiced legally in the early United States was technically illegal in Spanish-controlled lands, but Spanish administrators devised cunning ways of overcoming this legal restriction. After the reconquest of the Acoma Pueblo in January 1599, the Spaniards sentenced males and females above the age of twelve to twenty years of personal servitude. Males above the age of twenty-five endured the additional punishment of having one foot amputated by a Spanish sword before beginning their servitude (Forbes 1960, p. 91). The church distributed children under the age of twelve to work as servants for families of Mexican Christians in the area.

The captured Indians became servants without liberty for life. The legal distinctions between such servants for life and slaves did little, however, to change the living conditions of the Indians. An Indian working as a servant without liberty in a Mexican silver mine or on a Mexican ranch differed little in the quality of life from one working on a cotton plantation in Georgia or a sugar mill in Jamaica.

As control tightened over the Pueblo Indians, the Spaniards extended slave raiding to the capture of nomadic Athapaskan peoples, the ancestors of the modern Navajo and Apache. They also preyed on the farming peoples, including the Yuma, Pima, and Papago. The slave trade pushed ever farther north into what became the states of Utah, Nevada, and Colorado through the eighteenth century, and in the more remote areas until the dawn of the twentieth century.

Mission control over the Indians of California was legally terminated between 1833 and 1835, when the Mexican Republic declared all Indians free and independent. Much of the impetus for this emancipation came from the Mexican colonists moving into the area and finding that the clergy at the missions monopolized Indian labor. The new ranchers wanted the Indian labor for their own endeavors. The legal emancipation of the Indians changed their masters from the Spanish friars to the Mexican ranchers, who treated them no better than the clerics had done. In 1836, one California Mexican rancher, Francisco M. Alvarado, justified the continuation of the harsh treatment of Indians by explaining that the "Indians cannot be controlled except by flogging" (Forbes 1964, p. 93).

Indian slavery, both *de jure* and *de facto,* continued even after Abraham Lincoln's Emancipation Proclamation freeing the slaves in the Confederate states. The United States Congress outlawed the enslavement of Navajos by Americans and Mexicans through a joint resolution of July 27, 1868, and slavery of Alaskan natives did not legally end until even later.

When control of California passed from Mexico to the United States, the position of the surviving Indians improved only gradually. From 1850 until 1869, Los Angeles maintained an Indian slave market on Monday mornings. The Mayor's Court sold the labor of Indians convicted of offenses, the most common of which was drunkenness. By paying an Indian's fine, an Anglo or Mexican rancher could require that the Indian work for him for twice the length of time to which the Indian had been sentenced to prison (Forbes 1964, p. 94).

When the Indian completed his sentence, he often found that he now owed the rancher for his food or other services, and thus still could not be freed. The ranchers periodically supplied liberal amounts of alcohol for their indentured workers, and if a worker ever attained his freedom, the ranchers found it easy to have him rearrested for drunkenness. This started the cycle again.

Ranchers in California and other parts of the West maintained virtual enslavement of Indians through various legal charades, such as "debt peonage," in which the peon owed the rancher for food and other services provided at high prices that the peon could never afford to pay. The courts offered little recourse for Indians, since the Supreme Court ruled in *Elk v. Wilkins* in 1884 that the Fourteenth Amendment to the United States Constitution freed the African slaves but did not grant citizenship or constitutional rights to American Indians, even to those who had surrendered their tribal status and joined the larger society.

Even after emancipation of all slaves in the United States and its territories, agents of the federal government frequently conspired in the virtual enslavement of legally free Indians. Through legal devices that allowed them to confine Indians to reservations and to compel them to perform various types of unpaid labor, the Indian agents harnessed Indian labor and allowed it to be used for the profit of farmers, ranchers, and business, both on and off the reservation. Many reservation Indians had a status little higher than that of an indentured servant or a prison trustee. Some such practices continued until the United States finally conferred citizenship and full constitutional rights on all Indians in 1924.

When the morning fog lifts off Santa Barbara, and the imported cars of commuters snake down the mountain in long, slow lines, young Chicano men gather along Mission Street, which runs below the mission for which it is named. These young men, often mere boys dressed in blue jeans, pullover shirts, and old tennis shoes, line the streets waiting for an opportunity for day labor. They pace restlessly along the edge of the street, smoking cigarettes, drinking coffee from Styrofoam cups, and talking intermittently with one another, but they constantly watch the traffic for a signal from one of the drivers for them to jump into the back of a truck or crawl into a van. The one who first spots a potential employer and who moves fastest is the one most likely to earn a day's pay.

The young men will haul lumber, pick broccoli, cut grass, pour cement, transplant tomatoes, clean floors, carry bricks, chop weeds, wash trucks, stack wood, move garbage, water lawns, sort avocados, scrub grills, trim bushes, pack kiwis, or do almost any other legal labor for a day's pay. Of the many young men who line the street on any particular day, only a few will find work; the rest will have to move faster tomorrow.

Most of them have straight black hair, dark eyes, copper-colored skin, and beardless faces. They come from Mexico, speaking Spanish and bearing Christian names, but they are the survivors of the ancient Indians. With little if any European blood flowing through them, they continue today the long tradition of hard labor begun by their ancestors when Columbus first sailed to America. These young men now search for work in the same place where their native ancestors built the Presidio and the mission, cleared the land for farming and ranching, and laid the foundations for the prosperity so tastefully apparent in modern Santa Barbara. They are the people who built the city, and their strong backs, legs, arms, and minds still keep it clean and running today in the shadow of the old mission where the bones of the Chumash lie buried in their unmarked graves.

11

FISHING
FOR FOOD
AND PROFIT

Life on earth thrives where land and water meet—along the coasts of the oceans, the banks of the rivers, and the shores of the lakes. This holds true for terrestrial as well as marine life. Nowhere does this abundance of marine and terrestrial life show more vividly and dramatically than along the Pacific coast of southeastern Alaska, British Columbia, and Washington. The trees lap up the moisture of the perpetual fog, and in turn the trees nourish a variety of birds and animals. The larger mammals live in the water, where whales migrate in great herds among thousands of otters, sea lions, and seals.

Sailing into Alert Bay, off the eastern coast of Vancouver Island near its northern tip, one sees more telephone poles than totem poles. They clutter the water's edge as they run along the one main road that parallels the shore. The village of 1,300 people stretches out in a thin line following the curve of the bay. Seen from the water, the whole island appears to be nothing more than a bay. The island forms a crescent that offers a sheltered and secured port between Vancouver Island and the mainland of British Columbia, and with easy access into the Queen Charlotte Strait to the north and the Strait of Georgia to the south. Although the island bears the name of Cormorant Island, most people call it simply Alert Bay, both names deriving from the British ships HMS. *Alert* and HMS. *Cormorant,* which charted the area in the eighteenth century.

Viewed from any angle, Alert Bay still appears as a community built around the commercial fishing industry. Fishing boats with miles of nets fill the harbor; ancient canneries line the shore. Even the air carries the distinctive fragrance of large catches of fish freshly hauled in from the cold water.

Alert Bay boasts the world's largest totem pole, which can be seen rising from the hill behind the community. The Nimpkish Indian band erected the pole in 1973, and it rises 173 feet and contains twenty-two figures carved onto a red cedar log. The summit portrays a radiant sun with large rays stretching out into the crisp, humid Pacific air. At the other end of the community, a handful of older, comparatively shorter poles rise up in the Nimpkish cemetery.

Totem poles as large as these seem perfectly in keeping with the landscape of the northern Pacific Coast, where huge mountains loom over the cold, deep waters. Between the islands, massive clumps of rocks rise up out of the water, and with the surf swirling and surging around them in a thick foam, they look like mythological monsters emerging from the depths.

Even the flora and fauna of the area assume gigantic proportions. The tall cedar, fir, and spruce tower over humans. Between them grow tree-sized ferns that wave their huge fronds, making them look more like giant green machines than like animate beings. A spruce tree has been recorded at three hundred feet, but today the trees rarely reach their full height before loggers chop them down for lumber. Across from Alert Bay, one can see the once-forested mountains of Vancouver Island now absurdly dressed in alternating strips of barren and still forested lands. The lumber corporations have clear-cut large sections, leaving the majestic mountains looking foolish, as though they were wearing the punk haircuts of rebellious teenagers.

In the springtime, the swamp cabbages push up out of the ground in clearings and along the roads. Looking at first like a large shoot of stripped asparagus, the plant produces a deep yellow flower that resembles a giant easter lily, then it unfolds large, broad leaves. The leaves resemble the ornamental hosta that gardeners use to trim their lawns, but the plant served the ancient native peoples as a traditional food and material to make large mats with which to line their earthen ovens for feasts.

The exotic plants brought into this area by European settlers either die quickly as they are overtaken by the hearty native plants, or else they too must reach sizes not matched in their homelands. The quick-growing and hardy dandelions, which invaded from Europe, strain to mature before the swamp cabbage smothers them; thus the dandelions here generate flowers the size of carnations and leaves like twisted hacksaws. The dogwoods grow as large as maple trees, and the tulip blossoms approach the dimensions of cabbages.

With such abundant vegetation in and out of the water, the animals here also assume grander proportions. The bald eagles grow strong and large on a diet of giant salmon. The sea gulls look like flying turkeys, and the ravens tower over the gulls. Large black bears thrive in the forests of the islands, and huge grizzly bears thrive on the mainland coast. Fat skunks waddle through the bushes with little apparent fear of humans.

In the water the plants and animals grow even larger than their counterparts on land. The kelp rises up in the ocean, creating an underwater thicket as dense as the tall grass of the Argentine pampas. In this cool nutrient soup, oysters grow broader than a person's hand. Unlike the more southerly oysters, which are of a dainty size and can easily be swallowed in a single gelatinous slurp, these firmer, more flavorful creatures need to be cut with a knife even when raw. Alaska king crabs grow bigger than most lobsters and offer legs filled with succulent white meat.

Firm prawns grow nearly as large as bananas and can be just as easily peeled and eaten. Sockeye, coho, and dog salmon commonly reach nearly three feet in length, and the chinook salmon can reach five. They produce a rich, pinkish meat that offers a gourmet meal when eaten fresh, but can easily be preserved by the traditional technique of smoking or by modern canning and vacuum packaging.

Cod and trout grow almost as big as the salmon. But no matter to what size these fish grow, they look like little more than ornamental aquarium fish compared to the sturgeon, which sometimes exceed eighteen feet in length.

The rich and luxuriant plankton attract herds of migrating whales that congregate around rocks along Vancouver Island, across from Alert Bay. There the whales sing their deep, melodious songs and scratch themselves on the large rocks. Local legends say that the killer whales scratch themselves so that they can turn into wolves, their terrestrial counterparts, and then search for food in the thick forests the same way they do in the water.

Despite the large animals in the water and on the land, one need have little fear of them. The greatest danger to humans today comes from the thousands of logs that float through the water and line the shore, making piles of artificially uniform driftwood. A few of the tree trunks have a tangled hydra-head of roots sticking out, indicating that they fell into the water by a natural process of wind and water erosion, but most of them have been neatly cut in timbering operations that strip-mine the forest. The renegade logs somehow escaped while being floated down one of the rivers or while the logs were boomed up into the mile-long rafts that ply these channels.

While such logs pose a great nuisance in the day to fishing and ferry boats, the greatest danger comes during the night. The night hours last so long in the winter that it is hard for everyone to be off the water before dark, but any boat, even a large one, on the water at night rides in great danger of hitting one of these renegade logs. Every Indian family seems to have had a member killed in such an accident, or knows someone who has been—a lone fisherman coming in with his haul, parents and a baby returning from a late-night feast, or teenagers coming back from the high school on Vancouver Island.

Sailing into Alert Bay, one notices that most of the houses look reasonably modern, and the small Victorian church gives the village an almost Atlantic Coast look more characteristic of the Maritime provinces. Old and decaying canneries hover along the dock, and the brick structure that once housed St. Michael's boarding school for Indian children still stands stiff and erect on the northern end of the community. The modern structures protrude from the land and are easily seen from miles away over the water. It takes longer and closer inspection to discern the traditional structures of wood that blend in with the surroundings, and quickly age in the humidity and rain to weak, neutral colors.

As one enters the bay on a quiet day, it is possible to hear the drumming coming from the direction of old St. Michael's school. The rhythmic beat of the drums and the chanting voices drift over the waves, disappearing for a few moments but then reemerging in its rhythmic beat. The drumming and voices come from the children who troop regularly into the U'Mista Cultural Centre for their lessons in traditional Kwakiutl music.

The U'Mista Centre now houses some of the ancient masks, cloaks, and blankets of the Kwakiutl people, which were seized by the Canadian government to punish the people who carried on their traditional potlatch on Village Island at Christmas 1921. After holding the native treasure for sixty years, the museums of Canada finally returned the artifacts to the people of Alert Bay, who had built a traditional home for them. Under the direction of Gloria Cranmer Webster, the building now serves as both a museum and an active learning center to encourage the study of the Kwakwala language and arts.

The old people named the new cultural center *U'Mista,* which means approximately "homecoming" and had been applied in ancient times to people who returned home after a long absence, often in captivity. When the masks were returned after sixty years in government captivity, it was a true *u'mista,* and for that reason the people displayed the masks without glass boxes around them to separate them from the people. They said that the masks wanted to be free and not boxed in. Because the building now houses so many sacred items, the old people also call it "the box of treasures."

As one sails into the bay, the tall poles rising up along the edge of the water turn out to be the masts of the boats in the fishing fleet. For most of the twentieth century, Alert Bay has formed the economic center of the Kwakiutl territory. The fishing industry centered at Alert Bay, and the government and church administration for them also centered there, replacing the nineteenth-century focus of Fort Rupert and the Hudson's Bay Company at the northern tip of Vancouver Island.

For the peoples of the northern Pacific, fishing functioned as more than an economic activity or a subsistence pattern; it formed the cultural core of life on which their whole civilization arose. Their technology, myths, communal activities, rituals, ceremonies, religion, and art focused on marine life. They caught fish in every way known to the Old World, and in many ways unknown to the rest of the world.

The native people used wood and some metal to construct a variety of fish hooks for angling. These varied from small hooks for kelp fish to giant ones larger than a man's hand for halibut. They used the hooks individually or in complicated sets of baited hooks attached to a frame and anchored with weights or allowed to float on air-filled bladders. These sets of hooks floated in the water like large mobiles hanging in a modern art museum. In addition to curved and angled hooks, they used straight bone gorges that were baited and dropped to the bottom of the water to be sucked up by bottom-feeding fish, which then could not free themselves from the slender gorges that lodged in their throats.

Bait such as small fish or strips of octopus served to attract most large fish, but for some fish the natives used lures made of wood, and even complicated designs of feathers. One of these wooden lures looks like the shuttlecock used to play badminton. When put down deep in the water with a long pole and then released, the lure twists and turns as it makes its way back toward the surface, moving through the water in much the same way that a poorly hit shuttlecock might fly through the air. The shape and motion of the twirling lure attract the curious attention of ling cod, who follow the lure to the surface where the waiting fisherman spear them.

The fishermen made other wooden lures in the form of small fish, or used strips of white willow that could be pulled through the water in such a way that they reproduced the characteristic motions and ripples of a wounded fish and thus attracted larger prey (H. Stewart, pp. 48–62). At night the fisherman used fire to attract the attention of curious fish, which the men speared when they came to the surface.

Even the spears used in fishing came in great varieties depending on the type of prey, the time of year, and the precise location of the fishing. The simple wooden or bone point could be notched or barbed to make it more lethal, and the craftsmen often added two prongs to the side of a point to hold the fish in place.

The natives crafted detachable points for their spears to make them into harpoons that proved important in hunting larger prey. The Nootka, on the western coast of Vancouver Island, and the Makah, from the Olympic Peninsula of Washington, both used such harpoons to hunt whales, as did the Aleuts in the Alaskan islands farther to the northwest. Ropes attached to the points permitted the hunters to keep a whale on the line while minimizing the risk of being hit by the violently swaying harpoon shaft. The men quickly retrieved the shaft after it freed itself from the point, then loaded another point onto it and thrust it again.

The Coast Salish manufactured some of the longest harpoons in the world to use on sturgeon. These harpoons reached fifty feet in length and terminated in a forked end. In the winter the fishermen used the gigantic harpoons to probe the cold water for the sluggish sturgeon resting on the bottom. Once the fish were located, the fisherman speared them by aiming straight down with their lance harpoons. The wounded sturgeon, which could be as large as six hundred pounds, often pulled the canoes on an erratic and terror-filled ride toward the deep ocean, but repeated harpooning and fatigue soon overcame the giant beasts (H. Stewart, p. 68).

Fishermen sought the bottom-dwelling flounder in much the same way that they searched for the sturgeon, but with a different tool. Instead of a harpoon, they used a spear with several points that made it in effect a pitchfork, which they thrust deep into the water to probe the ocean bottom until they snared the flounder.

For herring they made a rake similar to the pitchfork, but from six to twelve feet long. When the herring ran, they came in such numbers that a fisherman could dip the rake into the water like an oar and impale the fish on it. With this tool they literally raked the herring, and, at times, other fish, into their boats.

Tightly woven baskets with narrow, inverted necks served as crab pots, which the Indians filled with bait and let rest on the bottom. Crabs crawled into the trap to feed, but could not crawl out again. The owner of the basket would pull it up after a day in the water and have a basket filled with crabs.

Men and women both participated in various methods of netting fish. The nets they used might be nothing more than small hand nets to scoop up fish such as smelt along the shoreline, or they could be larger ones attached to poles and used to scoop up salmon. Larger nets required the cooperation of dozens of people to spread them and haul them in. Some nets were made specifically for fishing at the mouths of rivers and others were used farther out at sea.

Native nets provoked one of the first technological changes in the fishing practices of non-Indians. Commercial fishermen coming into the area eagerly adopted the Indian gill nets, which the Indians manufactured with various sizes of mesh based on the size and type of fish they planned to snare. As early as 1873, non-Indians on the Fraser River in British Columbia and the Columbia River along the Washington-Oregon border used such nets in preference to the traditional European ones (Boxberger, p. 37).

The natives used a more permanent type of net to construct weirs, large underwater fences that guided and trapped the fish. The fishermen opened the weirs at high tide and then closed them at low tide, capturing thousands of fish in small estuaries and pools. The complexity of weirs and traps required the building of log dams and permanent stone foundations for them. The construction of these dams and weirs gave fishing among the coastal Indians a level of technological and engineering sophistication usually associated with agricultural people who must make terraces and irrigation systems for their crops (H. Stewart, p. 99).

The Indians built various types of structures to take advantage of the precise behaviors of specific fish, such as for collecting the annual herring spawn, which could be dried into a tasty food of high protein content. To harvest the millions of spawn, fishermen built rectangular frames that they suspended in the water and from which they hung kelp or tree branches to dangle below the water's surface. This submerged vegetable matter attracted the herring, which mistook the dangling leaves for natural vegetation and then deposited vast numbers of their eggs on them. The fishermen later retrieved their kelp or branches for drying in the sun, and hung more kelp on the same frames (H. Stewart, p. 125).

The fishermen further manipulated the environment by cutting paths through the thick kelp jungles. Lazy salmon readily followed the path of least resistance, which meant that they eagerly swam through the cut paths rather than forging their own way through the thick kelp. Like the hedges and fences used to herd deer in the east or caribou in the north, the kelp paths led the salmon into small, confined areas where they provided easy prey for the waiting fishermen.

In a division of labor similar to that of the hunting peoples in the interior and among foraging peoples throughout the world, the men did most of the fishing, and the women processed the catch. Women also specialized in the gathering of the abundant sea life closer to shore. They collected oysters, crabs, sea urchins, mussels, abalone, and clams, which they could gather while remaining close to their children. The marine life harvested by the women not only provided food, but also supplied more of the raw materials for making tools than did the fish gathered by the men. Of particular importance for the native tool kit before the introduction of metal was the wide knife made from the larger mussel shells, and a variety of cutting edges that could be made from other marine shells.

The women used their tools to process all of the fish and marine mammals brought in by the men. They gutted, scaled, and cleaned the fish, and dried vast quantities of them for the winter. They sun-dried fish when practical, but in the rainy climate of the coastal area, they also used smokehouses to preserve tons of fish and other seafood annually. Each product had its own peculiar characteristics that demanded a particular way of cutting or drying the meat, and each task required its own cutting blades and other utensils.

After drying the fish, the women pounded some of them into fish meal, which was an easily transported food used in soups, stews, or any other dishes to provide protein and thickening in the absence of fresh fish or while on long trips. The women also made a type of "cheese" by aging fish and roe. One method for doing this was to store salmon roe inside the stomach of a deer, which was then hung in the storehouse. Periodic kneading of the stomach as it dried would produce, after a few months, a cheeselike substance inside. Similar foods were made by burying roe in wooden boxes or in pits lined with rocks and maple leaves (H. Stewart, p. 146).

One of the most important technologies developed by women allowed them to extract oil from the fish. The women boiled and pressed aged fish such as the eulachon, the fish containing the greatest amount of oil, then stored the oil in wooden boxes and in long tubes of hollow kelp gourd, which hung in their storehouses looped like a garden hose in a garage. The oil made up an important part of the yearly diet of the coastal people, and they traded it inland in so-called "grease trails" that stretched for hundreds of miles into British Columbia, Washington, Oregon, and Idaho. Traditionally the oil together with the fish meal provided two of the most important trade goods that the coastal Indians used for commerce with the interior tribes.

The people of the north Pacific Coast created one of the most complex maritime cultures in the world. They invented and adapted a technology and modes of production unique to them and their special environment. In addition to their sophisticated technical culture, they attained one of the most complex social organizations of any nonagricultural people in the world.

Large-scale commercial fishing in America began as early as the arrival of the first European sailors on the eastern Atlantic Coast. They tapped the rich resources of the North Atlantic, where the cod ran as thick as the salmon did in the northern Pacific. By the sixteenth century, the Atlantic Coast of North America became a major fishing and whale-hunting area for European ships.

Off the northeast coast of America, when the passages between the Arctic islands thawed during the summer, Dutch and English whalers combed the waters for whales, which they butchered and processed on the shore. They packed their casks with oil from the sperm whale and from the Greenland right whale or Arctic bowhead whale. Occasionally the native people also hunted for whale, which they traded to the sailors for European metal and trinkets, but the native contribution to the whaling and fishing industry remained marginal compared to the role of the English, Scandinavians, and Dutch.

Native Americans of the islands and coast along the North Atlantic had little permanent impact on this fishing and whaling industry because the Europeans sailed in their own boats and brought with them an Atlantic-based technology that had been hammered out slowly over thousands of years. That Atlantic fishing complex developed gradually along the coasts and in the fjords and inlets of Europe, and slowly spread to the outer islands before being used to launch fishing expeditions onto the high seas.

Some evidence indicates that the rich fishing grounds of this area may have attracted English and perhaps Scandinavian fishing fleets before Columbus sailed into the Caribbean in 1492. North European fishing boats were venturing farther west and bringing home rich catches of fish, but like good fishermen anywhere in the world, they did not advertise their fishing grounds. Thus, today it proves difficult for historians to document the exact areas where they sailed.

By 1497 the English King Henry VII had commissioned the first systematic exploration and survey of the coast by sending out the Italian navigator Giovanni Caboto, whom the English called John Cabot. Cabot and subsequent explorers marveled at the vast number of codfish. The supply seemed inexhaustible, and the demand for fish in protein-deficient Europe seemed equally insatiable.

For the first century after the European discovery of North America, it appeared that the most important resource of North America lay not in the land but off the coast, in the cold Atlantic waters of Canada and New England. Fish teemed in these waters that had been exploited by the Indians only for their own subsistence. Old documents and maps named this coastal area the land of cod, a name still reflected in Cape Cod, Massachusetts, which lies south of the best fishing areas.

The cool, rich waters off the coast of Newfoundland and Labrador make ideal feeding for the cod, which reproduce and grow with abandon. A female can lay more than nine million eggs a year, and she can easily exceed fifty pounds. In addition, fishermen preserved the flesh with salt and sun, making it ideal for shipment over long distances and for sale throughout Europe.

We know there was a steady flow of European fishing vessels in and out of this area after 1500. Dried cod became a staple protein of the growing numbers of urban poor in Europe. Cod also became a common food for the populations of Catholic countries on Fridays and other church fast days when they could not eat meat.

One of the meager contributions of Inuit and Indians to the fishing industry of the North Atlantic came not from their culture but from their brute labor. From the earliest days of the fishing and whaling industries, European ships kidnapped and impressed native men, and sometimes women and children, into service. This practice continued long after the fishing and whaling industries relocated from European bases to the newly emerging Atlantic ports in New England, Nova Scotia, Newfoundland, and Labrador.

Even into the nineteenth century, Indians and Inuit commonly served on fishing and whaling ships in the Atlantic. They occur in almost all nineteenth-century descriptions of fishing communities such as the harpooner Tashtego in Herman Melville's novel *Moby Dick,* first published in 1851. Indians and Inuit found or were forced to assume a place in the fishing industry, but they did not change that industry and its already well established system of operation in the Atlantic.

Although the European fishermen arrived on the Atlantic coast of North America with a workable and transferable technology base, the settlers who began to colonize the land did not share the fishermen's knowledge. Just as the colonists arrived with little knowledge of hunting, they arrived with only slightly more knowledge of fishing. But while aristocrats claimed a monopoly on hunting in Europe, fishing was primarily an activity practiced by a lower class of specialists. Fishing in European ponds, creeks, and rivers never carried the prestige of hunting on the large, private game preserves.

The European specialization of labor and strict division into occupational guilds did not encourage people to undertake new activities outside of their limited professional areas. Peasants grew crops; they did not hunt, fish, mine minerals, work metal, or sell market produce. They did not even mill the grain they grew, or bake it into bread; both of these jobs belonged to separate crafts. Similarly, shepherds tended their goats and sheep, while herdsmen and dairymen cared for the cattle; they did not grow crops, make shoes, weave wool, or impinge on anyone else's craft. Fishermen fished.

* * *

The northern Pacific was the last coastal area of America to be conquered by the Europeans. After a scramble between the British, Spanish, and Russians, the United States bought Alaska from Russia and divided the rest of the area with Britain along the forty-ninth parallel. The fur trade attracted the initial interest of whites like John Jacob Astor, but as the trappers exhausted the fur, the bountiful marine resources of the area became increasingly important.

The first attempts to exploit Indian fishing along the northern Pacific Coast originated with the Hudson's Bay Company, which sought to market salted salmon in the 1830s. The North Pacific proved too distant from most markets for even salted salmon to survive the voyage in edible condition. To reach Europe or the East Coast of the United States, the ships had to sail south through the tropical Pacific, around Cape Horn at the southern tip of South America, through the tropical Atlantic, and finally on to a European port. The trip proved too costly and too uncertain, and in any event the Atlantic fishing grounds seemed ample to supply European needs. The Hudson's Bay Company did find a ready and eager market for its salted salmon in nearby Hawaii, but this market proved too small to sustain a viable industry of commercial fishing in the Northwest (Boxberger, p. 35).

With the invention of the canning process and the availability of cheap and plentiful tin from Cerro Potosí and the other mountains of Bolivia, new possibilities arose for commercial fishing in the North Pacific. Hapgood, Hume and Company opened the first commercial salmon cannery at the mouth of the Sacramento River in 1864. It failed because of improper canning procedures and because industrial effluents from adjacent gold mines killed the salmon in the river. Even though the location of the first cannery proved poor and the technological procedures needed improvement, other companies found better locations and technology; they opened canneries on the Columbia River, in Puget sound, and along Vancouver Island. Soon commercial fisheries and canneries stretched from Monterey, California, to Alaska. The major boom for the industry came in the First World War with the great military demand for easily transported protein.

The fishing companies relied heavily on Indian labor and technology such as the gill nets, and on the traditional skills of the Indian women in processing the fish. Despite the heavy dependence on Indian women in the early stages of the fish canneries, the companies found cheaper labor in Asia. The canneries gradually replaced many of the Indian women employees with Chinese and, later, Japanese workers imported into the area.

As the commercial fishermen switched to power boats and ever-larger nets and more-expensive equipment, the canneries relied less on Indian labor. The new boats employed seines, large nets used in open water to surround great numbers of fish of all kinds. Some Chinese men also replaced Indian men working on boats. In fishing communities such as Alert Bay, where the fisheries did not have enough imported labor, the Indians entered financial relations whereby the company supplied the boats and gasoline while the Indians managed them and took most of the financial risks. This system operated by rules similar to that of sharecropping in the old plantations of the South after the freeing of the slaves.

By the middle of the twentieth century, some Indians, such as Billy Assu of Cape Mudge and James Sewid of Alert Bay managed to buy their own modern power boats and became successful entrepreneurs within the new commercial system (Spradley). These men combined the traditional fishing systems based on kinship with their new requirements as commodity producers for an international system of corporations and markets. Native entrepreneurs such as Sewid and Assu formed the Coast Native Fisherman's Association and later the Native Brotherhood, organizations that helped to preserve and restore native fishing rights.

In Seattle, Victoria, Vancouver, and other urban areas, the immigrant non-Indians quickly pushed the Indians out of their traditional fishing enterprises. Despite the objections and resistance of the Bureau of Indian Affairs, the Lummi of Puget Sound went to court in 1897 to plead for a halt to the encroachment of their treaty rights by commercial fisheries. The long legal struggle of the Lummi met one legal reversal after another, until finally, in 1974 federal judge George Boldt ruled that treaties of 1854 and 1855 guaranteed the Lummi their historical rights to half the salmon harvest. Since then the courts have upheld the fishing rights of other tribes as well, but the people have had to struggle against tremendous corporate and political pressure to exercise those rights.

In places such as Alert Bay, the Lummi reservation west of Bellingham, Washington, and other coastal communities scattered from Alaska to Oregon, the Indians continue their traditional livelihood of fishing. They now use satellite communications to connect their computers to international markets, but underneath the new technology, the native tradition continues. They do not fish today with the same tools they used a century ago, any more than today's farmer would walk behind a plow pulled by a mule.

The Indians of the Northwest Coast are some of the very few native people who have managed to maintain a large part of their traditional subsistence pattern. Despite conflicts among themselves as well as with the outside society, they found ways to merge their traditional way of life with the marketing requirements of the modern economy. Long after their cousins on the Great Plains have had to give up the buffalo hunt, after the farming Indians of the East Coast have lost their fields, and after many other Indian nations have become extinct, the native people of the north Pacific Coast continue the work of their ancestors. At the opening of the twenty-first century, they seem to be entering a cultural, artistic, and economic renaissance based on the same maritime resources that sustained the culture and economy of their ancestors over the past several thousand years.

12

GUERRILLAS AND WARRIORS

E ach year on the last weekend of September, the Dakota host the Mah-kato Powwow for all nations at Dakota Wokiksuye Makoce, the Land of Memories Park, just south of Mankato, Minnesota. For three days the singing groups drum and sing on the side while the people dance in an eternal circle. Between dances, elders and whole families step forward to host meals for all participants in honor of one of their members, to record a family event, or to thank the assembled people for some favor.

The event focuses on family and community ties. It is a time for socializing, good food, good music, flirting, catching up on gossip, or comparing new camper vehicles. In some regards it resembles a family reunion in the South, an ethnic festival in a Northern metropolis, or Cinco de Mayo in San Antonio.

Despite these similarities, the Mah-kato Powwow is more than a people's celebration of themselves. The deeper significance impressed itself clearly on my mind a few years ago, when the weather turned unseasonably cold even for a Minnesota autumn, and a stormy rain alternated with light drizzles. It was the kind of day that drives picnickers and football players inside. By any measure, the weather was both too wet and too cold for any outdoor activity, much less a dance. Women carefully folded their embroidered shawls. Men put away their delicate moccasins and feathered bustles. With great disappointment the children had to put away their headdresses and wash off their face paints, which smeared in the rain. The visitors and onlookers who wanted to watch the colorful dancing packed up their minivans and station wagons to drive home.

The Mah-kato Powwow had been rained out. Something persuaded me to wait and not go scurrying home after such a long drive to get there. I huddled in a small shed around a kerosene heater with a handful of other folks, and in silent boredom we watched a man repair a pair of moccasins made from elkhide by his grandfather.

After everyone had put away all the valuable and delicate Indian clothes, they returned to jeans, flannel shirts, heavy sweaters, bowling jackets, boots, and tennis shoes. A man found a large plastic sheet and spread it over the drum. The sheet proved large enough for the young singers and drummers all to huddle under it around their drum, and they began to beat the drum in unison and sing.

As the pounding beat spread out over Dakota Wokiksuye Makoce, the dancers slowly returned from the sheds, campers, and cars where they had taken refuge. They brought out other large sheets of plastic and held them high so that a line of five or six people could share it as they slowly drifted back toward the drum and began to dance again. Soon people had filled the muddy arena. Old ladies danced beside their granddaughters, men beside their wives or children, and teenage "fancy dancers" twirled and stomped in the rain without a plastic sheet over them and without the colorful swirl of their traditional costumes.

Not a feather could be seen at that powwow as the dancers continued for hours in their everyday clothes. I realized then that the colorful costumes—bright fancy-dancer feathers, somber traditional feathers, elk's-teeth dresses, and embroidered shawls—and all the other props were not the heart of the powwow. The essence of the powwow lay in the beat of the drum, the high-pitched men's voices, and the dance itself. The essence of the powwow was in the ephemeral acts and not in the permanent objects that accompanied those acts. The powwow was the dance.

As I watched the dancers moving beneath opaque sheets of plastic and the steady rain, I saw that this moment could just have easily been a hundred years ago or a hundred years in the future. The Dakota had always danced, and in repeating the identical motions for generation after generation, all the Dakota merge in one continuing dance for a thousand years into the past and a thousand years into the future.

The people came there to dance, and they would not leave until they had done so. They had not come there to dance for entertainment or fun, but for a serious and even sacred purpose. They had come to Land of Memories Park to remember and to dance in honor of the thirty-eight Dakota patriots hanged there by the government of Abraham Lincoln on the day after Christmas in 1862. No matter how cold the wind or how persistent the rain, they had come to honor their fallen warriors.

In Mankato the United States hanged thirty-eight men in the largest mass execution in North American history. To heighten the drama of the executions, the government constructed a special scaffold for all thirty-eight gallows. After the guards covered the condemned men's heads with hoods, the cutting of a single rope released all thirty-eight trapdoors and thus hanged all the Indians simultaneously. The sight of so many bodies dangling in the air made a dramatic display to show all Indians what would happen to them if they gave the United States government any trouble while it was fighting its war against the Confederacy. To stress this point, newspapers throughout the frontier regions reproduced engravings of the mass execution on their front pages, and pictures of the event were posted all over Indian territory.

For the memory of those men who died in Mankato, the Dakota must dance. In addition to honoring those thirty-eight men, the Mah-kato Powwow also honored other Indians who have fought and died in war. The United States flag occupies a central place at the powwow, and every part of the powwow begins and ends with honoring ceremonies for that flag. This may seem contradictory to many people who cannot understand honoring both those who died fighting against the United States as well as those who fought for it, but the people at the powwow honor the bravery and sacrifices of all of their warriors.

Every powwow I have ever attended in any part of the United States also flew a special black flag to honor the prisoners of war and those missing in action who never came home from Vietnam. A quarter of a century after that war ended, the native people still remember and mourn those who never returned. They never forget a service done or an honor owed.

It is not only the Indians but all Americans who owe a debt to these fallen warriors. The debt of modern North America to the Indian warriors derives not merely from the large number who died in service to the United States and Canada in overseas battles, but also from the military tactics that the army learned from the Indians. The Indians taught the colonists how to fight a guerrilla war, and its knowledge proved to be the decisive factor that allowed the thirteen small colonies of only about three million people to wrest their independence from the largest and best-armed empire in the world.

The colonists recognized from the time of the first settlements that Indians fought differently from European soldiers. The Indians did not line up in formation and march onto a large field to meet a similarly organized group. As described by one of the Jamestown colonists, the "Savages" came "creeping on all foure, from the Hills, like Beares, with their Bowes in their mouths" (Leach, p.2).

The natives of America often fought wars in the same way that they hunted, stressing strategy and technique more than technology. Traps, lures, decoys, and calls were used as effectively in warfare as in hunting. A particularly effective lure was to set out a small party of warriors as bait to attract the attention of the enemy. As the enemy pursued the smaller party, a larger group encircled and attacked the enemy from all sides. This strategy was very similar to luring deer or caribou into a surround and then slaughtering them.

Both the fur trade and the wars over it depended on Indians. The Indians did the trapping, and when it came time to fight competing colonial powers, the Indians did the fighting. The Indians allied with the Dutch fought against the Indians allied with the English. When the English took over the Dutch lands, the Indians who had been allied with the Dutch then fought for the British against the French Indians. The colonial powers soon divided the Indians into two major factions. The six nations in the League of the Iroquois lived in the area of New York State and maintained a long neutrality that ended in an alliance with the British. The French in Quebec, along the St. Lawrence River, depended mostly on an alliance with the Hurons.

The insatiable European market soon depleted the furs of New England, the St. Lawrence River, and all the lands of both the Iroquois and the Hurons. By 1660, within forty years of their first shipment of furs from New England, the Puritans had exhausted the beaver supply in their area (Cronon, p. 99). The animals died because of overhunting and because they lost their habitats as European settlers chopped down the forest to plant crops and make pastures for their livestock.

Each Indian group had to move deeper into the continent by heading west. This quest for furs set the Hurons and the Iroquois into direct competition for these new lands. By the 1640s the Iroquois had reached a state of near-permanent hostility against the Huron, who controlled a fur-trading empire across southern Canada and the Great Lakes.

During the spread and growth of the fur trade, warfare became as much a part of the business as trapping and trading. War became big business for the Indian tribes, whose members accepted large payments and trade concessions in return for alliance with one or another of the European powers. During the seventeenth and early eighteenth centuries the French showed greater success at obtaining Indian allies than did the British, but the British moved in a steady stream into New England, New York, Pennsylvania, and Virginia. The French therefore encouraged the Indians to make war on the English colonists.

From this phase of colonial history we acquired the image of the Indian as the bloody savage attacking bucolic cabins by surprise, killing the men, women, and children except for a few taken as prisoners for a life of hell.

Often the settlers' scalps were sold to the occupying European power that had offered a bounty for them. Scalptaking had a long history in native America, but it also had a narrow, prescribed position. The Dutch at New Amsterdam became the first to offer bounties for scalps, and from the Dutch the practice spread to other Europeans and to Indians who had not previously taken scalps.

Scalping is a modified form of headhunting, and people have practiced headhunting on every continent, including Europe. The ancient Celtic warriors of Europe chopped off heads and strung them on their steeds like a gory necklace when they returned from battle. Of course, by the time the European colonists arrived in America, the tribal practice of headhunting had already died out in Europe.

The taking of heads and using them for religious purposes seems to have arrived late in North America, but it certainly arrived before the Europeans did. Evidence suggests that head taking became more widespread in the southern and eastern part of North America at the same time that a whole complex of Mexican images, including that of the feathered serpent, moved around the Gulf of Mexico and north up the Mississippi River.

Archaeologists today refer to the similar sets of items found across the area as "the Southeastern mortuary complex" or "the Southern ceremonial complex." The largest cache of artifacts associated with this complex was found in Spiro, Oklahoma.

Among the most intriguing motifs in artifacts found in the Spiro mounds are the frequent portrayals of heads. As distinct from the simple portraits and silhouettes found among the Hopewell artifacts mentioned earlier, these faces frequently show bared teeth and often have eyes or mouths that appear to have been sewn shut. One such striking piece, a jar found near Paducah, Kentucky, stands only sixteen centimeters high and is made in the form of a head with the eyes sewn shut to mere slits. The mouth was not sewn, but the lips seem to have shrunk, revealing the teeth clenched in an expression of apparent pain. Another jar, found at Fortune Mound, Arkansas, has a closed mouth with lips sewn together. Such depictions look very much like trophy heads gathered in war.

Similar heads can still be seen today in parts of the Amazon, where warriors traditionally gathered them from their slain enemies and used them in religious ceremonies. Particularly in the jungles of Ecuador, the Shuar (Jívaro) shrank heads with their lips sewn shut to prevent the spirits of the slain from harming their killers.

In the southern United States, such trophy heads appear in shell and ceramic artifacts. Sometimes they were engraved on round shell gorgets; others were carved from shell. They often occurred with drawings of human bones, which were sometimes themselves incised with designs.

From the Spiro mounds, a sequence of engraved conch shells depict what appear to be dancing warriors, shamans, or gods. In their hands they carry trophy heads, usually held by the hair. Sometimes the dancers appear to be holding snakes or to be wrapped inside a large figure of a snake. In addition to these two-dimensional representations of head-taking, a sculpted pipe depicts a warrior, dressed in full regalia and wearing large earspools, severing the head of a man with a large curved blade. The objects found around Spiro and related sites include a large number of monolithic ceremonial axes, ceremonial flint knives, and maces or batons. Skulls were often found in the graves of high-status individuals. Such graves also contained the skeletons of infants.

In at least some of the native languages, warriors used the word for *head* rather than *scalp* in discussing what they did, and in the Iroquois pictographs used in wampum belts, the symbol for *scalp* was a headless body (Axtell, p. 214).

Even in the early colonial era, the emphasis remained on taking heads from enemies rather than mere scalps. As early as 1637 the English colonists of Connecticut offered the Mohegans a bounty for every Pequot head delivered to them; the Dutch of New Amsterdam made a similar offer for Raritan heads in 1641. Soon the commercial flow of heads reached such a level that the colonists needed to simplify it; they could not handle so many heads. The simplification seems to have been inspired by the fur trade. We find that by 1675, during the time of King Philip's War in Massachusetts and Rhode Island, the colonists no longer paid a bounty for heads; instead, they offered the Narraganset a bounty merely for the "Head-Skin" of their enemies (Axtell, p. 223).

The simple expedient of substituting the crown of the scalp for the entire head permitted a sustained commerce in scalps over longer distances and longer periods of time. Heads had to be delivered fresh, before they began to rot and stink, but a properly treated scalp could be preserved for months or even years. After the transition from head bounties to scalp bounties, the colonists commissioned campaigns that penetrated deeper into enemy territory, making the short raids for heads into ever-longer scalp-hunting expeditions.

The colonial powers quickly transformed a gruesome but infrequent act of war into a whole industry. After eliminating enemy Indians around the European communities, the colonists then offered bounties for the more distant allies of other European powers. By 1688 this escalated another step when the French offered bounties not only for the scalps of the Indian allies of the British, but for the scalps of Englishmen themselves. To stop British colonization of New England, they offered ten beaver-skins for every settler's scalp. In 1696 the British responded with a counteroffer for French scalps (Axtell, p. 224).

As long as the native warriors took heads in combat, they only wanted the heads of other warriors, but the trade in scalps ignored age and gender. The scalp of a young girl could bring as much on the French or British scalp market as that of a seasoned fighter. The scalp market essentially destroyed the distinction between warrior and noncombatant, an unfortunate development that plagued European-Indian combat for the next two centuries.

As the American frontier pushed westward, the practice of scalping spread quickly before it. Indian nations that had never practiced scalping learned it as they acquired other parts of the newly emerging frontier trade. The scalp trade became as much a part of the West as the sport of buffalo hunting, the commerce in furs, and the spread of corn liquor.

The accumulation of scalps in colonial settlements presented a problem. In the early years the colonists eagerly displayed the scalps in public squares or in public buildings. But in time this practice came to be considered distasteful. In 1785 the village of Salem, Massachusetts, stopped displaying scalps when it built a new courthouse. Many scalp collections ultimately passed into the hands of museums and local historical societies.

In their wars against the Indians, the settlers of New England and Virginia quickly learned that the only way they could avoid Indian traps was through the use of Indian guides and scouts who would help them (Leach, p. 61). To defeat the Indians, they had to be able to think and act like the Indians. When the colonial armies stood in ranks on the battlefield, the Indians stood behind trees and slaughtered the exposed and brightly dressed soldiers. Since the Indians refused to stand in formation, the colonial soldiers had to learn to take refuge behind trees.

The French learned the lessons of Indian warfare faster than the English, and put those lessons to good use in the protracted imperial wars in America between the two nations. The turning point came when the British drillbook general Edward Braddock tried to take the French-held Fort Duquesne, which guarded the convergence of the Allegheny and Monongahela rivers into the Ohio at what is now Pittsburgh. Because Braddock had the superior firepower, he went to battle with great confidence that his men could easily bombard and then seize the fort. On July 9, 1755, before his army could reach the fort, the Indian allies of the French slaughtered Braddock's army in the woods.

After this bitter defeat, the British authorities recognized what the colonists already knew—that they had to change their European fighting style in America. Benjamin Franklin pointed out that "the manual Exercise and Evolutions taught a Malitia, are known by Experience to be of little or no use in our Woodes . . ." (Leach, p. 407). Similarly, General John Forbes wrote, "[We] must comply and learn the Art of Warr, from Enemy Indians . . ." (Leach, p. 440).

In the following year the colonists began wholesale training in Indian styles. Robert Dinwiddie, the lieutenant governor of Virgina, wrote to George Washington urging him "to teach them as much as possible Bush fighting." In the same year the British Parliament created a regiment of "Royal Americans" to specialize in forest warfare. In New Hampshire, Robert Rogers organized a troop of rangers skilled in Indian techniques of warfare (Leach, p. 370).

Having learned the techniques of Indian warfare while fighting the French, the colonists applied these same lessons to their ensuing struggle for independence against the British crown. When the colonists decided to launch a strong public protest against the British tea tax, they chose to dress in Mohawk clothing and stage attacks on cargo ships carrying tea. The rebels darkened their skins, carried tomahawks, marched in single or "Indian" file, and even communicated among themselves with phrases and sign language from unidentified Indian tribes. The most famous such "tea party" rocked Boston Harbor in December 1773, but rebels throughout the colonies undertook similar protests. They always dressed as Indians to do so. This was not done haphazardly or by chance; the colonists had already begun using the Indian as a symbol of resistance to authority and as an icon of liberty (Johansen and Grinde 1989).

In South Carolina, Francis Marion, a Berkeley County plantation owner, first learned about warfare in successive campaigns against the Cherokee in 1759 and 1761. The importance of what he had learned did not become evident until after a series of defeats of colonists by the British in the War for Independence. After the fall of Charleston to the British in May 1780, and the fall of Camden in August, the fledgling American army in the South seemed on the verge of annihilation. At that point Marion took what men he could find into the swamps and attacked the British in surprise raids. His men hit loyalist strongholds and harassed the British supply and communication channels, but in the style of guerrillas, they usually avoided full battles against a much larger and better-supplied army. Francis Marion and his men lived off the land without expensive supply lines, and he became known as "the Swamp Fox" for using essentially Indian-style tactics against the British. In recognition of his success with this style of warfare, the Continental Congress promoted him to brigadier general in 1781.

In Vermont, Ethan Allen organized his Green Mountain Boys to fight against the British and to push for Vermont independence. Like Francis Marion, Ethan Allen had also learned many of his fighting lessons in the French and Indian wars.

The American Revolution did not achieve the scale of guerrilla war that we associate with twentieth-century wars such as the protracted struggles in Algeria against the French, in Vietnam against the Americans, or in Afghanistan against the Soviets. For the most part, the colonists fought a traditional war using a regular army in the European style, but guerrilla warfare often made the crucial difference in cases where the Americans lacked a regular army. Indian-style fighting probably tipped the balance in a war between a small and disorganized group of colonists and the premier military power of the world.

In the nineteenth century, Indian-style warfare continued to be important to the struggling United States against European powers. The United States had to use these tactics in the War of 1812, when Britain controlled the seas and again invaded the United States with an army strong enough to capture and burn the new capital at Washington, D.C.

During most of the nineteenth century, however, the United States grew and built an army and navy largely following European models. If guerrilla warfare was the native influence of the eighteenth century, then fighting on horseback proved to be the major influence of the Indians on the developing American cavalry in the nineteenth century.

Ironically, it was the Europeans who introduced the horse to the Indians, but the Indians of the northern frontier, the Southwest, and the plains invented a new style of fighting on horseback. They adapted their traditional style of bush or guerrilla fighting to horseback, and the resulting armies of Indians probably resembled the ancient equestrian fighters of Central Asia and Arabia more than they did the European models derived from Roman cavalry technology and tactics.

It might be historically more precise to consider the arrival of the horse in European ships as a *reintroduction* of the animal, since the horse originally evolved in America and wandered to Asia, before becoming extinct in America during the Pleistocene era. From Asia the horse spread into the Middle East and Europe. Every great conquering empire of Asians or Europeans relied heavily on the horse. The Arabs who conquered North Africa and Iberia introduced some of the fastest horses and some of those best adapted for warfare. These Arab and Moorish horses formed the basis for the Spanish steeds brought by Columbus and the subsequent conquistadors of the Caribbean and then the Mexican mainland.

The repopulation of the horse in North America began from the Mexican coast, where Cortez and his men landed. Despite Spanish efforts to keep the horse out of Indian hands, the Indians quickly learned how to handle the animal. The launching of Spanish exploration into the north by Coronado and others introduced the Indians of the southwestern United States to the horse, which quickly became a highly valued and rapidly traded commodity in a market well beyond the power of the Spanish authorities. Horses thrived in the lush grazing lands of North America, and their herds grew so large that many escaped and formed new wild herds that proved an open resource for anyone, including Indians, who wanted to capture and tame them.

Early in the eighteenth century, the horses burst upon the open plains of the modern United States, which provided grazing territory matched only by the vast plains of central Asia. By 1722 the first horses reached the northern plains and the Dakota people, who had just suffered a great loss of land to the Ojibwa, who themselves had been pushed westward by the expanding Atlantic colonies.

The horse dispersed northward from Mexico during the same years that the gun traveled westward from the Atlantic Coast and the Great Lakes area. The acquistion of these two items by plains tribes in the 1730s produced a whole new culture.

The Indians who lived on the plains, and the neighboring tribes who lived on the prairie and on marginally agricultural lands, quickly adopted the horse and, in doing so, changed their traditional subsistence base. The horse allowed them to pursue the buffalo, rather than hunt it only when it passed through their homeland in its seasonal migrations.

Hunting proved so lucrative and easy compared to the older farming-and-foraging life-style that whole tribes, such as the Cheyenne, gave up growing crops and turned to hunting almost exclusively. When they needed food, tools, or other goods that the buffalo did not supply, they traded their vast harvest of buffalo meat and hides for what they needed.

Riding their fast horses on the open plains gave the Indians their first real chance to resist the onslaught of white settlers from the East. Throughout the nineteenth century, great nations of horsemen—Dakota, Lakota, Crow, Cheyenne, Assiniboin, Comanche, Arapaho, Blackfoot, Kiowa, and Apache—used the horse as the basis of their struggle against the invaders. The horse allowed them to strike deep into white territory at designated targets, and the horse provided quick and easy flight for warriors and their families from the white armies (Crosby, p. 172).

Along with the Arabs and the horse tribes of central Asia, the Indians became some of the best horsemen in history. Unlike these other groups, however, the Indians used the horse for hunting and not for herding. The Indians borrowed some of the Arab knowledge and horse technology brought by the Spaniards to America, but they also had to invent much of their own. They operated largely as self-taught horsemen.

Pioneers encountering the Plains Indians adopted horses from them. The English and German settlers arriving in America had little experience with horses beyond the workhorse that pulled the plow or wagon. The use of horses in European combat had been mainly the privilege of the aristocratic elite, and the knowledge of how to handle such animals did not come over to America with the peasant farmers. They knew relatively little of the swift fighting steeds of the Indians, and they didn't bring with them the rider-warrior mentality of nomadic hunters.

The new settlers and the soldiers sent into the plains quickly recognized the superiority of the Indian horses for speed and agility in long-distance travel as well as combat, and they began adopting the Indian mounts. The appaloosa, with its mottled brown and white coloring, its blotch of white hair on the rump, and its vertically striped hooves became one of the best-known breeds of so-called Indian ponies in the American west, but the settlers adopted many other breeds as well. Cavalrymen and cowboys both depended greatly on Indian horses.

The increasing numbers of the whites and their steadily developing technology allowed them eventually to defeat the plains warriors. In the end, the train, more than any other weapon, defeated the Plains Indians. The United States cavalry and the Royal Canadian Mounted Police never became as skilled or quick in handling the horses as the Plains Indians, but the train enabled them to transport large armies of men and horses faster and farther than even the fleetest Indian band on horseback.

The railroads also disrupted the migrations of the buffalo and permitted their wholesale slaughter. Without their source of food, the hunting tribes became hungry and filtered into mission stations, Indian forts, and finally reservations, where they could find food. Hunger delivered the final blow to the Indians of the plains.

In a long sequence of campaigns during the nineteenth century, the United States honed the cutting blade of its army on the Indians. The ultimate results could not be in doubt to anyone. By 1890 the practice was over. The army had done all it could to the Indians, but by this time the United States no longer needed the Indian for practice; it was ready to use its army on the world stage.

In the twentieth century the American Indian community again offered great service in the defense of the United States. To forestall any attempt by the enemies of the United States to try to make alliances with the native people, the Navajos reaffirmed their allegiances to the United States and denounced Adolf Hitler, whom they called Man-Who-Smells-Moustache. On June 3, 1940, a full year and a half before Japan attacked Pearl Harbor, the Navajo nation passed a resolution asserting the independent and democratic culture of the "First Americans" and proclaiming their willingness to fight against all foreign invaders who threatened the United States.

Coming from such a small and seemingly unimportant nation as the Navajos, the resolution might have seemed farcical to some people of that time, but the Navajos were to play a unique and often overlooked part in the struggle against the Axis powers. At that time even the Navajos themselves did not know what they were about to accomplish.

The small Navajo nation alone sent a relatively high number of 3,600 men and 12 women off to fight in World War II, including 420 Marines with a unique function. Spread across the Pacific, these men were responsible for encrypted radio communication among American forces. Rather than devise a special new code, the United States Marines depended on the Navajo "Codetalkers" speaking in their own language, which they encoded in special ways, so that for example, "dive bomber" became *ginitsoh*, which meant "sparrowhawk," a bird that could swoop down quickly like a dive bomber (Iverson, p. 48). Through a long list of such word substitutions and word associations, the Codetalkers created a code that the Japanese never broke.

The spirit of men like the Codetalkers and other veterans of the two world wars, the Korean War, and the Vietnam War, as well as the wars of the eighteenth and nineteenth centuries, still live in the powwow. The native people do not forget these warriors, and it is for them that the people of today must continue to dance.

On the night of October 30, 1987, a small group of people gathered beneath the Mendota Bridge over the Minnesota River, directly beneath the flight pattern of airplanes into the Minneapolis–St. Paul International Airport. It was only a month after the Mah-kato Powwow, and the early cold that had bedeviled the powwow had intensified and the rain had hardened to become a driving snow.

The Dakota minister Dr. Chris Cavender and Mdewakanton Dakota spiritual leader Amos Owen opened the ceremonies with traditional and Christian prayers. Only about a hundred people could endure the cold darkness, and many of these were elderly Dakota women and their families. In a ceremony reminiscent of the powwow, but distinct from it, they had come to honor the Dakota women and children interned on that spot during the winter of 1862–63, when the Dakota warriors were held and then executed at Mankato.

In 1862 the United States Army erected a civilian internment camp on the banks of the Minnesota River, just below Fort Snelling. The military authorities wanted to hold the women at least a day's journey from the men as hostages to ensure the good behavior of the captured men. The army also held them in fear that the women might strike back and somehow incite their warriors to fight again.

The men marching to Mankato and the women dragging their children to Fort Snelling had to pass through many small Minnesota towns and settlements where the townspeople lined up to form a gauntlet of hate. Fifteen of the Dakota women received serious injuries from the attacks of the settlers, and the settlers snatched one infant from the arms of its mother and smashed it to death. Exhausted and abused, the Dakota women limped into the camp that was to be their involuntary home for a year.

The black-and-white photographs that survive of the internment camp show a stark image of hundreds of seemingly identical tepees set up to house the 1,600 civilians. The uniformity of the arrangement seems almost too modern for the picture to be from the nineteenth century. At first glance, a viewer might easily mistake the rows of tepees for a Boy Scout encampment or a modern survival camp. But the high wooden stockade around the camp reveals a more sinister intention. Ice covers the river beside the camp, the trees stand bare against the winter, and the thick, hanging smoke that covers the camp indicates the deep cold.

Those old photographs have an eerie quality. The tepees seem so traditional, yet the identical appearance of the tepees, neatly arranged within an enclosure, offers a strange glimpse of a form that was to haunt the twentieth century. The pictures show us the birth of an institution, the beginning of a whole new social practice of concentrating innocent civilians into an area and imprisoning them for protracted periods without charging them with any crime. The British used the same type of camp to intern Boer women and children during their war in South Africa. By the middle of the twentieth century, the concentration camp had spread virtually around the world. The French used them in Algeria, the Germans constructed them in Europe, and the Russians built them in Siberia.

The Americans had chosen to build their fort at the strategic spot where the Minnesota River flowed into the Mississippi. The Mdewakanton Dakota, however, had a different vision of that spot. For them the confluence of the rivers was where their ancestral grandmother and grandfather first emerged from *Ina*—their mother, the Earth. Mendota marked the sacred place where human life was created.

The weather in the old photographs seems as cold as the night we all gathered on the same spot, 125 years later. Rose Bluestone, Naomi Cavender, and other elders rose one at a time to tell what each knew of her own ancestors who survived and some who died at the internment camp. Bundled in heavy coats and kerchiefs tied tight against the Arctic wind, the women spoke softly and slowly in English mixed with Dakota. The whining automobiles on the bridge overhead and the buzzing airplanes sometimes drowned the women's voices, but they persisted late into the night. They had come to speak, and they had come to stay the entire night in honor of their ancestors.

They spoke of hardships, such as that of the mother who buried her baby and then saw it again the next day, in the jaws of a starving dog who dragged it through camp. They spoke of the grave injustices of the government against the women, such as the reduction of their food rations, and they spoke of the little injustices and insults to human dignity, such as the soldier guards who urinated on the womens' tepees during the night. They spoke of great kindnesses, as when townspeople brought food and blankets. They spoke of great achievements, as when the interned women quickly and laboriously taught one another to read the Dakota language using an adapted Latin alphabet and orthography devised by missionaries. The men learned the same system at Mankato, and thus the men and women in families that had never before been separated could still communicate with one another by writing letters, copies of which Dakota people still cling to today as memories of the most trying episode in Mdewakanton history.

As each woman finished speaking, she asked the Mazakute Singers, huddled around their drum, to play an honor song in memory of a grandmother who survived the camp, a grandmother's sister who died there without children, and the other women who died without anyone to remember their names.

At each request the men sang out loudly, as though determined that the Dakota voice would again fill the valley, no matter how many cars and airplanes might fight to stifle it. As they sang, the old women climbed slowly down from the small podium and shuffled around in a slow dance of honor on the frozen earth. After completing one circle alone or leaning on the arm of a family member for support, each old woman's descendants and other relatives came out one by one to dance behind her. When they had completed another circle, friends of the family joined them, and finally other people who simply wanted to add their dance of honor for the women of Fort Snelling. The dances seemed to be as much for the old women who led them around the arena as for the long-dead ancestors to whom the honoring songs and dances were dedicated.

Throughout the night, as snow occasionally drifted through the trees, the women continued their speeches and dances of honor while the men drummed and sang. Finally the airplanes stopped landing and taking off, and the cars ceased to pass overhead as commuters all reached the safe warmth of their homes, and the cities went to bed. The women danced on, and when they had said all they had to say about their ancestors, when they had read the names of all the people they knew who had been interned there, they gathered in the still, tight darkness of the sweat lodge to purify themselves for the next morning, when they would smoke the sacred pipe and sing a Dakota hymn.

The Dakota women were making peace, seeking to restore the balance and harmony of the world, to reconcile a history of pain. They danced to bring peace to the people who died there. They danced to bring peace among themselves as well as peace with the white society. They danced to make peace with Ina, the Earth Mother, whose act of creation at the confluence of the two rivers had been desecrated by the internment camp built upon it.

America has learned much about fighting from the ancient Indian warriors, but we have barely begun to learn the elders' lessons for making peace.

13

AMERICA'S PATRON SAINT

Macon, Georgia, lies a little too far south of Atlanta to be a suburb, and yet a little too close to be a full city in its own right. It enjoyed a brief prosperity during the cotton days before the Civil War, and the perpetual poverty since then has preserved its handful of antebellum homes clustered on a hilltop overlooking the downtown area.

Across the tiny Ocmulgee River from downtown Macon, a poor district sprawls along the river. Small wooden houses with rickety old porches lie interspersed with cement-block houses sealed with air conditioners plugged into their windows. The small communities cluster around convenience stores that offer the coolest reprieve of any spot in the blistering and seemingly eternal summer of Georgia. The poverty of Macon has an anonymous and hard-to-identify quality—neither urban nor rural, not completely black but certainly not completely white; not hopeless, yet with no apparent remedy.

On the poor side of town, on the plateau overlooking the river, a scattering of what appear to be small, wooded hills crop up out of the ground. These artificial hills turn out to be a series of temple mounds put together in a configuration much like those of Cahokia and other Mississippian sites, even though Macon, Georgia, lies a long way from the Mississippi River.

Archaeologists found something unique here that distinguishes the Ocmulgee site at Macon from other Mississippian sites. One of the structures that looks as if it could be a truncated pyramid or a small temple mound turned out to be a large room built into the earth and covered with wood, thatch, and dirt. The upper part of the structure suffered severe damage from an ancient fire, but that same fire helped to preserve the lower part of the building. From that base, modern archaeologists have been able to reconstruct the entire structure.

To reach the room, one must walk though a long, low entry tunnel. After walking only a few feet, the visitor experiences a marked change between the outside and the inside. One moves from the bright Georgia sun into near darkness, from the loud birds, chirping insects and other distracting noises into absolute silence muffled by layers of mud and earth, from the searing hot summer air to cool, refreshing shade.

It takes a few moments for the body and eyes to adjust to the new surroundings, but gradually the features of the circular room emerge. In the middle, the clear markings of a large hearth remain as evidence of the ancient council fire that provided light for the activity of the subterranean chamber. A circular platform follows virtually the entire circumference of the room, and on the platform one clearly sees the impression of a series of forty-seven seats. The focal point of the room faces directly across from the entrance, in the most brightly illuminated spot in the great room. Rising up from the platform, a clearly visible eagle emerges with a large, almost square body. Its head has an oversized forked eye, shaped like an upside-down V, a particular motif found on birds and even humans in the late Mississippian sites and artifacts.

This ancient room has stood on this site for at least a thousand years, and it is now reconstructed to the form that it had in about the year 1000. The room obviously served as a meeting room for the community. It may have hosted a combination of religious and secular meetings as well as various ceremonies through the year or in the life cycles of community members.

In the southwestern United States, many such rooms are still visible in the Anasazi ruins. There again, we find a proliferation of small, circular underground chambers or kivas. Like the earth lodge at Ocmulgee, these kivas frequently have platform benches on the sides, and focus on a central, recessed hearth.

The kivas provided one of the most distinctive architectural characteristics of Anasazi ruins. They form the central meeting place of the ancient people who lived there. The number of kivas indicates that many different small groups met in them. Whether organized around kinship, gender, religion, or some other principle, the number of kivas built over thousands of years shows the abiding importance of the activities within them.

Whether we are looking at the earthen lodges of the Mandan on the Missouri River in North Dakota, at the longhouses of the Iroquois confederacy, at the plank houses of the Northwest coast, or the earth lodge on the Ocmulgee River in Macon, Georgia, we see the importance of meeting houses for the natives across the North American continent. Natives in almost all parts of North America built structures for community gatherings. Even the Inuit of the Arctic built a large communal igloo where they held their winter ceremonies.

Throughout North America, the native people organized themselves into a great variety of lodges and small, locally based organizations that cut through kinship. Frequently these organizations were restricted to men, but some were for women only, and some included both males and females. Some of the groups, such as those of the Great Plains, served as warriors' societies for the protection of the group; others, like those in the Southwest, served ceremonial and sacred purposes associated with the continued health and well-being of the community.

In Europe, voluntary organizations such as the Masons resembled the Indian lodges in some respects, but the European groups usually had a decidedly hierarchical organization. The European organizations often modeled themselves on a military or aristocratic sequence of ranks and offices with elaborate titles.

In twentieth-century America, civic organizations and men's lodges acquired a reputation as primarily social institutions often associated with rowdiness, excessive drinking, and escape from familial duties. This twentieth-century denigration of the lodge tradition obscures the much more serious purposes and origins of these groups, which often had a direct involvement with the American struggle for independence and with the effort to shape a unique American identity separate from that of the disparate nations of origin of the settlers.

Describing the Americans of the early nineteenth century, Alexis de Tocqueville wrote in *Democracy in America* that in "no country in the world has the principle of association been more successfully used or applied to a greater multitude of objects than in America." In addition to the ones directly connected with government, "a vast number of others are formed and maintained by the agency of private individuals."

De Tocqueville had no ready explanation for this odd American trait, but at places in his writing he seems to hint at it. In general he despised the Indians of North America, but he admired some of their qualities as free citizens in their own land. He wrote that "Indians, although they are ignorant and poor, are equal and free." He even recognized their influence on Americans when many "Americans of the West are born in the woods, and they mix the ideas and customs of savage life with the civilization of their fathers."

During the struggle for independence, colonists organized themselves in ways that frequently imitated the councils and groups of the Indians. One of the earliest groups organized by the rebellious colonists to pursue independence was the Tammany Society, named for the chief of the Lenni-Lenape (Delaware) who greeted William Penn when he arrived on October 27, 1682, to found the colony of Pennsylvania. Whether or not Chief Tammany appeared on that particular day under a fabled elm tree, he did sign two important treaties with Penn in June of the following year and a decade later, in June 1692. Chief Tammany entered history as one of those Indians, like Squanto and Powhatan, who helped the European colonists to survive in the North American environment for which their European cities had not prepared them.

During the eighteenth century, after Chief Tammany died, he became the hero of many dubious tales and apocryphal histories as well as the reputed utterer of more words of wisdom than he ever could have imparted. He became a great judge and lawgiver of colonial mythology. One story even claims that he once went to Mexico to meet with Manco Capac, the ruler of the Incas in Peru. At this meeting point, halfway between Pennsylvania and Peru, Chief Tammany gave Manco Capac advice on how to organize Inca society. Colonial legends falsely credited Tammany as the originator of many of the Indian gifts such as corn, beans, tobacco, the crabapple, and even the canoe (Werner, p. 3).

With so many different stories and so much false information about Chief Tammany, it becomes difficult to sort out the actual details of his life. One tradition claims that Chief Tammany lived for a while near Scranton, Pennsylvania, and another maintains that he built his primary wigwam in New Jersey on the site where Princeton University later arose (Myers, p. 4). After a long and productive life, legend says that Chief Tammany had accomplished everything that he could do. He then wrapped himself in his blanket and set himself on fire.

In addition to being a great lawgiver, Chief Tammany acquired an intimate connection in the colonial mind with nature and eventually with the month of May and the opening of spring and the fishing season. The first day of May became his special day, and colonists combined the European tradition of the maypole with Indian traditions and created an amalgamated day of Indian-European frivolity and merriment to welcome spring. In some states they celebrated his day a little later, on the twelfth of May rather than the first.

As relations between the colonists and Britain became increasingly hostile in the late eighteenth century, the frivolous celebrations around the memory of Chief Tammany assumed a more serious note. Tammany became increasingly associated with the rights of the American colonists. The colonists themselves took on the identity of *Americans*, a term previously applied to the Indians, while the colonists had called themselves by the name of their country of origin.

Loyalist groups had already formed organizations named for the patron saints of their original homelands. Englishmen formed the St. George Society. The Scots organized into the St. Andrew Society, while the Welsh venerated St. David, and the Irish honored St. Patrick. To show their strictly American identity, colonists adopted *Saint* Tammany as their patron. Tammany offered a strictly American symbol around which all colonists could unite, no matter what their original European heritage.

Through the American Revolution, the celebration of Tammany Day continued each year on the first of May. Even when George Washington bivouacked his troops at Valley Forge, they observed the end of the harsh winter with a celebration of Tammany's Day on May 1, 1778. The enlisted men raised maypoles, dressed a sergeant in Indian costume to play the role of Chief Tammany, and the whole army celebrated their American identity, their survival through the harsh winter, and their determination to continue fighting the British.

Soldiers and common men sang songs to Tammany, and poets composed long odes in his honor. The playwright Ann Julia Hatton wrote a play *Tammany; or, the Indian Chief,* which became the hit of the New York stage in 1795.

In honor of Tammany, the revolutionary Sons of Liberty took him as their "patron saint," and by 1772 they had changed the name of their organization to the Society of King Tammany. Revolutionary societies from Georgia to Massachusetts sprang up as the Society of Saint Tammany, the Society of Chief Tammany, the Society of King Tammany, or even the simple Society of Tammany in New York.

While the nomenclature varied from one colony to another and even from one community to another, all the Tammany societies followed an Indian, particularly an Iroquoian, model of organization. They formed thirteen tribes to represent the thirteen colonies, and each tribe had its own totem. The eagle represented New York, the otter New Hampshire, the panther Massachusetts, the beaver Rhode Island, the bear Connecticut, the tortoise New Jersey, the rattlesnake Pennsylvania, the tiger Delaware, the fox Maryland, the deer Virginia, the buffalo North Carolina, the raccoon South Carolina, and the wolf Georgia (Myers, p. 5).

A Grand Sachem presided over thirteen other sachems, who led the general members, called "braves." Other titles represented other Indian offices, and they acknowledged the President of the United States as the Great Grand Sachem over them all. Just as the Iroquois considered themselves united by the "chain of friendship," the Sons of Tammany formed a "chain of union" that championed the principles of fraternal union and patriotic nationalism (Mushkat, p. 11).

They called their meeting house a "wigwam," and they filled it with Indian paraphernalia including bows, arrows, and calumets, the sacred tobacco pipes. The society in New York collected Indian artifacts and created the first museum of American Indian works at its earlier wigwam on Broad Street from 1790 to 1798.

After the American Revolution, the Tammany societies became the first veterans' organization of men who had fought in the war. In support of the newly formed American government, they again changed their name, to the *Constitutional* Sons of St. Tammany. They formed centers of strong patriotic fervor committed to spreading the spark of revolution to other countries, and to fighting monarchy and tyranny in every guise. They ardently supported the French Revolution.

The members of the Tammany societies came from the strengthening middle and skilled working classes of urban and rural America. They were craftsmen: upholsterers, paperhangers, carpenters, small merchants, and farmers. Most of them fought in the Revolutionary War as common soldiers, not as officers. They were men without sophisticated polish and education, but they were devoted to liberty and freedom. The Tammany Society gave them a patriotic focus, but it also provided them with a social organization. The Tammany Society functioned as a political party, a social club, and a trade union.

The Sons of Tammany worked hard to maintain their Indian—and thus their American—identification. Although at times this verged on the farcical, it had a serious and frequently important aspect, particularly in negotiations with the Indian nations. During the Revolution, they often entertained American Indian visitors and delegations as a way of maintaining good relations with the Indians tribes while the colonies fought the British. As early as May 1776, the Tammany Society of Philadelphia hosted a visiting Iroquois delegation that had come to inquire about the plans of the colonies for a war with England. During the negotiations, the visiting Iroquois lodged on the second floor of Independence Hall.

After the Revolution, George Washington faced the difficult task of winning back the friendship and allegiance of several defeated

Indian nations who had sided with the British against the colonists. When he invited Alexander McGillivray and the other Creek chiefs to New York to negotiate a new treaty in 1790, Washington asked the Tammany Society to host the chiefs and to build informal and formal ties with them. This started a new tradition of the Tammany societies serving as the urban hosts for visiting Indian delegations, particularly for ones conducting peace negotiations with the United States government.

In the early decades of American independence, the Tammany societies played key roles in organizing public celebrations and parades in honor of the new American republic. They sponsored the celebration of the ratification of the Constitution by the states, and in time their efforts for national commemorations focused on the annual twin celebrations of St. Tammany's Day in May and the Fourth of July. They always wore Indian dress and danced in the Indian style just as they had done during the Boston Tea Party and at similar acts of early rebellion against George III. Those who did not wear full Indian regalia pinned the tail of a buck deer to their hats because Chief Tammany had supposedly used the deer as his personal totem.

The more staid upper class never approved of these public spectacles of patriotism. One writer in *The American Citizen and General Advertiser* of July 6, 1809, complained bitterly about such displays; "Instead of commemorating the birth of the nation with that manliness and dignity which the occasion calls for and inspires, we see them with pain and disgust daubing their faces with paint, crowding their heavy heads with feathers; making savages in appearance more savage; representing, as they term it, the genius of the nation in the person of someone who has no genius. . . ."

The Tammany societies stood in contrast to the higher-class membership of the Masons and the Society of Cincinnati of the same time. The Society of Cincinnati limited itself to officers of the Revolutionary War, and still today it admits only descendants of officers of that war. In selecting the name Cincinnati, they emphasized their ties to the Old World and to the Roman tradition of the fifth-century general Lucius Quinctius Cincinnatus, who always fought for the patrician interests against the plebeians. As an elite organization of lettered men, they maintained close ties with the French officers who had fought with them in the American Revolution, and when the French Revolution came, they sided with the aristocracy against the French masses (Mushkat, p. 11).

The Society of Cincinnati limited membership to inheritance through firstborn sons only. This rule of primogeniture would provide only the firstborn of the firstborn with the right to wear the society's insignia. After ardent resistance from George Washington, who feared that this might create an incipient American aristocracy of the officer class, the society dropped its primogeniture rule (Myers, p. 4).

The middle- and working-class people following Chief Tammany contrasted decisively with the elite aristocrats following the Roman general and dictator Cincinnatus. The two groups offered competing versions of what American patriots wanted to create in their newly independent nation. In the days before the firm formation of political parties, organizations such as the Society of the Cincinnati represented the aristocratic or federalist interests, while the Tammany Society represented the Democratic Republicans.

With renewed British aggression against the United States in 1812, many of the Indian nations sided with Britain against the fledgling American government. This break between the United States and the Indians caused a permanent change in the Tammany societies. In anger at the Indians who had deserted them, they stripped the society of all Indian regalia and dropped the Indian titles. They broke the bonds of friendship that had bound them to the Indian nations. The War of 1812 ended America's initial glorification of the Indians, who were transformed from the Noble Savage and Champion of Liberty to the bloodthirsty savage of the forest, waiting to scalp American men and abduct their women and children. The change in perception of Indians from nobles to savages coincided with the start of the great trek westward and the opening of the plains and Pacific areas to settlers.

After the War of 1812, the New York Society of Tammany resurrected a few of its original Indian trappings and titles, but the close identification between the society and the Indians had been permanently severed. The members even sold the Tammany Museum collection of Indian artifacts. By the end of the nineteenth century P. T. Barnum had bought the American Indian collection that the Tammany society had owned, and he incorporated it into his "Greatest Show on Earth."

In the nineteenth century the United States became a more serious nation, and much of the revolutionary ardor of the eighteenth century slipped away as the prosperous middle class sought a return to the traditional European activities of earning money, and to the values and religion that supported this quest. The Deism of the previous century lost favor as Americans of all classes embraced powerful fundamentalist movements. Most of the societies drifted into obscurity and disbanded as the members joined overtly political organizations and parties.

Mockery of religion and the honoring of a secular saint such as St. Tammany, a man renowned for his pagan life-style, retreated from the front parlor to the back room. Andrew Jackson was the last President of the United States to bear the title Great Grand Sachem of the Society of Tammany. The organization's ties to the revolutionary tradition and to the highest organs of American government grew steadily weaker and more frayed.

The New York Tammany Society continued as a strong but local political organization having merely nominal association with liberty, Indians, and revolution. Politicians of the Democratic Party became particularly powerful within the Society of Tammany and eventually took it over and ran a corrupt political administration from Tammany Hall. When the politician William Tweed became the Grand Sachem in 1868, the Society of Tammany had become a mere front for the corruption of the Tweed Ring, which siphoned off tens of millions of dollars before *Harper's Weekly* magazine and the *New York Times* exposed them. The courts convicted "Boss" William Tweed and some of his cronies in 1873, and left the name of Tammany associated in the minds of most Americans with political corruption rather than with Native American liberty and independence.

The Tammany societies became the best known of the early Indian lodges organized by whites, but others arose as well. During the American Revolution, at the same time that some members of the Sons of Liberty formed the Tammany Society, more adamantly revolutionary members of the group formed the Improved Order of Red Men. Like the Tammany Society, the Red Men organized themselves into "tribes," met in "wigwams" under a Grand Lodge, and reproduced or invented Indian rituals at their meetings around a campfire. Sachems presided at their initiation ceremonies.

Despite superficial similarities to the Tammany societies, the Red Men advocated a more radical and even more strongly American ideology. They maintained that the European settlers in America had learned democracy from the American Indian, and that they could improve that democratic strain by further emulating the Indians. They explained that the early settlers "never knew what real American liberty was, they having lived under kings all of their lives, and having no vote or voice in . . . their own government. Their first vision of real freedom was caught from the wild savages, who roamed the forest" (Johansen and Grinde). By changing the name from the Sons of Liberty to the Improved Order of Red Men, the fraternal members recognized the role of Indians in the development of American democracy.

Rather than adhering to traditional Christianity, the Red Men offered prayers to the "Great Spirit" whose light filled the forest (Carnes, p. 58). The Red Men in their early years had a decisively anticapitalist ideology that called for their members to emulate the Native Americans, who held property in common (Carnes, p. 32). They also favored the abolition of alcohol and advocated complete abstinence from strong drink for all of its members. Unlike other fraternal organizations, which met in taverns whenever practical, the Red Men eschewed meeting in places that served alcohol. As the nineteenth century progressed, the Red Men become more concerned with ritual and less with ideals. While the Tammany Society became a corrupt political machine, the Red Men became a men's social and fraternal group.

The fraternal organizations based on Indian themes shared a common commitment to liberty and to the basic principles of democracy. This contrasted greatly with the fraternal organizations based on authoritarian patterns of learning from masters and blind obedience to those with more knowledge. Organizations such as the Odd Fellows had a strong overt strain of partriarchy that also appeared in the organization and rituals of the Masons, the Knights of the Golden Circle, the Knights of Pythias, and the Order of Good Templars.

Even the shrouded Knights of the Ku Klux Klan glorified the authoritarian social systems of the Old World in their medieval nomenclature, costumes, and ceremonies. The men who formed the first Klan in Pulaski, Tennessee, in 1866 borrowed apparel, ceremony, and insignias from the older Sons of Malta (Carnes, p. 8).

By the second half of the nineteenth century, fraternal orders of all types had fallen on hard times. New civic groups for men sponsored community services such as hospitals and orphanages, and acted as booster clubs to support local businessmen. The men's societies opened up to lower-middle-class and working-class men, but they had to fight newly emerging labor unions for the loyalty of these workingmen.

About the time that the Indian and classical fraternal orders reached a nadir, the Indian spirit found a rebirth in boys' organizations. The impetus came from the artist Ernest Thompson Seton, who was born in 1860 in England but grew up in the Canadian backwoods between 1866 and 1870, and lived on the western prairie from 1882 to 1887. Seton wrote and illustrated books about the natural life of Canada's backwoods and prairie. He published *Mammals of Manitoba* in 1886, followed by *Birds of Manitoba* in 1891.

Seton also worked to form boys' clubs based on Indian models. After much discussion of the idea, he started the first group in 1902 with the backing of the *Ladies' Home Journal*. His Woodcraft Indian societies used much of the terminology of the earlier men's groups. A boy entered as a Brave, worked up to Warrior, and could eventually become a Sagamore. But Seton sought a more realistic approximation of Indian life than the fraternal orders had advocated. He strove to purify the Indian strains, to return to the original ideals behind these Indian names and titles.

He wanted the Woodcraft Indians to give boys a chance to learn self-reliance and to organize their own activities, albeit with adult supervision. For this purpose the boys organized into self-governing tribes, each with its own animal or plant totem as a group emblem.

Seton also wanted to minimize competitiveness among the boys by having them work to fulfill absolute standards rather than to vie with one another. For each achievement, such as running one hundred yards in twelve seconds, making a tepee or a bow and arrow, or tracking an animal, the boy earned a feather and a small "wampum badge" to be worn on a special sash. Seton derived this system of honor from the Plains Indians, who awarded coups for particularly brave deeds of young men. The boys never won the badges by having to defeat another boy or team; instead they won them only from their own efforts competing against themselves toward an absolute goal.

Through the Woodcraft Indian movement, Seton sought to build character through the virtues of honesty, thrift, and helpfulness. For Seton the ideal man was Tecumseh, the Shawnee leader. According to Seton, "Tecumseh was a great athlete, a great hunter, a great leader, clean, manly, strong, unsordid, courteous, fearless, kindly, gentle with his strength, dignified, silent and friendly, equipped for emergencies, and filled with a religion that consisted not of books and creeds or occasional observances, but of desire to help those that had need of help. . . ." He was "the model of perfect manhood" (Rosenthal, p. 65).

Seton attempted to export the Woodcraft Indian model to England, but despite having an interest in nature and outdoor activities for youths, Britons had little interest in the American Indians. A British officer and veteran of the Boer War, Lord Robert Stephenson Baden-Powell, took the basic framework of Seton's idea, stripped away most of the Indian characteristics, and made a paramilitary organization called the Boy Scouts, which he created in 1908. In 1910 he and his sister Agnes organized a corresponding Girl Guides for females.

The Boy Scout model spread much faster than the Woodcraft Indian model, but in North America the two merged. Seton worked with the first Boy Scout groups in America, and they quickly absorbed many of the characteristics of the Woodcraft Indian movement. Seton's handbook *The Birch-bark Roll of the Woodcraft Indians* in time gave way to *The Boy Scout Handbook*, which reflects the same organization, ideals, symbols, and activities. This made the Scouts in North America more Indian in orientation, whereas the Scouts in Britain remained a paramilitary organization.

At about the same time that the Scouts began growing in America on Indian models, social fraternities grew in importance on American college campuses. Based on classical models, these organizations eschewed any Native American trappings in favor of Greek mottoes, Roman togas, and other classical trappings, down to Greek columns on the porches of their residence halls. Scouting, based on Indian models for middle-class children, as opposed to Greek fraternities, based on classical models for the educated upper class, reflected in the early twentieth century the rivalry between the Indian-style Tammany societies and the classical Society of Cincinnati in the eighteenth century.

In each of these historical episodes, Americans consciously modeled modern social institutions on those of the Indians. They saw in Indian society ideals and behaviors that all people should emulate. As America moved away from its rural heritage and into the industrial era, Americans became even more aware of the need for these Indian models for modern youth.

Whether these groups helped their members work for social or personal aims, over the past three centuries they have consistently played a major role in inventing American identity. They helped the American people discover who they were, and shaped the image of who they wanted to become. Through such groups, Indian values and ideas exerted an influence on middle-class urban and industrial America in the twentieth century in much the same way that they did on frontier and rural America in the eighteenth century. The Indians continued as a source of inspiration and social models for new generations of Americans.

The meeting chamber in Ocmulgee, Georgia, or a kiva in New Mexico still speaks to the American psyche. One feels a certain connection and sense of belonging in such a chamber. It represents a part of many things in our collective social life, from the town meeting to a Scout jamboree, from a nation's quest for independence to a young child's quest for adulthood.

14

AMERICAN-IZATION OF THE ENGLISH LANGUAGE

WOJB radio broadcasts daily across the Ojibwa territory of northern Wisconsin. The station originates from Lac Coutre Oreilles Reservation, just sixty miles south of what the Ojibwa call Lake Gitchee Gumi, which we know as Lake Superior, the largest freshwater lake in the world and a traditional focal point of Great Lakes Ojibwa culture and mythology. The nonprofit station operates as one of the most important Indian stations in the nation, and one of the few native stations to broadcast east of the Mississippi River.

WOJB occupies a plain, windowless building. The structure looks more like a warehouse than a broadcast studio, but parked prominently in front of it is a large white satellite receiving dish bearing a black drawing of a stylized thunderbird, the sacred symbol of the messenger. The station fills the air with national and international news, information about upcoming ball games at the reservation high school, Ojibwa language classes from Lac Coutre Oreilles Community College, health and nutrition information, announcements of powwows, and fishing updates, as well as tribal myths, drum songs, and talks by the elders. Over the Labor Day weekend, each year for three full days, the station broadcasts the drum groups, singers, and speakers of the Protect the Earth Pow Wow.

"Woodland Community Radio," as its name implies, reflects the life of the woodland people who live in the heart of North America. They live in the forests surrounded by tens of thousands of lakes dug out of the earth during the last glacial retreat. Most of the Ojibwa reservations, such as Lac du Flambeau and Fond du Lac, have French names that reflect the Indian heritage of the area. WOJB broadcasts from Lac Coutre Oreilles, which means Lake of the Short Ears, and is pronounced in modern English as "La Coot Oray" or reduced to its initials, LCO.

To reach the radio station, one must drive between a series of lakes and rows of small tourist cottages and A-frame structures marketed rather euphemistically as chalets, villas, or "hobby farms." The lakes outnumber the small towns with their white-owned businesses catering to the two major industries, tourism and timber. The largest businesses seem to be bait-and-tackle stores, usually located close to warehouse liquor stores. In addition to the traditional taxidermists and canoe shops, the towns offer boat-repair services, hot-tub salesrooms, video rental stores, and the usual lineup of fast-food restaurants.

The Lutheran churches seem to come in about a half-dozen different sects, but the real religion of the area is high school ice hockey, which the locals pursue with a zeal that professional teams must envy. Ice hockey only barely takes precedence over ice fishing, cross-country skiing, and snowmobile driving in the winter, and canoeing, motorboating, and fishing in the summer.

Even after the ice-fishing houses legally have to be removed on the first of March, solitary fisherman squat over the holes in the ice until virtually the last possible day before "ice out." Many of the communities have a simple and effective way of determining the exact day when "ice out" occurs. After driving over the frozen lakes and rivers with their cars and four-wheel-drive vehicles all winter, they park a rusty old clunker of a car on the ice in March. Locals then take bets and organize gambling pools on the exact day in April when the weather will warm up enough to melt the ice and send the hulk crashing through to the cold bottom of the lake.

Even though the radio station is very much an Ojibwa institution, it maintains a certain pan-Indian atmosphere. The walls of the station bear paintings, photographs, and craft objects from Indian nations across North America. The radio programming also reflects a multicultural world, with music from Hopi drummers and Inuit singers as well as interviews with Indians throughout America.

Despite the Indian orientation and Ojibwa focus of the radio station, it broadcasts its programs primarily in the English language. Aside from native songs and an occasional tribal elder speaking in Ojibwa, the announcers use English, the language most commonly understood by the native and immigrant audiences of Wisconsin. To use only the Ojibwa language would cut off virtually all the non-Indians, all the non-Ojibwa Indians, and even most of the Ojibwa, who now function better in English than in their ancestral tongue.

The common use of English by North American Indians leads some people to the conclusion that Indian languages have died. At Lac Coutre Oreilles, however, students from kindergarten through college study the Ojibwa language. Indian languages live often as a ceremonial or family language, but in public most Indians speak English.

Some languages, such as Navajo in the southwestern United States, Cree and Dene in northern Canada, and Inuit across the Arctic, still live as the common tongues of daily life. Other languages, like many of the Algonquian dialects of New England, have now become virtually extinct. In classrooms and night schools throughout Indian territory today, native speakers teach classes in Cherokee, Choctaw, Creek, Dakota, Lakota, Ojibwa, and dozens of other languages, but these languages show no signs of replacing English or of taking over again as the mother tongues of the people who lost them.

Although English has become the common language of Indians in North America, they have not abandoned their native tongues completely. Indian people have carried parts of their languages with them into English, and in the process they have helped to make English a more vibrant and important language. The English language has changed the lives of Native Americans, but they have also changed the English language.

Europeans, upon first arriving in America, lacked the words to name what they saw in the new environment. As Thomas Jefferson explained their plight, the "new circumstances . . . call[ed] for new words, new phrases, and the transfer of old words to new objects" (McCrum, p. 111). They recognized some of the animals, such as deer, bears, and wolves, and misapplied European names to some creatures, such as buffalo and robins, but even when they exhausted all of these names, America had strange animals, plants, geographical configurations, and weather that needed new words. From the beginning the Europeans had to use Native American words to name animals such as *moose, caribou, raccoon, opossum, chipmunk, barracuda, manatee, cougar, puma, jaguar, terrapin, chigger,* and *skunk.*

They also had to use Indian names for trees and plants such as *hickory, pecan, persimmon, mahogany, mangrove, maypop, mesquite, yucca,* and *saguaro.* Particularly in the area of food plants, the colonists took many of the Indian names, including *maize, hominy, squash, avocado, pemmican, manioc, cassava, papaya, pawpaw, tapioca, succotash,* and *scuppernong.*

Even the topography of the continent appeared strange and alien to the Europeans, and they had to adopt Indian words such as the Choctaw *bayou* and the Taino *savanna,* the latter identifying a grassy plain with few trees, a concept also expressed by the Quechua word *pampas.* In the Canadian tundra, explorers adopted the Cree word *muskeg* to denote the sphagnum bogs of decaying vegetable matter. The upland coastal swamps usually found in wooded areas of the southern Atlantic Coast became known as *pocosin* from the Delaware word for such areas. The Algonquian word *podunk,* meaning a corner of isolated land or a small neck of land, passed into English as the name of a Massachusetts community, but came to signify any remote locale.

Spaniards brought up from South America the word *chaco* to apply to treeless savannas. Although some dictionaries give a Basque etymology for the word, it probably comes from the Quechua people, who use *chaqo* to describe a place that once had trees but no longer does. The word derives from the verb for communal net hunting for small animals, which the Quechua people did in open, treeless areas. The word became the name of a large part of Bolivia and Paraguay—the Gran Chaco—as well as the name of a canyon in New Mexico and other sites across the southwestern United States.

As America became more urban, many of these words denoting various kinds of rural environments became less common, but they could play a lifesaving role for early colonists and pioneers unaccustomed to the country. The words told them which areas they could pass through and which to avoid. In this way Indian terms formed the linguistic map of the new territory.

Even the weather of the Americas called for new words. The Europeans immediately recognized that the giant storms that blew up from the Caribbean in the late summer and fall far surpassed in scale and ferocity the simple squalls and rain showers implied in the English word *storm*. They had to use a Carib word, *hurricane*, to name the fierce storms of the Caribbean. Similarly, white settlers applied the Salish word *chinook* to both the moist, warm winds that blew in from the Pacific and the warm, dry winds that blew from the Rocky Mountains onto the northern plains of the United States and Canada. From the Paiute language the settlers took the word *pogonip* to describe the ice fog or clouds of ice crystals common in the western mountains.

The word *blizzard* probably derives from an Indian word, although its origin is now lost. According to the *Oxford English Dictionary*, the first written record of *blizzard* comes from the frontiersman Colonel Davy Crockett in 1834. Since Crockett used it without explanation, as though the reader would already know the word, we may assume that *blizzard* had already attained common usage by that time.

A concept in anthropology called *naïve realism* assumes that the words people use reflect the world around them precisely as the world is. A person, no matter what language used, perceives the world in fairly much the same way as any other person.

Even if we admit that all humans have the same basic potential for perception, the actual perceptions vary. An Arctic Inuk can judge the thickness and stability of sea ice much better than almost anyone else in the world. Bushmen of the Kalahari know how to track animals and humans over vast expanses of territory by seeing traces of evidence that would baffle anyone else. The footprint of a giraffe might be barely visible to a European, but the

Bushman sees that the giraffe is a pregnant female listing slightly to the right from a flesh wound to the right hind leg.

Any human can learn to judge ice or track giraffes with the right teaching, but one needs the language to explain it. Europeans arrived in America with languages well suited to European geography, land, weather, animals, plants, seasons, and social structure. Words such as *storm, tempest, squall,* or *gale* perfectly describe European conditions, particulary coastal ones, but they do not convey the information needed to describe such things as an American hurricane, blizzard, or chinook. When William Shakespeare used the word *tempest* to describe a South Atlantic storm, it would not be the same if he had called his work *The Hurricane.* Someone who equates a tempest with a hurricane might mistake the calm eye of the storm for the end of the storm, a mistake that could have disastrous results.

Indian words invaded the English language well before the first English colonists came to settle. The colonists arrived in North America already using Indian words that had entered English via the Spanish language acquired through British trade and piracy in the Caribbean. These included words such as the Mayan *cigar,* Arawakan *tobacco,* Taino *potato,* and Nahuatl *tomato.* It even included the Taino word *hammoc,* the name for the Indian sleeping device eagerly adopted by British sailors for use on board ship.

Many South and Central American animals retained their original Indian names in Spanish and in English. From Quechua came the name for the llama, which English-speakers adopted with Spanish orthography and therefore mispronounced as *lama* instead of *yama*

Quechua also supplied the names for the *vicuña* and the *condor.* From Tupi languages, spoken throughout large parts of the Amazon basin, came the names for the *piranha,* with its razor teeth, the colorful *toucan* with its oversized bill, and the *capybara,* the world's largest rodent, which swims in the waters of the Amazon. From Guarani, a language still spoken today as the second official language of Paraguay, came names for the *tapir,* a piglike creature, and the fierce *jaguar.* From the Aymara language spoken around Lake Titicaca in Bolivia came the names for the *alpaca* and the *chinchilla.* Even the word *shark,* which entered English late in the sixteenth century, probably came from an American language.

Many of the native American medicines had no counterparts in European languages. Particularly medicines from the tropical zones entered English through Spanish and kept their Indian names. These included *quinine* from Quechua, *curare* and *tonka* from Carib, *ipecac* and *jaborandi* from Tupi, and *mescal, peyote,* and *tacamahac* from the Aztec language of Nahuatl.

In the material culture of the Americas, English-speakers found even greater challenges. The English concept of the house simply did not adequately convey the variety of residential structures used in various ecological niches of America. The colonists learned to use the Algonquian word *wigwam* for homes made of bark on an arched, wooden frame; they also adopted the Algonquian *wickiup* for a similar temporary structure. On the plains, American settlers encountered the Dakota word *tepee* for the large, conical tent pavilions made of bison hides. In the north, the unusual domed ice houses required the Inuit word *igloo* to describe them. The Navajo homes built partially into the earth retained their Navajo name of *hogan.* The Nahuatl word *jacal* was used for the wattle-and-daub houses with thatched roofs found in Mexico and around the Caribbean, and the Nahuatl *teocalli* signified both the sacred mounds and the temples often built on them.

The material artifacts and clothing of the Indians required new words, since they came in forms unknown to the Europeans. The soft-skinned foot apparel of the Indians differed so much from European shoes that the settlers adopted the Algonquian word *moccasin.* For the same type of footwear made into a boot of deerskin or sealskin, they adopted the Inuit word *mukluk.* The natives of the Arctic also gave the world hooded jackets and the Aleut word *parka* to name them, which, when lined with fur, were sometimes also called by the Inuit *anorak.* The soft and exceptionally warm wool of the musk ox became known by the native name of *quiviut.*

The brightly embroidered smocks commonly worn by women in the Yucatán and Central America acquired the Mayan name *huipil.* From the Spanish language, English acquired *poncho,* which referred to an Andean garment with a name derived from the Araucanian or Mapuche nation of Chile.

Indian inventions included the *toboggan,* a Micmac word for a sled with a curved front. In Alaska and northern Canada the Inuit people used similar sleds pulled by special dogs, which they called *huskies* in the Inuit language. In New England the natives often slung a rope around the forehead or chest to ease the weight of a heavy loads on their backs; this rope bore the name of *tump* in Algonquian and came into English as *tumpline*.

By the time the English and French arrived in North America, they already used the Arawak or Carib word *canoe* for the light boats of the Indians. Christopher Columbus himself had introduced that word to Europeans after his first voyage, making it one of the first Native American words to become part of European languages and eventually an internationally used word. Other native words for water transportation included the Mosquito word *dory* for a dugout with high sides and a flat bottom, and the Inuit words *kayak* and *umiak* for two different kinds of boats made of skins.

The natives of America also used new weapons such as the war club with a stone or metal blade inserted into it and called *tomahawk* in Algonquian. From the Nahuatl language we took the much less commonly used word *atlatl* for the spear-thrower used to hurl spears with greater force and accuracy than throwing them by hand would permit.

Many Indian ceremonial and religious objects had no counterparts in Europe, and thus retained their traditional names. This applied to the Algonquian *wampum*, which consisted of a string of woven beads made from welk shells and used to record important treaties and events in pictographic writing. The Hopis of the Southwest made small dolls called *kachinas* to represent spirits in their ceremonies. Many groups in the Southwest conducted their religious ceremonies in the underground rooms for which the Hopi word *kiva* has generally been used. Dried gourds containing seeds, shaken to provide rhythmic accompaniment in many religious ceremonies, kept their Tupi name *maracas*, although in English the word became more associated with nightclub entertainment and Caribbean bands playing on the beach than with a religious ritual.

Indian social life seemed organized on principles much different from European models, and often required new words to designate the people and their social roles. Even what it meant to be a woman or child varied from the European system, and English speakers began using the Algonquian words *squaw* and *papoose*, a linguistic distinction that shows the degree to which the colonists saw an Indian woman or infant as different from a European woman or infant. Nowhere did Indian social terms assume greater importance than in the political sphere, where settlers and natives had to conduct commerce, make bargains and agreements, and negotiate treaties. Various words came into use to designate the different kinds of Indian leaders. In the Southern States, *cacique* became common after the Spaniards learned it from the Taino. In its feminine form, *caciqua*, the word found use in describing women leaders such as the Lady of Cutifachiqui, but the word found little acceptance in common English.

In the Algonquian-speaking areas, *sachem* became the most common term for a leader, with the Abnaki word *sagamore* used to designate a lower chief. The Natick term *mugwump* came to signify an independent-minded politician who did not follow the party line, and the Chinook word *muckamuck* found its place in English as a mocking term to describe any high official or pomp-ous person. The New England colonists used the Narraganset word *netop* as a synonym for friend, especially when referring to a friendly native, and they used it as a friendly term of address.

Because they came from a political system just emerging from feudalism and still based on authoritarian control, Europeans had little experience in making decisions by consensus. When they sat down with Indians along the East Coast, they learned the concept of group meetings, which the Algonquian-speaking peoples called *caucus*. A holy man called a *powwow* often accompanied the meetings. Because such holy men often danced, the English began applying the word to any celebration of the Indians, but they also applied it to their own celebrations.

One of the strangest events that the Europeans saw was the ritualized giving away of possessions that commonly occurred among Indians on the plains and along the north Pacific Coast. No such concept existed in any European language, and the set-tlers adopted the Chinook and Nootka word *potlatch* for it. Even after the word was adopted into English, however, the Canadian government outlawed any such unproductive activity and impris-oned native people who sponsored or even attended a potlatch.

In total, the Indian languages of the Americas gave English

approximately two hundred relatively common words, of which about eighty came from the Indian languages of the United States and Canada, and the remainder from the Caribbean, Mexico, and South America. In addition to the daily words of common English, Indian languages supplied more than a thousand words that have more specialized and less commonly known use. These include many of the plants and animals that have limited habitats and thus a more limited use for their names. They include words from a variety of languages, such as the Catawba word *yaupon* for a type of evergreen holly; *wapiti*, a Shawnee word for a deer with a white rump; and *titi*, the Tupi name for a small monkey.

Scholars Latinized many of the Native American names so that they could be used as scientific terms and names. Altogether, counting common and scientific words, English now contains about 2,200 words taken directly from the native languages of America.

Through thousands of years of linguistic evolution, the languages of Europe grew rich and heavy in nouns, but poor in verbs. English, like the other European languages, shows a strong proclivity toward naming *objects* and thus easily takes in foreign words as nouns. It borrows far fewer verbs. Instead, English speakers seem content to use weak verbs such as *to be* and *to have*, both of which are vague almost to the point of meaninglessness. The verb *to be* serves as little more than a linking verb joining two nouns or a noun and adjective. Some European languages, such as Russian, have gone so far as to drop the verb *to be* in the present tense and simply string together nouns and their modifiers.

In adopting Native American words into English, the colonists usually made the word into a noun, no matter what type of speech part the word may be in the native language; thus virtually all the Indian words came into English as nouns, the names of things. English speakers adopted virtually no native verbs, adjectives, or adverbs.

Frequently, English speakers could not find a single noun for an Indian concept, and they had to take in a small phrase or string of words that could be translated into English. A new richness came into English through the translation of these Indian phrases and concepts. Often these phrases related to war, such as "going on the warpath," "scalp hunting," or "putting on warpaint." Just as frequently they related to the termination of fighting through the peacemaking process, in phrases such as "burying the hatchet," a phrase that came from the ancient legend of how the five tribes of the Iroquois confederacy united by burying their weapons beneath a tree. Similarly, "smoking the peace pipe" comes from an important social practice found commonly among native people throughout the plains, the Great Lakes region, and the eastern United States and Canada. Although humor usually ranks as one of the most difficult things to translate, a certain lighthearted quality also crept across the language barrier with phrases such as "playing possum."

From early colonial times, spiritual translations also passed into English with references to "the Great Spirit" and "the Happy Hunting Ground." The latter phrase possibly originated as false Indian translation of something invented by a missionary, but it made its way back into English as well as into diverse native languages.

Many of the native American languages lacked the flexibility of English in admitting foreign words. These agglutinative languages added meaning through the extensive uses of prefixes, suffixes, and even infixes, which could be lumped together in long trains of syllables. Because the precise placement and sequence of these syllables bore such importance, speakers of many of these languages found it almost impossible to adopt European words or even other Indian words with the same facility that English incorporated Indian words.

In an agglutinative language such as Paiute, spoken in Utah, a single, albeit very long, word could convey what requires a whole phrase in English. The phrase "they who are going to sit and cut up a black cow" becomes a single word, *wii-to-kuchum-punku-rugani-yugwi-va-ntu-m*, which literally means "knife-black-buffalo-pet-cut-up-sit-future-participle-animate plural" (Sapir, p. 30). In Chinook the word *i-n-i-a-l-u-d-am*, meaning "I came to give it to her," consists of a root word (*d*, "to give"), six prefixes, and a suffix. The whole sentence "I will go" in Hoopa, a language of northern California, becomes a short word, *te-s-e-ya-te*, consisting of a root, three prefixes, and a suffix (Sapir, p. 68).

Because of the difficulty in taking foreign words into the agglutinative languages, most of the native languages invented new descriptive terms that combined older words in new ways. Thus, in the Paiute phrase mentioned above, the Pauite-speakers used their native words for *buffalo* and *pet* to name the unusual cows brought by the settlers into America. It was easier for them to put together two old Pauite words than to borrow the English *cow* or Spanish *vaca*.

A train could be an "iron horse" in one language and a "fire wagon" in another. In Menominee, for example, the modern idea of "telephoning" was translated into the Menominee word sequence meaning literally "little-wire speech" (Bloomfield, p. 455). American Indian languages had a highly metaphorical aspect in which a fish might be known as a "deer of the water," or thunder could be called "his glance," referring to some unknown entity in the sky.

Many Algonquian languages expressed a new concept by combining apparently opposite entities such as water and fire to make the word *scoutiouabou*, "firewater," for the whiskey introduced by the European settlers. The Ojibwa people, who also spoke an Algonquian language, made *wabinesiwin*, or "paleface," to represent the people of European descent.

In an unusual boomerang effect, these descriptive terms made their way from the Indian languages back into English in translation. They became so much a part of American frontier speech that it is difficult to ascertain which came originally from a native language and which may have been invented by native English speakers in imitation of the Indian practice.

English-speaking settlers soon adopted the Indian practice of combining opposing concepts or highly implausible combinations of words to make new words. Thus, such very different creatures as the frog and the bull became *bullfrog*, or "fish" and "cat" became *catfish*.

English already had the capacity to make compound nouns, but the transplanting of English to America intensified and expanded this linguistic trait. Settlers often signified bad things simply by attaching the word *poison* as a prefix to a standard noun. Thus the colonists quickly learned to avoid poison ivy, poison oak, poisonwood, poison dogwood, poison elder, and poison sumac. In a parallel development, many of the Africans brought to America applied the English word *snake*, instead of *poison* to signify something that should be avoided. On Daufuski Island, one of the Sea Islands off the coast of South Carolina, islanders warned their children about snakebush, snakeweed, and snakeroot, a common plant that, if eaten by a cow or goat, will make her milk deadly to humans as well as to calves and kids.

Other English word combinations were used to describe new things in America, such as *rattle* and *snake* or *prickly* and *pear*. New double words included *live oak, June bug, red cedar, bloodroot, chokecherry, sugar maple*, and both *peanut* and *ground nut*.

Sometimes Indian words combined with English words to create bilingual compounds as in *pokeweed* and *pokeberry*, which made a virtual prefix from the Algonquian word *pak*, meaning "blood." One plant with a similar name was the *puccoon*; settlers translated it into English literally as *bloodroot*, which looks like it could have been in the English language for millennia. Scholars then translated it into Latin as *Sanguinaria canadensis* for its scientific name. Through similar fashion, many Indian words show up in English and even in other languages in direct translation. Such transformations keep their meanings but change the sounds, thus leaving little evidence of their native etymology.

The Indians who lived on supposedly alcohol-free reservations called the liquor that had to be smuggled into them *bootleg* because of the manner in which it was smuggled. This term eventually spread to general use throughout America. Similarly the translated Indianisms of *firewater* and *joywater* enjoyed a wide usage. From the Chinook trade language, the word *hooch* or *hootch* spread as a term for a particularly cheap form of liquor named for the Hochinoo (or Hootznahoo) tribe of Alaska.

New words and phrases opened a rich vein of linguistic development in American English. The mixture of this new descriptive speech pattern and traditional English appreciation of such linguistic devices as alliteration and rhyme inspired whole new vocabularies. A place that sold "hooch" was likely to have all manner of illegal, particularly lewd, activity around it, and this became *hootchy-kootchy*, a word popularized by the gyrating gymnastic dances that Little Egypt performed at the 1893 Columbian Exposition in Chicago, a world's fair in celebration of the four-hundredth anniversary of Christopher Columbus's voyage to America.

Respectable people who shied away from *hootchy-kootchy* joints called the men who frequented them *punks*, a word with a twisted origin from the Delaware language, where it signified "touchwood," the pieces of fast-burning wood used to light fires. The word transferred from the lighting mechanism to the cigars or cigarettes being lit with them, and finally, in the late nineteenth century, to the people who smoked such cigarettes in public. Eventually it merged with an older English usage to mean any delinquent lower-class person who violated the norms of the middle class. The earliest connotations of the word still linger in the image of a punk leaning on a street corner with a cigarette dangling from his lip. The evolution of the slang word *fag* for a cigarette closely parallels that of *punk*. The English word *faggot* referred to bundles of twigs used to start fires and eventually became a slang term for a cigarette.

The etymology of colorful slang words such as *hooch* and *punk* traveled a more easily detected path than a more prosaic verb like *honk*, as in the simple sentence, "the goose *honked* as she flew over the pond." It is hard to visualize a time when we did not have a way of describing the sound made by the great flocks of Canadian geese that annually migrated north and south over America. Prior to the nineteenth century, however, English speakers, being attuned to the sensibilities of peasants rather than foresters, woodsmen, hunters, or environmentalists, called the sounds of geese and ducks by the single term *quack*.

The first recorded use of the verb *honk* comes from Henry Thoreau's 1854 description of birds flying over Walden Pond. The trail ends there. Did Thoreau invent the word after listening to what the Europeans called the "quacking" of the goose? With the heavy borrowing of words into English from the Indians of New England, it is no coincidence that *honck* is the Narraganset or Wampanoag word for Canada goose.

From simple beginnings the word *honk* has led a rich life after adapting to a more colorful environment of slang, music, and sex than Thoreau experienced around Walden Pond. With the invention of the automobile and the installation of horns on them, drivers drafted *honk* to describe the sound that their horns made, and thus the word became an important verb without which it is hard to think of how we would describe public life and places in twentieth century urban settings.

Another line of descendants from the word *honk* went underground in an etymology that becomes difficult to follow through the dimly lit world of nightclubs. Musicians applied *honk* to tinny, brassy music and to the places where it was played for poor, urban African Americans. Thus arose the *honkytonk*, from where the term gradually crept out to include similar nocturnal gathering places of poor whites. When African Americans moved on to jazz and a new argot invented for it, the word *honkytonk* clung to the music of the poor whites, and eventually *honky* itself became a mildly derogatory name for whites, who were also called *rednecks* or *crackers*.

Another long and imaginative history comes to light when we pursue the word *okay*. The stories behind it seem as varied as the imaginations of the lexicographers and etymologists who penned them. According to the *Oxford English Dictionary*, the first printed use of the word appeared on June 18, 1840, in the Boston *Atlas*. "The band rode in on a stage which had a barrel of Hard Cider in the baggage rack, marked with large letters 'O.K.'—*oll korrect*."

By September of that year the New Orleans *Picayune* had also given the meaning of *O.K.* as "oll korrect" in one of its articles, but the same newspaper also pointed out that the initials could just as easily mean "orful katastrophe" or "orful kalamity." Other newspapers gave the meaning as "Old Konnecticut" "Out of Kash," "Out of Klothes," "Out of Kharacter." The latter etymologies seem equally as valid as the first.

This cabalistic use of the word comes from the O.K. Club of New York City, supposedly organized in honor of Martin Van Buren, who was born in Kinderhook, New York, and thus acquired the nickname "Old Kinderhook." The group took the name "O.K. Club" in 1840, when they discarded their former name, "Old Butt-Enders." In addition to calling themselves the O.K. Club, they also advertised themselves with a banner reading "K.K.K.K.K."—"Kinderhook Kandidate Kant Kome It Kwite" (Read, p. 3). This use of alliterative *k*'s bears no relation to the post–Civil War *KKK* or Klu Klux Klan.

Despite all of the fretting over cabalistic uses of *k*'s in nine-teenth-century politics, none of these analyses offers any explanation for how that political usage of *O.K.* jumped to the common meaning ascribed to *okay*, meaning "everything is fine" or "no problems." The folk etymology of *okay* skips the politics and ascribes the derivation to egregious presidential spelling. According to this theory, the word *okay* came from poorly educated Andrew Jackson, who served as President from 1829 to 1837 and supposedly marked his presidential papers with the initials O.K. to indicate "ole kurrek" (all correct). The only problem with such a story is that we have many papers and letters written or signed by Andrew Jackson as general and president, but never do the initials O.K. appear.

A British etymology, while acknowledging that the term is mostly an Americanism, postulates that it derived from a brand of English sauce bottled under a colorful label that read "O.K." Sauce. Such an etymology hardly accounts for the finer semantic nuances of the word *okay*. A manufacturer might use adjectives such as *great, super, fine, elegant, royal, rich, creamy, smooth, delightful*, or even a simple *good*, but it is doubtful that many Americans would be persuaded to buy a product that described itself as merely *okay*.

A native American contender for the true etymology of *okay* comes from the Choctaw language, where the word *oke* meant "it is" or "it is so." The Choctaws inhabited the lower Mississippi River area until their removal to the Indian Territory by Andrew Jackson between 1830 and 1837. The Choctaws speak a Muskogean language, and it is from their words *okla homa* (which mean "red people") that comes the name given to the Indian Territory upon its entry as a state into the United States.

Prior to their removal and the colonization of the present states of Arkansas, Louisiana, Mississippi, Alabama, Georgia, and Tennessee, the Choctaws' language served as the general trade language of the area much the way Chinook served as a trade language in the northwestern United States. Like any trade languages used by foreign speakers, Choctaw offered an abbreviated vocabulary associated with barter and the exchange of goods. The word *oke* occurred frequently in such exchanges, signifying that the two parties were in agreement—a usage very close to what it still is in modern English.

The first half of the nineteenth century saw the opening of this area to settlement by colonists from the Carolinas and Georgia; this was the western frontier. Andrew Jackson himself fought repeated battles in this area against the Creeks in the war of 1812 and again in the interminable war against the Seminoles. After election to the presidency in 1828, Jackson also oversaw the removal of all the Southeastern tribes, including the Choctaw. During his two terms in office, the Southwestern states along the Mississippi River occupied a focal point in American domestic issues.

This Southwestern frontier produced many national heroes and politicians, including Davy Crockett, Daniel Boone, and the cronies who came to office with Andrew Jackson and his Democrats in the elections of 1828 and 1832. It should be of little surprise that, considering the national political focus on this area and its people, a frontier word such as *oke* would appear in New York and Boston newspapers by 1840.

The word filled an important void in the language. It spread quickly among the common people during the later nineteenth century, but the educated class fiercely and tenaciously resisted such street slang. Woodrow Wilson did much to popularize the term among journalists and more powerful people in the twentieth century by signing his official papers *okeh*, the spelling that he thought came closest to the original Choctaw. Despite this presidential endorsement and a common acceptance of the word in speech, academics and schoolmarms continued to wince at its usage in written language.

Undeterred by the preferences of schoolteachers, *okay* spread beyond America to other English-speaking parts of the globe, and then to other languages. Today, *okay*, pops up as frequently in German or Spanish as in English, and it has even entered common speech in Arabic, Russian, and Japanese. *Okay* may become the first truly international word understood in every country of the world.

Another international word that may have an Indian pedigree is *Yankee*, the name by which citizens of the United States became known throughout the world. Dictionaries cautiously offer a variety of potential etymologies that vary with the inclinations and imaginations of writers. Perhaps *Yankee* derives from the Dutch name *Jan* or its diminutive, *Janke*, both of which occurred frequently in the old Dutch colony of New Amsterdam. An alternative derivation posits the origin as *Jan* plus *kees*, the Dutch word for cheese, but it remains unclear why anyone would want to use such a combination of words.

In addition to the Dutch origin for *Yankee*, we have a French contender. This etymology surmises that *Yankee* might be a poor pronunciation of the French word *Anglais*, the name they applied to the English settlers. The Scottish theory proposes that *Yankee* came from the Scottish term *yank*, meaning a hard blow. The reasons behind such a possible use of the word remain as obscure as the Dutch-cheese etymology.

Before scholars proposed any of these origins from European languages, we already had a native American possibility. The oldest recorded etymology derives from the travel narratives of Thomas Anbury, who served as a British officer during the American Revolution. Writing in 1789, not long after the term became popular, he derived *Yankee* from *eankke*, a Cherokee word meaning "slave" or "coward" (Mencken, p. 110).

Whether or not this Cherokee origin represents the precisely correct etymology, Thomas Anbury's analysis seems to point us in the generally correct direction. *Yankee* probably descends from an Indian name applied with derision to the whites or perhaps to the English in particular, and it probably found wide usage among Cherokees as well as among other Indian nations. Examination of the historical record reveals similar usage of the term by other groups as well.

The Lenni-Lenape (Delaware) used a similar word to refer to the white settlers. In the *Walam Olum*, the written history of the Lenni-Lenape beginning about the year 1600 and continuing to the ninetenth century, they refer to the English as the *Yankwis*, but often they use the even more derogatory name *Yankwako*, meaning "English snake" (Spicer 1969, p. 150).

Since its spread into American English during the colonial era, *Yankee* has become an international name used to identify the people of the United States. Its use becomes particularly important when foreigners wish to distinguish people of the United States from Canadians and Mexicans, who are also North Americans, or from South Americans, who also share the name *American*.

Because English offers no other single word to designate the rather cumbersome phrase "citizen of the United States," the shorter word *Yankee* stepped in to fill the linguistic void.

No scholar of language writing in 1492 would have had reason to suspect that English might one day become an international language used throughout the world and spoken by far more people outside England than within it. The changes necessary to make this happen did not occur automatically. Before English could become an international language, it needed a tremendous expansion and revitalization that it never could have received in England. That change began in North America, where the provincial language of England was filled with new words, phrases, and concepts. The changes continued as English became the language of British colonial administration in India, Africa, and the South Pacific, but none of these other areas inspired the extensive changes brought about by the native languages of the Americas.

English survives today as a tribal language mixed together from the tongues of the Angles, Jutes, and Saxons, with some Gaelic and Norse additions. The tribal Norsemen who settled in France and became known as the Normans brought a heavy dose of French into English, and as the English incorporated the Gaelic peoples around them, they added a few of their words as well. When the language came to America, the Choctaw, Ojibwa, Cherokee, Muskogee, Seminole, and dozens of others added to the European tribal language of the Angles, Jutes, Saxons, Celts, Vikings, and Normans.

15

THE NAMING OF
NORTH AMERICA

Seattle points toward America's future. For a long time after its founding, Seattle must have seemed like the end of America, tucked far away in the northwest corner, accessible only by ship up the Pacific Coast or by arduous trek overland. The Northern Railroad reduced the isolation by connecting Seattle to St. Paul on the Mississippi River, and thus with the remainder of the United States. Seattle became the connecting port for people and supplies between Alaska and the lower forty-eight states; it served as warehouse and general store for the Yukon Gold Rush. It became a major point of exchange between the western United States and western Canada, and it was the United States' closest port to Japan, Korea, and northern Asia.

Everything about Seattle seems new. During most of the year, the frequent rains wash the dust and visible pollution off the buildings and the vegetation. Fresh green vines cover the cement walls of the freeway and make overpasses look like forest tunnels. The Space Needle gives the city's skyline a futuristic shape, jutting up beside Elliot Bay, while streamlined ferries crisscross the bay, connecting Seattle with the other side of Puget Sound as well as with Alaskan and Canadian ports. Even the older dock district and the renovated "nostalgia" zone date back only to the beginning of the twentieth century, built after the dawn of the modern era of electricity. Rather than showing the age of the city, such areas emphasize its newness.

As a settlement of a more modern and prosperous America, Seattle, more than any other city in America, shared the largess of the surrounding water and land with the indigenous people of the area. Sometimes under judicial and federal government control, but often of their own accord, the incoming settlers and the natives found a way to divide the bountiful fish harvest of Puget Sound and the adjacent ocean waters. Unlike many other parts of America that completely cut the native people off from the utilization of any natural resources, the natives of Puget Sound have managed to hang on to part of theirs, and thereby achieve a modest prosperity that allows them a more equitable position within the ranks of working people.

Seattle has many unique aspects, but perhaps one of the most interesting derives from the city's name. Seattle is the largest city in the Americas named for a Native American. Other cities, such as Miami and Chicago, also bear Indian names, but the city of Seattle was named in honor of a particular Indian, a man of peace and of wisdom gained in the forests and waters of Puget Sound.

Chief Seal'th lived in the area of the city named for him from about 1786 to 1866. In 1855 he signed the treaty with the white settlers that gave them ownership of the land of the Duwamish people, which today lies under Seattle's industrial zone. Even though he lacked the concept of *selling* land, he knew that his people were losing their land forever. A monument in Seattle commemorates his life, and books around the world have quoted him extensively on the subjects of the ownership of land, the way to treat the environment, how to assure equitable relations between ethnic groups, and the proper relationship of humans to the spiritual world.

In a speech to territorial governor Isaac Stevens in 1854, Chief Seal'th summarized with great eloquence the difference between the way his people thought of the land and the way the newcomers did. "Every part of this soil is sacred in the estimation of my people," he explained. "Every hillside, every valley, every plain and grove, has been hallowed by some sad or happy event in days long vanished. The very dust upon which you now stand responds more lovingly to their footsteps than to yours, because it is rich with the blood of our ancestors and our bare feet are conscious of the sympathetic touch" (F. W. Turner, p. 253). Even though the text of the original speech may have been greatly altered and romanticized, the sentiment appears to be particularly Native American.

The ways that people name their environments vary from one culture to another, and reflect many of the basic values of those people. Some places bear the names of generals, like Washington, D.C., or its Virginia suburb, Alexandria. Others bear the names of revolutionaries, like Leningrad, Ho Chi Minh City (formerly Saigon) and Juarez (Mexico). Or they use saints and gods, as for the cities of St. Augustine, Corpus Christi, or San Francisco.

The name of Seattle reflects a much different choice from Vancouver (named for an explorer), Victoria (named for a European queen), or Astoria (named for the New York millionaire merchant). Already, by the time of the founding of Seattle, whole countries had been named for Europeans.

Christopher Columbus himself had his name smeared throughout the Americas. The South American nation of Colombia bears his name, as does the city of Colón (the Spanish version of *Columbus*) in Panama. In North America his namesakes include British Columbia, the District of Columbia, and the Columbia River. Columbia became the name of cities in South Carolina, Maryland, Illinois, Kentucky, Louisiana, Mississippi, and Missouri as well as of counties in Arkansas, Florida, Georgia, New York, Oregon, Pennsylvania, Washington, and Wisconsin. Columbus became the name of cities in Ohio, Indiana, Kansas, Kentucky, Nebraska, Mississippi and Georgia, as well as a county in North Carolina.

When the European aristocracy and their paid explorers sat down to carve up the map of North America, they approached it with the vanity of schoolboys scribbling on bathroom walls. Each ruler wanted to leave his name or title, or perhaps the name of his wife, his children, or even his mistress on the map. America acquired names such as Charles Towne in the colony of Carolina (which was also Latin for Charles) and Baltimore in Mary Land, as well as entire colonies named Georgia, New York, New Jersey, and Delaware. Poor Virginia acquired its name in honor of the dubious sexual condition of England's Queen Elizabeth I.

Even the French and the Spaniards named places in honor of men, such as the colony of Louisiana or the settlement at Albuquerque, named for Francisco Fernandez de la Cueva, Duque de Albuquerque, who was viceroy of Mexico from 1702 to 1711. Often, however, they used a saint's name, which may also have been the name of someone's hometown or his royal patron.

In addition to making new names, the explorers and settlers recreated the geography of Europe in a jumbled way. Mexico became New Spain, the northern Atlantic Coast became New Scotland (or Nova Scotia), and just to the south of that, of course, came New England. In between New England and New Scotland came the French provincial name of Maine, which lay adjacent to a New Hampshire and a New Brunswick, which, of course, should not be confused with Brunswick, the city on the coast of Georgia.

Each cartographer used his own prejudices, nationalism, and simple fantasy to rename the various parts of North America. A Hondius map published early in the seventeenth century, about the time the Pilgrims sailed for America, gave only three names for all of America north of Mexico. *Nova Francia* appeared in the far north, *Florida* in the south, and everything in between was *Canada*. A century later, a Herman Moll map gave a much more detailed picture, but the details were confusing. California appeared as a large Pacific island. North of New England and Nova Scotia came New Britain, and nearby was the island of New Breton. On the western side of Hudson's Bay appeared New York, New North Wales, and New Denmark.

When all else failed, the colonists used some simple descriptive name such as *Vermont*, i.e. "green mountain," or simply Newfoundland. Even in the Spanish territories the interlopers seem to have run out of saints' names as they turned to simple descriptive names such as *Nevada* ("snowy place") or *Colorado* (meaning *red* and referring to the color of the river of the same name).

Through the power of the European monarchs, the early names stuck, but as the settlers moved into the interior of America, they followed Indian geography and used Indian guides. As the settlers arrived, they found that no matter what their maps and charts proclaimed, America already had its own names. The Indians had named the land, and the settlers learned the Indian names of the country.

Even though virtually all of the coastal states and provinces of North America have European names, most of the states and provinces of the American interior still bear Indian names such as Yukon, Ontario, Manitoba, and Saskatchewan in the north, and Alabama, Mississippi, Texas, and Arizona in the south.

Often these names reflect the tribal names of the people who lived in an area. Such names might be a tribe's own name for itself, or it might be the name given them by a neighboring group. We have states named for the Dakota, the Kansa, the Massachuset, the Illini, and the Utes. Some are names that describe the land or the water. *Iowa* is a Siouan word for "beautiful land," *Wyoming* derives from the Algonquian for a large prairie, *Michigan* is Ojibwa for "great water," and *Minnesota* is Siouan for "waters that reflect the sky." The original meanings are often rather straightforward, but translators and local boosters have usually worked to derive the most poetic name possible.

Nebraska means "flat" or "broad river" in the Omaha language; this makes it similar in meaning but not pronunciation to the Algonquian term for "long river" that eventually became *Connecticut*. *Ohio* means "good river" in Iroquoian languages, and *Oregon* means "beautiful water" in Algonquian. *Kentucky* has one of the more mysterious meanings: "dark and bloody ground."

The native people often gave such simple, descriptive names as these to places because such names had a greater utilitarian value than names of people. Because the native people rarely made or used maps, descriptive names helped native travelers to recognize places.

In addition, they used mythological names or stories that helped others to recognize and remember a long list of place names. In Inuvialuit, *Tuktoyaktuk* means "resembling a caribou," and refers to the ancient reef formations visible along the shore. One legend says the name came from some caribou who wandered into the area and became petrified. According to another story I heard from one of the residents, the first woman to come to the peninsula saw the reef formations from a distance and mistook them for caribou. Neither story is more "correct" than the other, but in any case, the formations readily identify the land for even a first-time visitor.

As mentioned earlier, the Inuit built distinctive piles of rocks in the shape of human beings. The name for these structures, *inukshuk*, means "something like a human," and derives from *inuk* meaning "a person." From this same root comes the singular of their collective name, *inuit*, meaning "the people." The modern town of Inuvik on the Mackenzie delta also derives its name from this root; *inuvik* means "the place of human," although it is more often translated as "the place of man."

Oddly enough, despite the stereotype of the Indians as bellicose people, three of the states have names that mean "friend." The name *Texas* comes from the Caddoan word for "friend" or "ally." The name *Dakota* has the same meaning in the Dakota language. For this reason, even today, many Dakota people prefer to be called *Dakota* or *Lakota*, meaning "friend," rather than Sioux, which is the French corruption of the name given them by their traditional tribal enemies, and probably means "snake." Today the Dakota live mostly in Minnesota, whereas their relatives the Lakota live in South Dakota; if names accurately matched he inhabitants, South Dakota would now be South Lakota.

The colonists followed the same naming pattern with rivers as with lands. At first they renamed them after Europeans, like the Hudson River in New York, the Ashley and Cooper rivers in South Carolina, the James River in Virginia, and the Mackenzie River in northwestern Canada. The Indian names of rivers, however, seem to have been even more persistent than the Indian land names. Most of the great rivers of North America still have Indian names, such as the Mississippi, Ohio, Minnesota, Illinois, Missouri, Arkansas, Tennessee, Wabash, Assiniboine, Ottawa, Saskatchewan, Athabasca, Potomac, Chattahoochee, Tallapoosa, Tallahatchie, Yukon, Kuskokwim, Congaree, Klamath, Sacramento, Quinnipiac, Suwannee, Oconee, Kennebec, Muskegon, Mohawk, and Catawba, as well as hundreds of smaller rivers, creeks, and streams in every state and province. In keeping with the persistence of Indian water names, most of the major lakes of America have Indian names, such as Ontario, Erie, Huron, Michigan, Nipigon, Baskatong,

Michikamau, Winnipeg, Eufaula, Iliamna, Tahoe, Shasta, Okee-chobee, and Winnebago.

The most expansive Indian place name in all of the Americas is *Canada*, derived from the Iroquoian word *kanata*, meaning "village," and now applied to a whole country. The name *Canada* first appeared in the 1534 narratives of Jacques Cartier describing a community at Stadacona (Quebec). From this minute origin as a place name, it gradually spread to all of northern North America, covering nearly 4 million square miles, one of the largest nations on earth.

The people of Mexico also chose a traditional Indian name for their country after achieving independence from Spain and freeing themselves from the name of Nueva España. *Mexico* means "the place of the Mexica," another name for the Aztecs. Mexico also preserved more of its native names than any other country in North America. Many of the Mexican place names include Nahuatl words such as *calli* (house), *co* (place), *tlan* (at), *pa* (in), *atl* (water), *tlan* (near), *tetl* (stone) and *xocitl* (flower).

The Mexicans also use *Mexico* as the name of the capital of their country, and the Canadians have the name *Ottawa*, derived from an Algonquian name meaning "trade" or "trader," referring to the activities of a native group who lived in that area. Other major cities in Mexico and Canada, including Manitoba, Saskatoon, Acapulco, and Oaxaca, show their clear native origins.

In his journal, on November 23, 1492, Christopher Columbus referred to the enemies of the Arawak people whom he had visited as the man-eating *canibal*. This one word eventually grew into a thick and tangled bramble of words, pronunciations, and meanings in many languages. From this came the Spanish word *canibal*, from which English speakers derive their word *cannibal*. The new noun generated its own offspring by begetting the verb *to cannibalize* as well as the adjective *cannibalistic* and the nouns *cannibalism* and *cannibalization*.

William Shakespeare derived the name Caliban from Carib and used it for the wild man in his play *The Tempest*. In keeping with the British view of the natives of the New World, Shakespeare portrays Caliban as stinking, immoral, deformed, alcoholic, violent, and superstitious, without redeeming moral qualities and ready to rape a white woman whenever chance provides an opportunity.

America almost acquired a native name for the entire northern and southern continents. As early as 1502 a map, known as the Kunstmann II map, depicted what was known of this New World and carried an illustration showing natives roasting one of Amerigo Vespucci's men on a spit over a raging fire. Illustrations for books on the New World frequently included scenes of the cannibals with parts of humans roasting on their fires or hanging for storage from a tree or post. This inclusion of pictures of cannibals on maps led to so persistent a connection of America with the practice of eating human flesh that the continent almost took its new name from this practice. The 1540 Swiss map of South America in Sebastian Muenster's edition of Ptolemy labels the northern coast of what is now Brazil with the simple word *Canibali*, a corruption of the name *Carib*, but at this time the name did not yet have the full modern meaning of *cannibal*. Other maps followed the tradition and referred to that part of the New World as simply "the place of cannibals" (Quinn, pp. 640–47).

With a slightly different pronunciation, *cannibal* and *carib* occurred interchangeably in early reports, but eventually the latter became the proper name for many of the inhabitants of the West Indies, including the native populations of Cuba and Haiti. When it became obvious that the islands were not a part of India and that they needed a new name other than West Indies, they became known as the Caribbean. Only a quirk of fate prevented this early label of Caribbean from being applied to all of the New World.

Not all of the American place names derived from native languages reflect names actually given by the Indians. Explorers and settlers often misappropriated Indian names or phrases and applied them seemingly without discrimination. In many cases the colonists adopted an Indian name such as *Massachusetts*, which referred to the rocky hills of the area, but, lacking knowledge of the Indian languages, the colonists applied this description of land to the water of the bay and eventually to the whole colony. The colonists often applied the native name of a section of a river to the entire river, as happened with the Connecticut and Penobscot. Some Indian languages offered a decisively different way of dividing up the landscape and applying names than did the European languages. The naming pattern varied from one native group to another, depending on the topography of their native landscape, on the kind of language they spoke, and on their own values. People such as the Kwakiutl, who live along the British Columbia coast and survive by harvesting the waters, consequently use many place names that indicate the relative position of upstream, downstream, seaside, inland, off a point, or in dangerous water. They also use names that reflect what happens there, such as "place of many salmon," "cedar bark on rocks," "small mussels," "finding whales," or "having elk." Living on the ocean and along rivers and scattered islands, the Kwakiutl used a variety of words for water, but they would not name a place simply for its water, springs, or river the way the Aztecs or Arabs would do, since they lived in areas where the location of water could be a matter of life or death.

Whereas Kwakiutl names describe the land, Dakota names sometimes describe the environment, such as *missouri*, meaning "water flowing along," but they also frequently describe historical episodes such as "buffaloes return running," "where Pawnee camped," "they who find a woman," or "jealous ones fight" (Boas, p. 20). They also named places for people, such as "Flying-By's camp" or "Four Bears' camp."

Many of the Indian names still in use simply described a place. An Algonquian description of a place where onions or smelly weeds grew became the present name of Chicago. The phrase for "abandoned town" or "old town" in Muskogean (Creek) became the name *Tallahassee* in Florida. The Papago description "black base," referring to a nearby mountain, became the name *Tucson*. The Algonquian description of "separated island" became Chappaquiddick Island in Massachusetts. The Cree words *kishiska*, meaning "rapid," and *djiwan*, meaning "current," became the name of the Canadian province of Saskatchewan. Similarly the Cree words *win* (dirty) and *nipi (water) became Winnipeg*, the name of a river and the capital of Manitoba province.

In addition to describing the place, Indian place names often described an activity done there. Pojoaque, New Mexico, derives its name from the Tewa language meaning "drink-water place." Manomet, Massachusetts, gets its name from the Algonquian word meaning "portage." *Minnehaha* comes from the Dakota for "falling water" or "waterfall"; contrary to some pseudo-poetic interpretations, it does not mean "laughing water." Auilby Creek, Alabama, despite its English sound, is a tranliteration of the Choctaw phrase *koi-ai-albi* meaning "panther-three-killed" (G.R. Stewart 1945, p. 7). The Wisconsin name *Weyauwega* comes from the Ojibwa meaning "he embodies it" and refers to a mythological action.

To understand the native names of America, one needs to understand both the geography and the culture. The heavy dependence on waterways for transportation in the eastern half of the continent meant that many of the native names described the water, but differently from the way the European settlers did. The European colonists named rivers and lakes, but often lacked a name for the outlet of a river. For the Europeans, the outlet did not seem to be a separate *thing* requiring a separate name.

By contrast, native cultures usually named the outlet of a lake, or named a river in parts, but did not use a single name for the whole body of water, which the colonists perceived as a single entity. For Indian canoeists on a lake, the outlet was the most important part, because that was the water exit from the lake. So long as they could identify the spots on the lake where water flowed in and out, they did not need a name for the remainder of the water. They emphasized the connection or edge of what Europeans saw as two separate things, a lake and a river.

In the Iroquoian languages, the outlet of a river was called the *oswego*, which meant literally "flowing out." This became a place name in New York and in several other states because it occurred so frequently in names within Iroquois territory, and can be found as far south as South Carolina.

Confusion sometimes arose over Indian naming practices in regard to mountains. Mountains occur mostly in large clusters or massifs where it is problematic to separate precisely one mountain from another. The shoulder of one seems to jut into the ridge of the next; one has three peaks, and the other appears to have no peak. Most Indian cultures did not try to name whole mountains or whole ranges; instead they named *features*. Each peak carried its own name, as did each ridge and hollow.

Despite this difference in naming pattern, mountains frequently have Indian names, even though they may not be the same names given to them by the Indians. When Cabeza de Vaca explored the Florida coast in 1528, he found a town known as Apalachen at the armpit of the Florida peninsula. The Spaniards applied this name to Apalachee Bay on the ocean side of Apalachen, and gradually the same name spread to the mountains found inland from the area. Over the coming century of European exploration, this name became *Appalachia*. The name became so important and widespread that Washington Irving proposed it was the name for the whole United States (G. R. Stewart 1970, p. 19). Not until the scientific work of Arnold Henry Guyot, published in 1861, did the name *Appalachian Mountains* come to apply to the whole range extending from Georgia north to Newfoundland and Quebec.

Mountains ranges and parts of ranges bear Indian names throughout North America. These include the Allegheny, Aleutian, Adirondack, Taconic, Ouachita, Pocono, Wasatch, Absaroka, Shenandoah, Hoosac, Skeena, and Caribou mountains.

The popularity of assigning Indian names varied with whims or fashions in North American literature, politics, and popular culture over the decades. In the eighteenth century, settlers favored classical names that harked back to ancient Greece, Rome, Palestine, or Egypt. They frequently mocked the Indian names, which seemed unusual to European ears. James Kirke Pudding compared the harsh consonants of native American names to the harsh sounds of "a catalogue of Russian generals." A similar thought was expressed by David Humphreys in 1794 when he proclaimed "CONNECTICUT! Thy name uncouth in song" (G. R. Stewart 1945, p. 275).

This view of native names contrasts starkly with that of the poet Lydia Sigourney as she expressed it in her romantic little poem "Indian Names":

> Old Massachusetts wears it
>   Within her lordly crown,
> And broad Ohio bears it
>   Amid his young renown.
> Connecticut hath wreath'd it

Where her quiet foliage waves,
And bold Kentucky breathes it hoarse
Through all her ancient caves.

By the nineteenth century, the newcomers to America had accustomed their ears and tongues to Indian sounds and had begun to use them more frequently and easily. Washington Irving wrote extensively in favor of Native American names, and Walt Whitman defended the use of native names in his *American Primer*: "[H]ere are the aboriginal names. . . . What is the fitness—What the strange charm of aboriginal names? . . . They all fit. Mississippi!—the word winds with chutes—it rolls a stream three thousand miles long."

American settlers became so enamored of Indian place names that they started inventing new names for areas and indiscriminately using names from eastern Indian places for places in the far West. By using primitive Indian-English dictionaries or simple word lists compiled by marginally educated missionaries and explorers, land developers and railroad companies put together Indian words to make names from word combinations never used by any Indian nation. Thus Oregon acquired a name that meant roughly "beautiful water" in the language of the Algonquian-speaking peoples who lived on the East Coast and around the Great Lakes, thousands of miles from Oregon.

Wyoming got an Algonquian name from Pennsylvania meaning "large prairie," but the adoption came only after a long fight. Decades before the settling of the present state of Wyoming, its name achieved popular acclaim after an 1809 poem, "Gertrude of Wyoming," by Thomas Campbell. The poem recalled the Iroquois defeat of a group of Tory settlers and the ensuing death of 350 of them during the chaos of the American Revolution. By the time Congress created the territory of Wyoming in 1868, ten communities in Rhode Island, New York, Pennsylvania, West Virginia, Kansas, and Nebraska had already claimed the name. The name had grown in popularity and was proposed for the new Western territory, even though it had no historical relationship to the area, to the native people who lived there, or to the languages spoken there. One anti-*Wyoming* group of congressmen favored the name *Cheyenne*, since that name referred to the native people living there, but Congress rejected *Cheyenne* for fear that Europeans might confuse it with the French word *chienne*, meaning "female dog." No one in the seemly Victorian era wanted a state whose name meant "bitch" (G. R. Stewart 1945, p. 312).

The explorer and writer Henry Rowe Schoolcraft invented a number of such names in his capacity as Indian agent for the territory of Michigan. He made *Algoma* from the *Al* of *Algonquian* and the Algonquian word for "lake," *goma*. Several towns took this name or a slightly different spelling of it, such as Alcona County in Michigan and a town in Iowa, where the post office accidentally changed it to Algona, the name that stuck.

Schoolcraft also invented the name *Iosco*, which he translated from the Ojibwa as "shining water." It became the name of towns in Michigan, Minnesota, and even New Jersey.

A bastaridized Indian name could be made by combining the Greek word for 'city," *polis*, with an Indian prefix such as *minne*, the Dakota word for "water." This produced "water city" or *Minneapolis*. A similar process created *Indianapolis* or "Indian city."

A more convoluted mixture of languages occurs in *Zumbrota*, the name of a Minnesota town between the state capital of St. Paul and Rochester. The Zumbro River received its name from the English pronunciation of the French name *aux embarras* meaning "at the obstacles," the obstacles being the jam of driftwood that accumulated annually on the river. The Dakota people added *ta* to *Zumbro* in order to signify a *place* on the river, thus creating an English-French-Dakota hybrid.

In 1874, settlers from Indiana founded a community in Los Angeles County, California, and named it Indiana Colony, but the following year the United States post office refused to accept that name for fear that mail carriers might confuse the state of Indiana with Indiana Colony. The settlers decided that if they could not have *Indiana*, then they wanted a name that still stressed an Indian connection, but they could not find a local name, since the community no longer had any speakers of the native language. Dr. T. B. Elliot, president of Indiana Colony, wrote to a missionary among the Ojibwa of Wisconsin for help in finding an appropriate Indian name. The nominations from the missionary included *Gishkadenapasadena*, "peak of the valley," *Weoquanpasadena*, "crown of the valley," *Daegunpasadena*, "key of the valley," and *Pequa-denapasadena*, "hill of the valley."

All of these names proved too long and cumbersome for ease of pronunciation or spelling, but since they all ended in the rather euphonious *pasadena*, that became the name of the new city meaning simply "of the valley" (Gudde, p. 239). Communities in Texas and Maryland later borrowed the name.

Wewanta, West Virgina, has a pseudo-Indian name that supposedly came from the phrase "We want a post office" (G. R. Stewart 1970, p. 531). Wewaset, in Pennsylvania, has a pseudo-Indian name invented by the railroad but having no known meaning in English or any other language.

Some American settlers used fictional Indian names for real places, and some American writers used real Indian names for fictional places. William Faulkner lived in Lafayette County, Mississippi, but he set fourteen of his novels and many short stories in the fictional Yoknapatawpha County. He borrowed that name from the original name of the Yocona River, on the southern border of his county. The Chickasaw phrase *yoknapatawpha* meant "flowing, muddy water," but through time it had been shortened to *Yocona*. Faulkner's Yoknapatawpha County bears a name in keeping with the real counties of Mississippi, including Yazoo, Tallahatchie, Coahoma, Oktibbeha, Pontotoc, Tishomingo, Itawamba, Noxubee, and Yalobusha.

Just as some apparently Indian names are not actually Indian in origin, some English, French, and Spanish names are direct translations of older Indian names. Lookout Mountain, Tennessee, originally had a Creek name that meant "rock rising to a point"; in its original form it became the name of Chattanooga (G. R. Stewart 1945, p. 231). Talking Rock in Georgia is a translation from a Cherokee phrase that essentially means "echo."

Translations from native languages are obvious in English names like Medicine Lake or Medicine Hat, where "medicine" is the usual English translation of the Dakota *wakan*, meaning "sacred," "holy," "mysterious," or "unusual."

Sometimes transliterations of Indian words into English make them sound English and thus obscure the native origins. No name could sound much more English than *Wheeling*, West Virginia, a city named for the Wheeling River. It orginated, however, from the Lenni-Lenape phrase *wih link*, which meant "place of the head," supposedly in reference to a captive whose severed head was placed on a pole beside the river at the spot where the community later arose.

French names such as Lac du Flambeau in Wisconsin come from Indian names that could just as easily have been translated into English as Lake of the Torches. Lac Qui Parle in Minnesota is a rough French translation of the Dakota name meaning "lake that whispers to itself." Fond du Lac in both Wisconsin and Minnesota is the French translation of Indian names specifying the head or source of lake, referring to their position at the head of Lake Superior.

The Platte River of Nebraska appears to have a good English name reminiscent, perhaps, of the River Plate in Argentina, but it comes to English from a French translation of an Omaha phrase, *ni*, meaning "river," and *bthaska* meaning "flat." This concept of the "flat river" eventually became the Platte. The original Omaha phrase *ni-bthaska* survives in the name of the state of Nebraska, giving the state and the river the same basic name in the Omaha and English languages.

Spanish names also frequently cover a native origin, as in the case of El Capitan peak in Yosemite National Park, even though the Spanish name was given it by English-speaking explorers in 1851. The Paiute name *Tote-ack-ah-noo-la* meant roughly "rock of the supreme one," referring either to a chief or to a supernatural being. The explorers rejected the native name and decided that the English translation from Pauite to "Chief Peak" or "Captain Peak" sounded too prosaic, so they gave it the Spanish equivalent, El Capitan, which resonated with a romantic image of conquistadors.

Tijuana, the name of a town and river in Baja California on the border with San Diego, appears to be a typically Spanish name. The name's origin appears to be *Tia Juana*, Spanish for "Aunt Jane," and from this arose many interesting stories about a mythical woman of that name operating a border cantina. Old Spanish maps, however, show an earlier Indian place name, *tijuan*, with a now-unknown meaning.

An Indian origin often lies behind a modern place name with the colors white, blue, yellow, or red in the name. This includes White Plains, New York, from the Weckquaeskeck name of the same meaning; White Earth Reservation in Minnesota; and Blue Earth, the name of a county and a river also in Minnesota.

The Yellowstone River (and the park named for it) derives from the Siouan word *mitsiadazi*. Similarly, Yellow Medicine County, Minnesota, is the English translation of the name of a yellow plant also called moonseed (*Menispermum canadense*) that grows in that area. Yellowknife, the capital of the Northwest Territories, is the English translation of a Dene (Athabascan) name for the native people who lived there and carried knives made of a yellowish native copper they mined in the north.

Indians frequently used animal names in making place names, such as Ecola Point, Oregon (from a Chinook word for "whale"), and Elwa Creek, Alabama (from Choctaw for "soft-shelled turtle"), a practice that continued much more commonly among European settlers in America than among the Europeans in Europe. Europe did have some animal names, such as Oxford and Frogmore in England, or the Teutonic names of Wolfsburg and Schweinfurt in Germany. The Canary Islands derived their name from *canis*, Latin for "dog," and in turn that became the name of a bird that lived there. Despite these exceptions, animal names occur much less frequently in the Old World than in America. The European settlers in America quickly assimilated the Indian habit of using animal names in their nomenclature.

The first known use of a Native American animal name in an English place name occurred in Virginia in 1607, when colonists started using the name Turkey Island. It is unknown whether they picked this name up from local Indians or whether the colonists invented it based on their own observations or hopes.

Buffalo, New York, derived its name from the name of an Indian who had been named for the animal. *Buffalo* also occurs in names such as Buffalo Leap (Nebraska), Buffalo Bull Knob (West Virginia), Buffalo Lake (Alberta), and in numerous towns that have *cow* or *bull* as a part of their names.

Many Indian nations held the turtle sacred as the emblem of a clan or, in the case of the Iroquois, as the name for all America, which they called Turtle Island. The name occurs in Turtle River

(South Dakota), Turtle Lake (Michigan), and the Turtle Mountain area of North Dakota.

Many animal place names come from native languages. Thus, Bear Creek, South Dakota, derives its name from a Lakota translation. In the case of Moquah, Wisconsin, the name of the town is the Algonquian word for "bear." Several hundred places in America have names containing the word *bear*, including Bear Lake and White Bear Lake (Minnesota), Great Bear Lake (Northwest Territories), Bear Gulch (Oregon), Bear Creek (Colorado), or simply Bear (Arizona). Sometimes the names come from English surnames or simply from English names given by settlers, so it is difficult to tell which are indigenous. Beeren Island, New York, comes from the Dutch word for "bears." The Spanish word for "bear," *oso*, also occurs frequently in names like Oso Flaco Lake and Canada de los Osos in California, as well as La Osa, Arizona.

Animal names occur in such places as Possumtown (Kentucky), Beaver Tree Canyon (Nebraska), Elkwood (North Dakota), Horse Head (Saskatchewan), Birdtail Creek (Manitoba), Raccoon Mountain (Georgia), Rabbithole Spring (Nevada), Coon Creek (Kansas), Frog Lake (Alberta), Pelican Rapids (Minnesota), Sturgeon Falls (Ontario), Thunder Hawk (South Dakota)), Wapiti Lake (Wyoming), Frogville (Oklahoma), Swan River (Saskatchewan), Pigeon River (Ontario), Blackduck (Minnesota), Rattlesnake Creek (Kansas), and Eagle Creek (New Mexico). Minnesota alone has ten Moose Lakes. *Caribou* occurs commonly in names across Canada and Alaska as well as New England and the Great Lakes area. *Coyote* occurs commonly in names across the southwestern United States.

Dog occurs frequently in names like Whitedog, Ontario, or Dog Creek, South Dakota, which comes from an individual's name. The French name of Prairie du Chien, Wisconsin, means "of the dog," and is a translation of the personal name of a Sauk chief. *Dog* also occurs in the name of the Dogrib people of northern Canada, who claim descent from a mythological dog who became a man.

Deerfield, Massachusetts, was one of the first places named for the deer, having received its name around 1677. *Deer* commonly appears in names across North America, such as Red Deer Lake in Manitoba, the city and river called Red Deer in Alberta, Red

Deer River in Saskatchewan, Deer River in Maryland, and Lame Deer, South Dakota. Variations such as *fawn, stag,* and *doe* also dot the map.

Not all names derived from animals actually refer to the animal. Dovesville, South Carolina, derived its name from the Dove family, and Cormorant Island, British Columbia, took its name from HMS *Cormorant*, which explored the area in the eighteenth century. Moose Jaw, Saskatchewan, had nothing to do with a moose or a jaw in its aboriginal form. The original name *moosgaw* merely described the warm breezes for the area, but when pronounced in English it sounded like, and thus became, Moose Jaw (Lowes, p. 21). By a similar process, Moosomin, Saskatchewan, (pronounced *moose-o-men*) has nothing to do with moose or men, but supposedly derives from a Cree name for a crossing of paths.

Some names in North America represent Indian objects or tools, such as Calumet, Wisconsin, named for the sacred pipe used to smoke tobacco. Dull Knife Community College in South Dakota has an obviously Indian-derived name similar to Cut Knife Hill in Saskatchewan or Knife River in northeastern Minnesota. We also find Fish Hook River (Minnesota), Kayak Island (Alaska), and Bow River (Alberta).

The European settlers frequently named places for people, a habit that they extended to naming places for Indians. After naming much of the coastal areas for themselves, the European settlers used a variety of Indian personal names, usually that of a person associated with a given area as a friend of the settlers, or in some cases as their enemy.

Michigan and Illinois both have communities named Pontiac, after the eighteenth-century Ottawa chief who fought diligently against the English. Similarly, Tammany became the name of a mountain in New Jersey and a parish in Louisiana, in honor of the Lenni-Lenape chief. Pokagon in Indiana and Michigan take their name from the nineteenth-century chief Leopold Pokagon.

After the American Revolution, Indian names became popular among the newly nationalistic American patriots as symbols of resistance to European domination and for defense of liberty. Even when Indian leaders fought against the settlers and lost, the settlers often perpetuated the memories of these men in place names. A

Ute chief gave his name to Ouray, Colorado, and Chief Yokum, an eighteenth-century chief, gave his name to both a pond and a mountain in Massachusetts. Pocatello, Idaho, was named for a nineteenth-century Bannock chief. Minnesota has a Wabasha city and county named for the hereditary personal name of a line of Dakota leaders. The Apache chief Geronimo has been remembered in Mount Geronimo, Arizona. South Dakota has a Crazy Horse Creek.

Most of the Indian personal names adapted for places came from males, usually great chiefs, but in a few cases the settlers used the names of Indian women. Thus a county in Iowa was named Pocahontas, after the daughter of Powhatan. Pocahontas County has a township named for her father as well as one named for her English husband, Rolfe.

The name of Sacajawea, the guide of Lewis and Clark, came from the Shoshoni, meaning "Bird Woman." Her name also became the name of a peak in the Wallowa Mountains of Oregon.

The Dakota commonly called a firstborn child Winona if female and Chaska if male. Both of these became place names in Minnesota. The town of Winona derived its name from a Dakota heroine. She was popularized in the 1881 poem "Winona" by H. L. Gordon, and several other communities around the United States adopted the name. It also found use among the general population as a personal name for a girl. This makes Winona one of the few personal names adopted by Europeans from the Indians.

In addition to places in almost half of the states in the United States bearing the name Osceola for the Seminole chief, towns in Illinois, Iowa, Kansas, Kentucky, and Missouri are named after Oskaloosa, one of Osceola's wives.

In the twentieth century a few Indian names have managed to defeat imposed names, especially when an imposed name had an insulting or negative connotation to the native people. British authorities named the long, narrow bay at the base of Baffin Island after the explorer Martin Frobisher, and the town at the head of the bay also bore the name Frobisher Bay, after the first Englishman to visit it in 1576. Before starting his search for the Northwest Passage from the Atlantic to the Pacific, Martin Frobisher had been an African slave trader. Aside from killing and kidnapping many Inuit and nearly inciting a mutiny among his own men, his only claim to renown came from his mining two hundred tons of supposed gold ore which he carried back to England, only to find that it was worthless pyrite, fool's gold. Undeterred he returned to the Arctic and mined another thirteen hundred tons of the stuff.

Frobisher's life might have been a farce had it not had such tragic consequences for Africans, Inuit, and his own sailors. The Inuit preserved the tales of his treachery and evil, and finally, after Canadian independence, they managed to change the legal name of their community from Frobisher Bay to the Inuit name *Iqaluit*. In neighboring Greenland, the Inuit still use the native name *Kalaallit Nunaat* in place of the Viking misnomer used by the rest of the world.

By a similar process, Tuktoyaktuk took back its native name after bearing the much plainer name of Port Brabant. In recent years the Dene natives of the Mackenzie River have been insisting on the use of the traditional name *Dehcho*, meaning "big river." Twenty-five-year-old Alexander Mackenzie named it Disappointment River in 1789, after he found that it flowed into the Arctic instead of giving him a direct passage into the northern Pacific. The British later changed the name to Mackenzie, an insult to the Dene who lived there and whom Mackenzie described as "meager, ugly, ill-made people, particularly about the legs which are very clumsy and covered with scabs." He went on to say that they "appear to be in a very unhealthy state, which is owing, as I imagine, to their natural filthiness" and were "covered with a coat of dirt and grease" (Mowat, p. 94).

The Indian names of America have deep roots that five hundred years of European colonization have not been able to eradicate. The European settlers wanted to make a New England, a New France, a New Spain, a New Sweden, a New Netherlands, a New Scotland, and indeed a whole New Europe in America. They succeeded only in part, and from Miami to the Yukon and from Arizona to Ottawa, Indian names still help us to understand where we are on this continent, and help give us our local identity.

16

North America's Inca Historian

Most records of the early life of North America's natives derive from archaeological excavations of mute objects and signs of human remains: bones, tools, weapons, marks of fenceposts in the soil, and art. Some wampum and pictographic texts have been preserved, and much information has been transmitted orally, but the oral tradition offers little information about the Indian nations that have disappeared leaving no one to pass on the spoken histories. We have no written records of these Indians that allow us to hear their own voices and explain to us their values, concepts, and beliefs. We can only piece together such cultural knowledge from the patches of information that we obtain from one source and the shreds of evidence from another.

We know much more about the Indians' material contributions to the world through their physical remains: their crops of corn, beans, cotton, and tobacco; their technology of snowshoes, rubber balls, and fur parkas; and their architectural constructions of pueblos, graves, temple mounds, and kivas. Time and neglect muffled the true voices of these people. Without voices and words, their civilization remains a still life, a collection of bones and rocks scattered among mounds of deteriorating adobe, a culture that no longer speaks to us today.

The intellectual history of American Indians has become obscured, and is hidden in some strange places, but none is stranger than the powerful opening chapter of North American history buried in a crypt beneath the floor of the cathedral of Cuzco in Peru, in the southern hemisphere, thousands of miles from the United States. It is here that we find the earthly remains of the first person to write a synthetic and analytic history of any of the native peoples of what is now the United States.

Cuzco has a strange blend of traditional Indian and European cultures. Many of the Spanish colonial buildings rise up from the monumental stone walls of Inca masonry, giving the buildings a schizoid appearance: massive stone foundations topped with Spanish tiles on the roofs; wrought-iron balconies jutting from the sides; and traditional Mediterranean courtyards.

The city centers today on the ancient Inca plaza formerly called Huancaypata, but now rechristened as the Plaza de Armas. For the Incas this spot marked the center of the empire and the center of the universe—the *Qusco*, the navel of the world. The Spaniards ripped down the Inca temples and palaces around the square to erect their own cathedral, churches, and palaces. The church took possession of the northern side of the square, a place called Quishuarcancha that had been the site of the palace and temple of the Inca Viracocha. After pulling down the great temples and parts of the great fortress of Sacsahuaman, the conquistadors used the stones to build El Triunfo—a church in honor of the Spanish Christian triumph over the pagan Incas. The larger cathedral built next door adjoined the church of El Triunfo, eventually absorbing the smaller as a subsidiary of the grander cathedral.

The expanded cathedral complex combines odd elements of Spanish, Inca, and even African civilizations. The two-hundred-year-old bell named Angola Maria contains a ton of gold, silver, and bronze, and is said to have been named in honor of an African slave woman. When rung, the bell can be heard for twenty-five miles and is reputedly the largest in South America. Paintings and tablets throughout the structure attest to the hundreds of miracles performed there: altars miraculously saved from fires, believers suddenly cured of diseases, nonbelievers stuck down in the prime of life, and earthquakes miraculously stopped (or even averted entirely) by the statue of Our Lord of Earthquakes, which is paraded throughout the city each Good Friday.

Indian artists used European models that they combined with their own interpretations to produce some occasionally unusual juxtapositions in the cathedral. The angels in the pictures look like Spanish noblemen and carry guns, while the cherubs around them all have Indian faces. A large painting of the Last Supper looks at first like many of the European models, with Jesus dividing food and passing it around the table to his gathered disciples. Closer inspection reveals the foods to be an assortment of tropical American fruits grouped around the main dish of roasted guinea pig, a favorite Indian food in the Andes. Even the altar of El Triunfo supposedly sits on the exact spot where the life-size gold statute of Inca Viracocha stood, thus making it hard to know which god the poncho-clad natives worship when they kneel there.

With this amalgamation of American, European, and African cultures, it should not be surprising to find the remains of an Indian who played a vital role in recording the history of North America. The crypt holds the bones of a man little known today in the United States. He wrote the first history of Indian and European relations of North America, and he was proudly an Indian. He is the father of American history, El Inca Garcilaso de la Vega.

He was born on April 12, 1539, to the Inca princess Chimpa Ocllo, a niece of the Inca Emperor Huayna Capac. Chimpa Ocllo had no legal husband; the baby's father was Don Sebastian Garcilaso de la Vega Vargas, one of the Spanish conquistadors who had no interest in marrying his Indian mistress. They gave the brown child the name Gómez Suárez Figueroa, later changed to Garcilaso de la Vega in honor of another Spanish ancestor.

The future historian grew up amid the disintegration of the Inca empire and the deterioration of the ancient Andean civilization that had slowly evolved over thousands of years in the relative isolation and protection of its mountainous homeland. As the son of an Indian noblewoman and a relative of the surviving aristocrats of the Inca empire, the young man acquired a thorough education in the history and culture of his people. He learned to interpret the *quipus*—the knotted strings by which the Incas maintained all of their records. His first language was the Indian language of his mother, Quechua, which is still spoken today by approximately 5 million Indians in Eucador, Peru, and Bolivia.

During this time the mixed-breed boy also witnessed the consuming greed and constant infighting of the Spanish conquerors as they quarreled over the great riches of Peru and forced an endless succession of Indian slaves into the mines to extract more gold and silver. Several times his family had to flee intruders and battles in the incessant plotting, fighting, and shifting of alliances among the Spanish conquerors. Spanish cannons besieged and then bombarded his childhood home, and although he escaped, many of his relatives died around him in the ensuing battle.

Many of the Incas still held out against Spanish rule during this time, and the young Garcilaso de la Vega witnessed with his own eyes one of the rebel Inca emperors still reigning in all of his pomp and glory. Not until 1572 did the Spaniards crush the forces of Tupac Amaru, the last independent Inca emperor, and a relative of Garcilaso de la Vega's mother. After capturing the emperor, the Spanish beheaded him and put his head on a spike in the central plaza of Cuzco.

By the time of that execution, young Garcilaso de la Vega had long since gone to Spain. Following the death of his father, this young mestizo followed the requests of his father's will by sailing to Spain to acquire a proper European education, learning to master Spanish, Latin, Italian, and probably classical Greek. He also went with the mission of clearing his father's reputation, which had been sullied by his joining the wrong side in the Peruvian civil war.

Apparently the young man threw himself into his own European enculturation with great zest, and disassociated himself from his Indian roots. As an exile living in Spain, he seemed to have been safely removed from the turmoil of Peru, but he had little chance to return. Under the Viceroy Toledo, Peru suffered a new round of persecutions in which the Spanish army exiled, imprisoned, or killed the surviving members of the Inca royal family. These persecutions spread to the mestizos, and at one point all the mixed-blood males of Cuzco were imprisoned as potential traitors because of their tainted Indian blood (Varner, p. 263). Had Garcilaso de la Vega returned to Peru, he may well have been killed.

Despite the turmoil of his distant homeland, Garcilaso de la Vega chose as his first literary project a subject that had nothing whatever to do with the Indians of America. He chose to translate from Italian to Spanish a work of essentially Greek philosophy of love written by a Portuguese Jewish physician, Judah Abarbanel, who published under the name León Hebreo. Garcilaso translated *Dialoghi d'Amore* (*Dialogues of Love*), and published it in 1590, but in 1612 the church placed the book on the forbidden *Index librorum prohibitorum et expurgatorum* and thus banned it. Even though the work achieved some popularity in Italian, it presented an unromantic and unerotic analysis of love very much in keeping with the technical ideas of Platonic philosophy. It consisted of a series of dialogues between Filon (Love) and Sofia (Wisdom) on the difference between desire (the feelings one has for something one does not possess) and love (the feelings one has for something one does possess).

The translation by Garcilaso de la Vega proved how well he, an Indian raised in America, had mastered the culture and languages of Europe. It demonstrated his grasp of the nuances of both Italian and Spanish and showed his ability to understand, analyze, and explain the intricacies of centuries of European philosophical thought. Garcilaso seems to have learned another important lesson from the author of *Dialoghi d'Amore*. Judah Abarbanel wrote at a time of great persecution of Jews and Arabs. His family had been expelled from Portugal and had sought refuge in Spain, only to see the Catholic monarchs Ferdinand and Isabella order the expulsion of the Jews from their lands in 1492. Rather than hide his Jewish identity, Abarbanel proclaimed it loudly in selecting the *nom de plume* of León Hebréo, which meant "Hebrew Lion" and echoed the notion of the Lion of Judah (Varner, p. 283).

Perhaps Garcilaso felt some identity with the plight of the Iberian Moors and Jews, since their plight paralleled in many ways that of the Incas and other Indian nations back in America. Since 1492 the Jews and Arabs had been forced to flee Spain or convert to Christianity, but even as Christians they faced great discrimination by a Spanish elite obsessed with racial purity. In his eager embrace of his father's Spanish culture, Garcilaso had found Spanish society closed to him. The government rejected his pleas to rehabilitate the soiled reputation of his father, and most of his father's relatives rejected the dark-skinned progeny of miscegenation. In Spain this descendent of Inca emperors was only a half-breed bastard, a person of mixed blood and therefore tainted with the suspicion of heresy among many other faults, sins, and crimes.

Despite the bitter climate of racial persecution, Garcilaso, apparently impressed by Abarbanel's defiant proclamation of his Jewishness, decided to declare openly his own ethnic heritage. On the title page of his translation, Garcilaso proclaimed it in letters even larger than the title as "the translation of an Indian ... Garcilaso Inga de la Vega." It was by this name, usually spelled *El Inca*, that he chose to be known for the remainder of his life.

We know little of El Inca's personal life, and can only speculate upon what motives drove him to the study and writing of history, but Garcilaso, like many other people as they mature, spent the second half of his life trying to recapture what he spent his youth escaping. His interest in Indian history apparently came after the death of his Indian mother, the execution of Emperor Tupac Amaru, and the ensuing persecution of the royal Incas and the mestizos.

El Inca began two major history projects that became the major works of his life and earned him the sobriquet of "Pliny of the New World." One massive work detailed the history and culture of his own people and family, the Incas, but because of opposition from the Spanish bureaucracy, it had to be published in two volumes. The *Royal Commentaries* appeared in 1609 in Lisbon, Portugal, but the *General History of Peru* did not appear until 1616 in Córdoba, after his death earlier that year in the same city. Even though this fifteen hundred-page text comprised a single work, the Spanish authorities refused publication under the name *Royal Commentaries* because they rejected the use of *royal* for anyone or anything not directly associated with their own crown. For them the word *royal* certainly could not be applied to Indians of America. Thus the two parts of one work appeared in separate countries nearly a decade apart, under separate titles.

After recording the history of native South America, El Inca turned his attention to a corresponding volume on North America. At the time El Inca wrote, the Spaniards called everything north of Mexico by the name *Florida*. At that time, Florida had not been reduced to the southeastern pennisula for which we now use the name; it included everything from Cape Cod to California. El Inca began researching and writing his history by 1567, but it took him more than thirty years to finish it in 1599. The government did not finally give permission for publication of the book until 1605, which was ironically on the eve of the English settlement of the continent, just when Spain was about to lose effective control of the area. His book subsequently became known by the somewhat misleading yet mysterious title *The Florida of the Inca*.

El Inca knew from his own experiences in Peru that the culture and history of the peoples of North America could easily be lost in the European conquest, but he also recognized that the conquest, inevitable as it appeared, was going more slowly in the north than it had in Mexico or in his own homeland. He therefore set about meticulously gathering all the information about North America that he could find in Spanish documents.

At this time in Europe, history consisted of the study and commentary of ancient texts, but as a native who had seen the rapid decline of Inca civilization, El Inca understood the importance of eyewitnesses and oral accounts. Like a modern journalist or anthropologist, he interviewed men returning from campaigns and expeditions in North America to learn firsthand from them what they had seen, heard, and experienced on this new continent.

Until this time the most important Spanish foray into North America had been the expedition of Hernando De Soto, and most of El Inca's book chronicles this trek with a summary of the prior, smaller expeditions. Several explorers had already published accounts of their personal adventures in North America, but El Inca did not give the account of merely one man. He combined a study of these published accounts with his own interviews of the survivors and, most important of all, with his own knowledge of America, of Indians, and of the Spanish conquest.

Like the Greek historian Herodotus writing about the ancient Mediterranean, El Inca sought to describe all the nations he could, but whereas Herodotus based much of his writing on his own travels, El Inca had to write without leaving Spain. Not wanting to present a history from only the official, Spanish view, he combined information from every perspective. After examining all the evidence, he presented his synthesized view of it, but he clearly informed the reader that this was the final perspective of only one man, an Indian.

Despite repeated literary genuflections to the authority of the Spanish crown and the Roman Catholic Church, El Inca wrote a book steeped in pride of Indian culture and civilization. On the title page itself, in addition to calling himself by his chosen Indian name, El Inca, he informed the reader that this history was written by a native of Cuzco. Repeatedly throughout the book he reminds the reader that his book was written by a native, an Indian, an "Antarctic Indian," a mestizo, a son of the Incas, the offspring of Peru, a child of the Americas. At one point he insists that in addition to using some of the native words of North America, he also uses terms in his native Quechua to remind the reader that this book was written by a Peruvian Indian and not by a European scholar.

El Inca never referred to the Indians of South or North America as savages or barbarians; he presented them respectfully in terms equal in honor to the Spaniards. The Indian leaders were nobles and gentlemen, and their nobility shone forth repeatedly. El Inca proclaims this equality of nobility on the title page with the inscription that this work is the history of "heroic Spanish and Indian cavaliers" (*heroicos caballeros Españoles e Indios*).

In one story after another about the Indians of North America, El Inca described the heroic nobility of even the lowliest Indian warrior. He wrote of an Indian farmer and his wife working in the fields when they were surprised by a squadron of Spaniards on horseback. Even though the man had time to flee, he took his wife to safety and then returned to fight singlehandedly against these strange men dressed in armor and riding on giant beasts.

He told of the Indians who ambushed another squadron of Spaniards, but when the Indians found that the squadron consisted of only seven soldiers, they permitted only seven of their number to fight to make it an even match. He told of the battle at Mauvila (Mobile) in Alabama, where all the Indians fought to the death rather than surrender. Then, when one wounded Indian warrior regained consciousness and saw that all were dead around him and only the Spanish survived, he quickly hanged himself with his bowstring before the Spanish could capture him.

El Inca showed that once the Spaniards were off their horses, the Indians always proved an even match for them. The Indians showed as much bravery and honor as the noblest of the Spanish. In some respects they outshone their captors, and El Inca took pains to show us the Indian perceptions of nobility by which they judged the Spanish. In this way El Inca serves as a mouthpiece that even now gives us some notion of what the native Americans of the sixteenth century thought and said.

El Inca quotes the Indian cacique Acuera's assessment of the Spaniards when he told them that they "wander from place to place, gaining [their] livelihood by robbing, sacking, and murdering people who have given [them] no offense." The Indian chief even knew how to enrage the Spanish nobles by reminding them that they were the mere servants of a distant king. Acuera concluded that "being so contemptible and as yet unable to rid yourselves of the stigma of servitude, you should never at any time expect friendship from me, for I could not use my friendship so basely." The chief reminded the Spaniards that he himself was a free king in his own right, and as a free man he had no desire to become the subject of the Holy Roman Emperor Charles V. "Therefore, all of you should go away as quickly as you can if you do not want to perish at my hands."

El Inca realized that his European readers might not believe that Indians could be so proud in the face of obvious European superiority. Knowing that some people would say "I exaggerate my praise of the race because I myself am an Indian," he swore that he was *under*stating it because "I lack sufficient words to present in their proper light the actual truths that are offered me in this history." With characteristic modesty he accepts the responsibility because of his deficient education in Peru when it was filled with schools for training in arms and horesemanship but not in letters.

El Inca did not hesitate to portray the horrors of the conquest from both sides, but when dealing with what might appear to be savage Indian behavior, he offered a perspective from which to understand it. He denied that they ate humans: "They on the contrary abominate this practice." El Inca turns the tables on the Europeans by explaining how horrified a group of Indians were when they found shipwrecked Spaniards who had eaten their comrades to stay alive. After denying that any Indians he had ever known were cannibals, he adds a note of scholarly caution: "It may be, however, that the Indians do eat human flesh in places where our men did not penetrate, for Florida [North America] is so broad and long that there is space enough within it for anything to happen."

He did not hesitate to record Indian atrocities committed against the Europeans, as well as European atrocities against the Indians. He related the story of Chief Hirrihigua, near Tampa Bay in present-day Florida, who killed three Spaniards with arrows while making them run around the plaza of the village. He then ordered the torture of a fourth Spaniard, a young man named Juan Ortiz, whom the Indians tied to a grill in order to roast him over an open fire. When the chief's wife and daughters pleaded for the life of the prisoner, the chief grudgingly relented and let him live.

El Inca does not shy away from presenting this cruelty, but he also offers the reader a context in which to judge it by explaining that the chief hated the Spaniards so desperately because they had cut off his nose and had thrown his own mother to the dogs to be disemboweled. "Outrage knows no forgiveness, and each time that Hirrihigua recalled that Spaniards had cast his mother to the dogs and permitted them to feed upon her body, and each time that he attempted to blow his nose and failed to find it, the Devil seized him with the thought of avenging himself on Juan Ortiz, as if that young man personally had deprived him of his nostrils."

El Inca balances the story of one Indian chief's anger by showing the kindness that Juan Ortiz received from the chief's family and how ultimately Juan Ortiz escaped to find refuge with another Indian chief, who showed him a decade of kind and generous treatment to atone for the months of suffering under Hirrihigua. El Inca used the concept of cultural relativity in a way that presaged its development in twentieth-century anthropology. In defending the Indians, he demanded that they not be judged according to "arts and sciences" that they did not have, since "it seems ungenerous to judge our deeds and utterances strictly in accordance with the precepts of those subjects which we have not learned. *We should be accepted as we are."* (Emphasis added.) He then asks the readers for goodwill and "to offer their favor most generously and approvingly to both my people and myself."

El Inca shows less interest in the military exploits of the Spanish expedition than in the way of life of the Indians of North America. He describes their temple mounds and the severed heads around them, their ways of farming, treating skins, getting salt, trading goods, making canoes, clothing themselves, and fighting, and their moral code concerning marriage and adultery. Like the Roman writer Tacitus describing the ancient Germans, El Inca gave us the most thorough and important portraits that we have of traditional Indian life in both Peru and North America. Because he was raised in Peru, his account of his home country is much fuller and richer than the information he gleaned about the people of North America. Yet in recognizing his common blood with the Indians of North America, he works with the motivation to look behind exaggerated anecdotes, religious zealotry, and European ethnocentrism to see the North American natives as a fully human people with a fully developed culture.

The Florida of the Inca described the place that was to become the United States before that territory contained a single European settlement, but we see repeatedly throughout the book names that have now become commonplace and familiar to us. Indian towns such as Ocali, Tascaluza, and Mauvila still live on today as Ocala in Florida and Tuscaloosa and Mobile in Alabama. Even the name *Alabama* came from the Indians; it is the *Alibamo* mentioned frequently by El Inca Garcilaso. Without this rigorous use of native terminology, the nomenclature of the southeastern United States may have ended as Spanish as the western part of the country or as Anglicized as the northwestern seaboard.

El Inca seeks first to be informative and only then to be judgmental. Even in his judgment, he condemns no one. Unlike the Spanish cleric Bartolomé de las Casas, who wrote a history of the West Indies that excoriated the Spanish for their cruelties toward the Indians, El Inca passes on the accounts of cruelty with no editorializing or moralizing.

The cold neutrality that El Inca often displays toward the Spanish conquistadors and their actions condemns them more than any editorializing he could have added. In a century when criticism of the government could easily have cost him his life, prudence dictated that El Inca stop short of open criticism. At times he posits explanations for Spanish actions, but even these seem to offer more condemnation. This shows most notably in his repeated mention of the failure of the Spanish to baptize the Indians, to save their souls or to further the interests of the Gospel, which they were supposedly spreading. Each time, El Inca assures the reader that the conquistadors had a primary obligation to conquer the land, and only then could they convert the people. He offers this explanation even for the Indian slaves and concubines kept by the Spaniards, and who obviously had already been conquered. One cannot help but wonder if he thought at these times about his own Indian mother, whom his Spanish father discarded when he tired of her.

Perhaps this identification with the suffering of his mother and her relatives served as an impetus for him to grapple with historical events from the perspective of women as well as men. The moral dimension of El Inca Garcilaso's writing about the relationship of males to females showed an oddly modern bent after he related at length the punishment of women for adultery in the Americas. He then inquired into the punishment for men, but the men whom he asked did not know. From this he concluded that "in all nations such laws are rigorous in regard to women and favorable to men," and he noted that such laws are always made by men. In the case of his own family, of course, those were Spanish men who made the laws and Indian women like his mother who suffered under the opprobrium of having a child out of wedlock.

El Inca Garcilaso seems at times to be questioning, through

veiled references, the authority of the Spanish government and the horde of bureaucrats at whose hands he felt grossly mistreated. He often followed his stories with a maxim about good government and just sovereigns. He said, for example, that sovereigns should not pass laws so strict that they encourage disobedience and rebellion, a passage that some interpreters have taken to be a reference to the rebellion in the Spanish Netherlands. He wrote that "experience has taught us that no kingdom rebels against its sovereign because of his good treatment, but because of his harshness, cruelty, and tyranny as well as an excess of taxes" (Varner, p. 313). Such a statement could as easily justify the rebellion of the Incas against the Spanish or the struggle of the Indians of North America. His words seem to presage the same arguments and language used more than two hundred years later by the North American colonists when they severed the bonds connecting them to King George III.

El Inca did not write a glorification of the Indians of North America, nor did he write about a golden age of noble savages. He seems far too pragmatic a person to have merely longed for a return to some romantic past. The Inca empire had ended, and he knew that the independent lives of the people of North America would also soon end. His history always seemed to look toward the future and what would become of these people. El Inca followed an agenda of practical prudence, and he saw only one hope for the Indians of the Americas. The crown and its soldiers had proven their dedication to greed, no matter what the cost to the Indians, and he knew that the Indians would find no salvation in them. The only hope he saw for Indian people was through the Christian church.

As he grew older, he apparently became more disillusioned with Europeans, but he recognized that European culture had some positive things to offer the Americas, and he wanted a future that combined the best of the Old World with the best of the New. For him, Christianity appeared to be the only part of European civilization that was superior to the Indian world. He claimed that only by adopting Christianity had his mother made herself any more noble than she already was by virtue of her Indian blood and Inca heritage. He also recognized the importance of writing as an Old World art, and claimed that if ancient Cuzco had developed writing, it would have been a more magnificent city than Rome itself.

When El Inca Garcilaso wrote, many people still saw the Indians as animals, little more than the monkeys and chimpanzees from Africa. When he started his work on Florida, the Spanish court was still considering the question "What is an Indian?" That question was posed in a royal order of the Spanish king and Holy Roman Emperor Charles V on April 16, 1550; the same order suspended further exploration of America until the matter could be settled (Horgan, p. 152). The issue was far more than an intellectual debate, for its answer would determine how the Indians must be treated. The conquistadors and the newly emerging class of European landowners in America favored the argument of Aristotle that some humans are "natural slaves." If their perception prevailed, then the subhuman Indians could be enslaved at will by the Spanish without regard for their souls.

On the other side were men, mostly clerics, who claimed that the Indians were fully human, capable of becoming Christians, and therefore could not be made into slaves. Instead they could be educated in schools, and could become priests and citizens. This was a position that had earlier been advocated by Queen Isabella, and also by Pope Paul II in his papal bull *Sublimis Deus*.

The debate raged on through the remainder of Charles V's reign and into that of his son, Philip II. In 1573 a new set of rules and orders for the Americas ended the debate granting the notion of Indian humanity, in principle. In fact, the authorities had reached something of an implicit compromise whereby the Church could proselytize among the Indians and have their souls, but the landowners kept the bodies during life in this world.

El Inca Garcilaso embarked on his books on the Americas in the midst of this debate. In advocating their Christianization, he took a firm stand on the side of the humanity of the Indians. He was trying to persuade his readers that the Indians possessed as much capacity for reason, love, understanding, and religion as did the Europeans. He took pains to show how eagerly some of the Indians sought the Christian faith even when the Spaniards refused to share it with them. By saying that they were fully human and capable of being Christians, El Inca Garcilaso was calling for Spain and the Church to treat Indians justly.

If the Indians could prove themselves capable of accepting Christianity, they should be able to master the other knowledge of the Europeans as well. "The natives of Florida have a great ability for these things, for without any instruction other than that of their natural intelligence, they have said and done such good things . . ."

Because El Inca lived as a dark-skinned half-breed in sixteenth-century Spain, where such people were often marked as Arabs, Jews, and religious noncomformists, El Inca Garcilaso probably wanted to avoid attracting attention to himself as a possible nonbeliever. He always stressed his Catholic piety. On January 1, 1567, about the time that Garcilaso began work on his history of North America, King Philip II issued a proclamation against the Moriscos, the nominally Christianized Arabs who had stayed in Spain. He forbade their speaking Arabic or using Arab names, wearing Arab dress, or engaging in celebrations or any display of their own culture. They even had to refrain from their traditional baths and circumcising their sons, and the proclamation ordered that they surrender all arms. When the Moriscos rebelled, a bloody war flared for a year.

El Inca Garcilaso wrote before the development of the modern division of labor between historians, journalists, moralists, geographers, propagandists, anthropologists, and storytellers. He contributed to the development of all these disciplines, but he should not be judged by the standards of any single one against the others. He wrote from a definite point of view, yet he tried to make sure that all the facts were accurate. He wrote about the past, but in doing so he tried to shape a better future, a future in which Indians would be fully human, and the accomplishments of Indian civilization would be acknowledged and not lost in the European onslaught.

On April 21, 1782, a century and a half after El Inca's death, the Spanish king Charles III inadvertently paid one of the greatest compliments one can pay a dead writer. The king banned the works of El Inca in America because they were inflaming the Indians (Castanien, p. 141).

The works of Garcilaso de la Vega had been very popular in

Peru, and in 1780, at the same time the English settlers in North America rose in revolt against Great Britain, the Incas revolted against Spanish rule in Peru. The leader of the revolt was José Gabriel Condorcanqui, a descendent of the royal Inca family and thus an indirect descendent of El Inca Garcilaso de la Vega. Condorcanqui had been affected by the works of El Inca Garcilaso and had used his books as a source of inspirational knowledge about the culture and history of his ancestors. He chose to fight under the name of Tupac Amaru II, his ancestor who had been the last Inca emperor and had resisted the Spanish during the lifetime of Garcilaso de la Vega.

At the end of the three bloody years of fighting, the Spanish army crushed the independence movement with great cruelty. Before executing Condorcanqui, the Spanish colonial authorities tortured him and cut out his tongue. They forced him to witness the torture and mutilation of his own wife and relatives before they were garrotted. On May 18, 1781, in the presence of his screaming ten-year-old son, the Spanish tied Condorcanqui to four horses and tried to quarter him. Failing in this, the authorities chopped off his head and put it on a pike in the square of Cuzco, as they had done to the first Tupac Amaru. The son was then sent to a life in prison in Cadiz—his only crime being that he was a descendent of the royal Incas (Varner, p. 380).

The following year, on April 21, 1782, the king issued the proclamation that banned the "history of the Inca Garcilaso where those natives have learned many harmful things." The magistrates were ordered to seek out in complete secrecy all copies of his books, without arousing the suspicion of the native population. The same proclamation forbade the Indians of the Andes to call themselves Incas. In order to break their bond with their glorious history, the Incas were to be called simply Indians or peasants. They were forbidden to perform their ceremonies and dramas, to wear their native clothes, or to possess any pictures or documents concerning their Indian history that might serve "to preserve the memory of their ancient pagan customs" (Varner, p. 381)

Despite the great popularity of El Inca Garcilaso among the Indians and whites of Latin America, his work on North America found only a meager audience in North America. Parts of it were translated, but not until 1951 did Americans have available the first full edition of his history of Florida, translated into English directly from the Spanish of El Inca Garcilaso by Jeanette Varner and John Grier Varner. With great vision and some risk, the University of Texas Press chose it as the first book it would publish. In part, this must have been because it dealt with Texas (in addition to other areas of the southern United States), and it combined Indian and Hispanic themes that continue to be important in the culture of Texas. In his writing, El Inca Garcilaso rather prophetically referred to the area that was to become Texas as the "Land of the Herdsmen."

El Inca Garcilaso de la Vega died in April 1616, in the city of Córdoba near the ancient mosque that the Spaniards had turned into a cathedral. On April 24 he was buried in an ornate chapel dedicated to the Blessed Souls of Purgatory within the cathedral of Córdoba. Thus he joined the numerous other Christians already buried there, as well as the Muslims buried before the Christians. He left behind a small household including one illegitimate son who became a priest.

Because he was not Spanish, El Inca Garcilaso's body was not destined to remain forever in distant Spain, buried in that amalgam of Arab and European architecture. In the twentieth century, Spain's new king, Juan Carlos, returned the body to Cuzco, the American homeland where El Inca was born and reared, back to the city of his mother and his royal Inca family, back to the city of which he himself had been the greatest chronicler. It seems only just that, buried in the oldest church in Cuzco, he is buried on the site of the temple of Inca Viracocha, one of the most sacred of Inca sites. His body now lies beneath the floor in the Inca foundations of the church, only a short distance from where tradition says the gold statue of Viracocha stood. Thus, El Inca Garcilaso de la Vega rests eternally in the navel of the universe.

The career of El Inca Garcilaso marks a unique juncture in world history because he was the greatest intellectual link forged between the minds of the Europeans and the American Indians. He helped to interpret the Indian culture to the world. He also helped lay the groundwork for the modern discipline of history by separating the role of historian as synthesizer and commentator from the roles of archivists, epigraphers, and paleographers who decipher and categorize old texts.

The modern historian Arnold Toynbee points out that although El Inca Garcilaso could not protect the New World from the shattering shock of the Old, he did perform an important role as intermediary between, and interpreter of, the New World to the Old. In this regard, Toynbee notes that El Inca Garcilaso follows an ancient intellectual tradition. "The Babylonian civilization was interpreted to the Greeks by Berossus, the Egyptian by Manetho, the Jewish by Philo and by Josephus. This is the distinguished company to which Garcilaso belongs."

17

INTELLECTUAL MINING

The Arkansas River twists across the state of Arkansas and through eastern Oklahoma. Barges chug down it carrying agricultural goods, coal, and the petrochemical products of Oklahoma's lucrative oil industry. In this setting, the prosaic name of the Pocola Mining Company sounds little different from hundreds of other companies started in this century to tap the rich natural resources of Oklahoma. Most of them disappeared with little interest to anyone other than the Internal Revenue Service, and a few of them grew into fabled multimillion-dollar fortunes that financed the skyscrapers, mansions, and magnificent art collections of Tulsa, Oklahoma City, and Bartlesville.

The Pocola Mining Company had a short life of two years from 1933 to 1935. It operated on one small farm along the Arkansas River outside of Pocola, Oklahoma, where the company dug several tunnels into a handful of hillocks. It made little money, and its owners left no fortunes to its heirs, created no museums, and endowed no foundations.

This mining company did not search for coal or metal or uranium or diamonds. The Pocola Mining Company operated as one of the few officially and legally organized mining companies in American history that did not seek to mine any natural resource. Instead, Pocola's founders created the company for the sole purpose of mining cultural resources; they mined the rich deposits of Indian artifacts made and buried in that area. The owners of the Pocola Mining Company dug up what was probably the greatest collection of artifacts and art objects ever discovered in North America.

In 1935 the *Star* of Kansas City compared the discoveries of the Pocola Mining Company to the recently completed excavations of King Tutankhamun's tomb in Egypt's Valley of the Kings. The mining company had tunneled into the largest of the mounds just outside Spiro, Oklahoma, and found a treasure of pearls, hand-carved beads, necklaces, earspools, carved pipes, and other goods carefully crafted from copper, stone, wood, and pottery, including effigy pipes, T-shaped pipes, shell and cedar masks, arrowheads, spearpoints, axes, blankets, flint knives up to three feet in length, and embossed copper plates and bowls. They also found hundreds of large conch shells and gorgets that had been carefully engraved. The gorgets were pendants worn about the neck, but larger than a modern saucer or small plate; they had been carefully carved from shells and incised with sacred images. The ancient craftsmen had carved many of them with cut-out designs that rendered the hard white shell as delicate and fragile as a lace collar.

The men who mined the Spiro mounds sold many of the artifacts at the mouth of the mine, where curiousity seekers and curio collectors came to purchase the pieces for a few cents, or a few dollars for the finest specimens. The miners loaded up crates of the artifacts, which they drove to the East Coast to sell to people from the trunks of their cars.

The Pocola Mining Company looted the mounds with no concern for archaeology or history, much less for the rights of the native people whose ancestors made and buried the objects. They did not record what they took, or where they sold it. What could not be sold had no value to them. They discarded the pieces of pottery, textiles, feathers, and fur for which they found no buyers.

They burned the wooden timbers that could later have been used by archaeologists to gain valuable information on the people who buried the artifacts. Frequently the miners broke up larger artifacts, such as the carefully engraved conch shells, because they could often get a few more cents for several interesting chunks than they could get for a whole piece.

The surprising find of artifacts by the grave robbers of the Pocola Mining Company revolutionized thought about North American Indians. No one had expected that such objects could have been created by Indians, and no academic theories of the time could explain the incredible funerary remains from Spiro.

After two years of looting by the mining company, the state and federal governments finally moved to protect what remained in the mounds. The Oklahoma legislature passed an antiquities preservation law, and the federal government sponsored a scientific excavation of the mounds through its Depression relief programs of the Works Progress Administration from 1936 to 1941. The archaeologist Forrest E. Clements of the University of Oklahoma visited the site and later wrote that when the looters realized that they would lose their primary site, they began working faster. By the time the archaeologist arrived, the "great mound had been tunneled through and through, gutted in a frenzy of haste." He said that "[s]ections of cedar poles lay scattered on the ground, fragments of feather and fur textiles littered the whole area; it was impossible to take a single step in hundreds of square yards around the ruined structure without scuffing up broken pieces of pottery, sections of engraved shell and beads of shell, stone, and bone." Tragically, "the diggers had completed their work" (Page, p. 5).

Before the Pocola Mining Company angrily surrendered its tunnels at Spiro, the looters perpetrated one final act of outrage and revenge on history by wiring the mine and tunnels with dynamite and blowing up as much of it as they could. In a sad testimony to the effect of their work, the dynamite did not do as much damage as the previous two years of indiscriminate tunneling and looting.

The Pocola Mining Company represents one of the most egregious examples of the wholesale looting of Indian artifacts for profit, but it is certainly not unique. Similar tragic stories could be told about the looting of Anasazi and Mimbres sites of the

Southwest, the theft of wampum belts from the Iroquois of New York, the seizure of Kwakiutl ceremonial objects and masks in British Columbia, and the theft of Dorset and Thule artifacts across the Arctic.

America has literally mined the ancient Indian cultures for artifacts. Not all of the mining has been as cruel as that of the Pocola Mining Company, but it has continued in more genteel ways up to the present. Some of this material is now on display across the world in museums from Leningrad to London and from Berlin to Los Angeles, but even more is hidden away or even forgotten in private collections, university warehouses, and the storage lockers of local history societies.

It is relatively easy to trace material objects, since they always bear the distinctive marks of the culture that created them. No matter where the artifacts travel, they can still be identified as American Indian. There is always the hope that one day they will be found, identified, and returned to their proper places.

We can trace Indian objects, but it proves much harder to trace Indian ideas, knowledge, and other parts of nonmaterial culture. Yet American scholars have mined the rich deposits of American Indian knowledge as much as native deposits of artifacts, but in contrast to artifacts, which usually reveal their origins, an idea or a bit of information can quickly be clothed in new garb that forever hides its true source.

Scholars and researchers, often with the best of intentions, have mined Native American thought in much the way that the Pocola Mining Company mined its artifacts. Digging through American intellectual development of the past few centuries does not always prove the Indian origin of an idea, but through an exercise in intellectual archaeology, we find native fingerprints and signatures throughout the work.

Ozhaw-Guscoday-Wayquay, whose name meant "Woman of the Green Prairie," was the daughter of Waub Ojeeg, the Ojibwa chief in the Lake Superior area of Chequamegon Bay. She married John Johnston, an American fur trader who had settled in the area around Sault Ste. Marie, in the Michigan territory, at the start of the nineteenth century. Ozhaw-Guscoday-Wayquay had several children whom she sought to educate in both the Indian and the white traditions. She raised her children to be fluent in French and English as well as Ojibwa. Her eldest daughter Jane showed particular promise, so the parents sent her to England for schooling (Mason, p. xi). They sent their son George for higher studies in Montreal.

In 1820 the Johnston family and their Ojibwa relatives played host to the visiting delegation sponsored by General Lewis Cass, who was the territorial governor and would become the U.S. Secretary of War and eventually Secretary of State. Cass brought a group to explore the western Great Lakes and search for the source of the Mississippi. Twenty-seven-year-old Henry Rowe Schoolcraft of Albany, New York, accompanied the expedition as mineralogist and geologist; this was to be his first trip of discovery to the source of the Mississippi River.

The intelligent and charming Jane Johnston captured the attention of the young mineralogist and changed his life. He married her and settled into the Ojibwa community as the government's Indian agent, a job he held for nearly two decades. The encounter between Schoolcraft and Johnston also redirected Schoolcraft's academic and scientific interests.

Schoolcraft worked hard to learn the Ojibwa language from his wife and her relatives. He began the task of learning what he thought was a very simple language as a "novel and pleasing species of amusement" (Bieder, p. 155), but the amusement soon turned to hard work as he found a language based on principles quite different from those of European tongues. Although Schoolcraft went on to become a scholar of American Indian languages, he relied upon his wife and her relatives to translate for him, since he never mastered the Ojibwa language. Like many academic linguists to follow him in the next century, Schoolcraft had an abstract understanding of the rules of grammar of the Ojibwa language, but he had difficulty applying them in daily speech. Convinced of the importance of the Indian languages despite his own shortcomings, Schoolcraft urged American colleges to begin teaching native languages as well as European ones (Bieder, p. 157).

Jane taught her husband much about her native heritage. Because she had a classical European education, she explained to him the delicacies and complexities of Ojibwa grammer by using

Latin declension and conjugation models. This collatoration eventually led to a six-volume analysis of the Ojibwa language. Despite
the creation of this monumental linguistic analysis, Schoolcraft
gradually realized that with his meager command of the Ojibwa
language he could never make his intellectual mark in philology,
but through his language studies with his wife, he gradually developed a new area of expertise.

In addition to historical and linguistic information, Jane Johnston Schoolcraft related to her husband the Ojibwa tales and
myths told to her by her mother. Through his wife, he also had
access to a small but highly educated circle of Indians who led
mixed lives combining white and traditional Ojibwa styles.
Schoolcraft collected information on a variety of Indian topics,
but his great "discovery" through his wife was that the Ojibwa
had an oral literature. Today we are so accustomed to the idea
that all the Indian nations had complex mythological traditions
that it is hard to imagine that English speakers at one time had
no knowledge of this. At the same time that Schoolcraft discovered
American Indian myths and folk tales, the German brothers Wil-
helm and Jacob Grimm of Hanau were also making the same
discovery of such tales among their own German farmers and
published their *Deutsche Mythologie* in 1836.

Henry Schoolcraft published his new discovery about oral litera-
ture as a two-volume set in 1839 with the title *Algic Researches*.
Schoolcraft himself had coined the pseudoscientific word *Algic* as
an adjective form of *Algonquin*, the language family to which the
Ojibwa language belonged. Schoolcraft had even formed his own
Algic Research Society in 1832 to further research into the
Ojibwa, and he had hoped to found the State Historical Society
of Michigan and the Michigan Territorial Library in 1828
(Mason, p. xi).

To comply with the newly emerging Victorian standards of
refined decency and modesty, Schoolcraft censored and rearranged
the tales in order to remove sexual references and any mention
of the more unseemly bodily functions. The tales achieved great
popularity with a large public audience and made an immediate
impact on other American writers of the era. Henry Wadsworth
Longfellow borrowed from this set of tales to write his popular
poem *The Song of Hiawatha*. This caused so much interest in the

tales that Schoolcraft published a new edition of his book under the more commercial title *The Myth of Hiawatha and Other Oral Legends*.

Despite, or perhaps because of, Henry Schoolcraft's dependence on his wife, Jane Johnston Schoolcraft, and her family, a tense relationship developed between them. As the racism of the Victorian era increased, Henry Schoolcraft found it increasingly difficult to face the world with his Ojibwa wife and their two mixed children, who were called "blacks" in the common terminology of that era (Bieder, p. 166).

Schoolcraft also felt himself pulled back into a rigid form of Christianity, which he thought should be imposed on his wife and on Indians in general. He criticized her for having been reared by such lenient parents, and wrote to her in a letter of December 8, 1830, that "it is the domestic conduct of a female that is most continually liable to error, both of judgement and feeling." He could not break her away from her own culture and the thick webs of kinship that united her to her family and people. He continued to remind his wife of her Christian duty, for "a woman should forsake 'father & mother & cleave to her husband, and that she should look up to him with a full confidence as, next to God, her 'guide, philosopher & friend' " (Bieder, p. 161).

Ten years later, Jane Johnston Schoolcraft died, freeing Henry Schoolcraft from the stigma of an Ojibwa wife, but also taking his most valuable source of information. Schoolcraft continued his studies of the Indians, but with far less sympathy toward them than he had shown in his writings while she lived. He reversed his earlier position in support of Indian land claims. He sided openly with the anti-Indian policies of Andrew Jackson, and with publication of an article titled "Our Indian Policy" in the *Democratic Review* in 1844, he supported removal of the Indians from their land.

As a prominently established academic and specialist in Indian culture and history, the elderly Henry Schoolcraft married again. Avoiding the mistakes of his first marriage, Schoolcraft chose a self-avowed racist white woman from South Carolina. Mary Howard Schoolcraft proved much more amenable to the religious and moral demands of her husband, but she also managed to outshine

him as a writer in her lengthy defenses of slavery, which she published under the name of Mrs. Henry R. Schoolcraft. Through her written criticisms of her husband's first wife, Mary Howard Schoolcraft helped to minimize the achievement and contributions of the Ojibwa Jane Schoolcraft while maximizing the originality and genius of Henry Schoolcraft.

Her magnum opus appeared as a thinly disguised autobiographical novel, *The Black Gauntlet*, which she dedicated to her husband, whom she called *Ne na baim*, which she said was an "Indian word meaning husband." The main achievement of Musidora, the main character in the novel, came when she "immortalize[d] the family by marrying a world-renowned genius, whose works could never die" (M. H. Schoolcraft, p. 478). In order to maximize the importance of this second marriage, she had to explain away the husband's first marriage to an Indian woman and their resulting mixed-blood offspring.

She characterized the genius's first marriage as an impulse of his romantic nature. He "idolized his Pocahontas wife with that patronage that a man feels for a woman who is a child in character and impulse, though he was, nevertheless often obliged to leave her, month after month, in his scientific explorations of various countries, and even when at home, he lived in his library fascinated with antiquarian and ethnological research; so that he only associated with his family at meals." (M. H. Schoolcraft, p. 495).

The marriage with an Indian woman so distressed the "fictional" professor's mother that she died of a broken heart, and the professor himself soon regretted the romantic, impulsive marriage of his youth. According to the second wife's account, the Indian wife died totally insane from opium addiction, a vice she shared with her son.

In conclusion, Mrs. Mary Howard Schoolcraft described the first marriage as something the professor had done in "ethnological enthusiasm" to unite "the American aborigines with the noble Anglo-Saxon" (M. H. Schoolcraft, p. 541). His marriage was a "suicidal . . . experiment to amalgamate in marriage with a race as inferior to his own as an ape is to Napoleon Bonaparte, or a Skenandoah is to an African cannibal negro (Mumbo Jumbo)" (M. H. Schoolcraft, p. 498).

Fortunately for historical accuracy, we do not have to depend solely on the descriptions and evaluations of Mary Howard to evaluate the genius of Henry Rowe Schoolcraft. She may have been able to obscure the contributions of Schoolcraft's Ojibwa wife, but she could not obscure the work of his second Indian assistant, a young Seneca, Ely Parker, because Parker quickly surpassed Schoolcraft in fame and respect.

In 1846, Schoolcraft published *Notes on the Iroquois: Or, Contributions to the Statistics, Aboriginal History, Antiquities and General Ethnology of Western New York*. Much of the information he gathered for the book depended heavily on the words and letters of Ely Parker, who obligingly wrote out answers to the incessantly demanding questions of Henry Schoolcraft. In keeping with his style, Schoolcraft neglected to make explicit his debt to Ely Parker. Perhaps if Schoolcraft had known then how prominent his young assistant was to become, he might have been more generous in allotting him credit for his early ethnographic work.

In a particularly Indian way, Ely Parker's mission in life began well before he was born in 1828 on the Tonawanda Reservation of the Seneca nation, near Buffalo in western New York state. His mother, Elizabeth Parker, was deeply troubled by a mysterious dream while pregnant with her future son. In the dream she saw a rainbow connecting the Seneca land with the white community at Buffalo, and beneath the rainbow hung the kinds of name placards that white merchants hung over their doors and put in shop windows. In traditional Seneca fashion, Elizabeth Parker took this troublesome dream to an elder for interpretation.

The elder explained that the "son will become a white man as well as an Indian, with great learning." He explained that the boy would become a chief among the Indians as well as the whites, and that "his name will reach from the East to the West—the North to the South, as great among his Indian family and the pale-faces" (Armstrong, p. 15).

She named the boy Ha-sa-no-as-da, which meant "Leading Name" because he was to be an important leader, but she also gave him the name Ely (rhymes with *freely*) for use in the world outside the Seneca lands. His father, William Parker, had assumed the name Parker in honor of a British officer, Arthur C. Parker,

who had been adopted into the tribe. Despite this English sur-name, Ely Parker grew up in the traditional Seneca cabin, speaking only the Seneca language.

The high expectations placed on young Ely Parker must not have seemed too strange for him, since he came from a family of illustrious achievement. His mother sat in caucuses as *ho-ya-neh*, an honored woman who nominated or impeached sachems of the Iroquois Confederacy. One of Ely's ancestors, Handsome Lake, started a spiritual and anti-alcohol movement in 1799 that became known as *Gai-woo* or "the good message." His mother's grand-uncle was Red Jacket, a great orator and leader during the War of 1812 (Armstrong, p. 16). Ely's own father served under Red Jacket in the war, and then became a chief of the Tonawanda Seneca.

True to the mission foreseen in her dream, Elizabeth Parker ensured that her son would receive both a white and an Indian education. She taught him much of the history and myths of her people, and she sent him to a Baptist mission school off the reser-vation. To ensure that he learned the masculine crafts of wood-working, archery, gunnery, spear fishing, canoeing, and tracking, she sent him to live with another group of Iroquois in neighboring Ontario.

Even though Ely showed little interest in English, he gradually began to master it, and then his mother sent him to learn Greek and Latin, which came much easier to him since he already knew one European language. By the age of fourteen, Ely was being used by the Seneca chiefs as a translator and scribe. Thus, at this young age he came into contact with high government officials and began, on behalf of the chiefs, to correspond with United States senators, cabinet secretaries, and even the President of the United States.

In April 1844, the elders called him out of school once again to accompany them to Albany for a conference with Governor William Bouck. Because the Indians had to wait many days for appointments and conferences, young Parker used his free time to roam the city. He particularly enjoyed the bookstores. While browsing through one of those bookstores, he met a young lawyer named Lewis Henry Morgan, who had come to Albany to do research in the state archives.

Morgan belonged to a lodge of young professional men in Aurora, New York. Under Morgan's leadership, the group had changed its classical name, the Order of the Gordian Knot, to the Grand Order of the Iroquois, and had elected Morgan sachem. Morgan wanted the practices of the order to follow as closely as possible those of the true Iroquois, but none of the young men knew any Iroquois. As a lawyer not adverse to research, Morgan made the trip to Albany from Aurora to examine the state archives and ferret out accurate information on the organization of the Iroquois Confederacy.

It was while browsing through the bookstore for information on the Iroquois that Morgan fortuitously encountered Ely Parker, a member of one of the nations of the Iroquois. Parker was the first Iroquois whom Morgan had met, and Parker agreed to spend most of the next two days talking with Morgan at his hotel and translating as Morgan talked with the chiefs whom Parker had accompanied. In Morgan, who was ten years older than he, the young Parker found an eager student who wanted to know everything about Iroquois ritual and formal organization.

For Parker, this was the first time he had met a white man who showed a genuine interest in the Iroquois. After years of studying the white man's ways and culture, the time had finally come for Parker to begin teaching the Indian ways to the whites. He was beginning to fulfill the other part of his mother's prenatal dream. Parker and Morgan formed an eager partnership in which Parker taught Morgan and the other white members of the Grand Order of the Iroquois, and they in turn helped to finance his continued education at the Cayuga Academy in Aurora, where Parker would be close to them for continued interaction.

In 1845, Parker took Morgan and the other members of the Grand Order to visit his home reservation. The Indians wore a mixture of traditional and modern clothes. In addition to planting traditional crops of corn and beans, they also grew barley, peas, oats, wheat, and apple trees. Most of their meat came from the hogs, sheep, and cows they now raised, since they no longer had access to the deer and other animals of the great forests of their ancestors. The visitors experienced some disappointment at the poverty of the reservation and at seeing that the Seneca lived in cabins much like those of the whites. To appease Morgan, William

Parker agreed to construct a traditional longhouse of the kind in which he had been reared.

This fateful visit could easily have been the end of the romantic dream of some young men who, having lost that dream, would settle into marriage, family, and a style of life appropriate to the nineteenth-century bourgeoisie of small-town America. Despite the disappointment, the interest did not lessen in Morgan. In his conversations with Parker he met someone who made him understand that no matter how much the Seneca grew to resemble the whites in the materials of their lives, they retained a substantially different culture. Their beliefs, ceremonies, practices, language, and whole way of life was based on principles different from, and often conflicting with, the larger society around them.

Parker taught Morgan that the main organizing principle behind the life of the Seneca and underneath all of these ceremonies was kinship. Such a notion seems deceptively simple, since most societies organize around kinship, but under Parker's tutelage Morgan realized that kinship was more than a mere biological given. Culture, not biology, constructed and organized kinship. The Iroquois concepts of kinship were constructed much differently from those of the Europeans. For the Iroquois, for example, the concepts of *brother* and *sister* included not only siblings but also parallel cousins (cousins related through two sisters or through two brothers).

Morgan realized that in order to understand so different a culture from his own, he had to be part of their society. He could not merely study it abstractly as an outsider; he had to *live* it. In 1846 the Senecas agreed to adopt Morgan into the Hawk clan as the son of Jimmy Johnson, one of the chiefs, but the adoption occurred on the condition that Morgan himself pay for the requisite feast and not put the burden on his new family. As a member of the Seneca nation, albeit through adoption rather than birth, Morgan felt the need to translate his new knowledge into help for the Seneca people. As a member of the state bar, Morgan represented the Seneca in their struggle to keep their lands from the Ogden Company, which was trying to develop those lands and push the Seneca westward.

The collaboration of Morgan and Parker in understanding Iroquois society resulted in the book *League of the Ho-de'-no-sau-nee, or Iroquois*, published in Rochester, New York, in 1851, only seven years after the meeting in the bookstore. Parker wrote long passages of the book and did all the transcription of political speeches, as well as all translations for the book. The book listed Morgan as author, but Morgan dedicated the book to Parker, asserting on the title page that "the materials . . . are the fruit of our joint researches," a point upon which he elaborates in the book's preface.

Ely Parker's sister, Caroline Parker, posed for the book's illustrations of the Iroquois woman draped in finely embroidered dress and shawl, and his brother Nicholson Parker appeared as a traditional Seneca man holding a war club. Morgan also filled the book with illustrations of household objects taken from the Parker home. He later persuaded Caroline Parker to copy articles of Indian clothing that Morgan obtained for the State Cabinet of Natural History.

The book on the League of the Iroquois stands today as the first book in American anthropology, and although it was Morgan who became known as "the father of anthropology," this first volume was very much the joint creation of Ely S. Parker and Lewis Henry Morgan. Anthropology came to life as the joint creation of an Indian and a white dedicated to helping their respective peoples better understand each other.

What we now think of as cultural anthropology or ethnology was largely invented by Morgan in his studies with Parker. It became the detailed study of a people and their way of life, and how these people connect with the whole pageant of world history. Using his newly acquired understanding of the Iroquois, Morgan reinterpreted much of classical and biblical history because he had the key of kinship analysis. He pushed scholarship to a new level by working toward a model of world history that included all peoples, not merely Western civilization as known in the European and Mediterranean world.

After publication of their book on the Iroquois, the lives of Morgan and Parker followed separate paths. Morgan moved deeper into tribal society, while Parker moved deeper into white society. Morgan continued his intellectual line of inquiry and his writing. His greatest achievement was *Ancient Society*, published in 1877. He became president of the American Association for the Advancement of Science in 1879–80, and he worked to finance the Bandalier expedition to the Southwest, which opened that archaeologically rich area to American as well as international scholarly attention.

Along with his intellectual work, Morgan led a full business life as a lawyer and investor. He accumulated a large fortune, most of which was dedicated to the creation of a women's college at the University of Rochester in New York following his death (Bohannan and Glazer, p. 31).

Ely Parker seemed at first destined to follow the intellectual and academic career of his friend Morgan, but the racism of the times intervened. Parker followed Morgan's example and studied law, but the state of New York refused to admit him to the bar because he was a Seneca and thus not a United States citizen. Lacking wealth with which to support himself and being barred from law, which was a primary entry into the legal and financial world of New York, Parker had to embark on a more practical profession. He became an engineer and worked on canal construction and designed federal government buildings in Illinois and Iowa.

When the Civil War erupted, Parker joined the Union forces and received an officer's commission. This presented a temporary conflict. Under the traditional Iroquois system, a man could not be both a sachem and a war chief. Parker managed to hold both offices since his military appointment was with the United States and not with the Seneca. He could be a war chief for the Americans and still be a peace chief among the Seneca.

He rose quickly and became the secretary and chief assistant to General Ulysses S. Grant. In this capacity, Parker wrote the terms of the surrender of Confederate forces at the end of the war. Parker appears clearly in many photographs of Lee's solemn surrender to Grant's forces at Appomattox Court House, but despite Parker's broad face and darker complexion, he looks much like any other union officer in the pictures.

Ely Parker rose to the rank of brigadier general in the United States Army, and he followed Grant on into public life in Washington. After the grant of citizenship to all taxpaying Indians at peace with the United States, Parker became an official citizen and thus qualified for public office. In 1869, Grant appointed him Commissioner of Indian Affairs—the first commissioner who actually was an Indian. During his two years in office, he opened a peace initiative to the Indians of the West, but after only two years in office he was brought down by one of the many procurement scandals that plagued the Grant administration. Parker was found not guilty of any offense, but he left public service disappointed.

Until his death, in 1895, Parker divided his time between homes in Connecticut and New York. A small income from a job as a clerk permitted him to pursue his interests in Indian history and culture, which he made better known to the larger society through public lectures, work with the Seneca, and collaboration with the author and poet Harriet Maxwell Converse, whom he described as "the best posted woman on Indian lore in America" (Armstrong, p. 175).

Harriet Maxwell Converse, like her husband and father before her, shared a strong interest in the Seneca and was herself adopted into the tribe. Despite their work together and their apparent affection for one another, the mundane demands of earning a living still prevented Parker from devoting himself seriously to intellectual pursuits.

Schoolcraft and Morgan are today recognized as the pioneers of modern anthropology. One can see in their early work the subsequent division of the field into field workers and synthesizers. Schoolcraft obtained a wealth of information through his wife Jane and subsequently through other Indian assistants, such as Ely Parker. Like many great gatherers of information, however, he never put it in good order. His major creation, the six-volume *Historical and Statistical Information Respecting the History, Condition, and Prospects on the Indian Tribes of the United States*, published between 1851 and 1857, was so chaotic that subsequent researchers could hardly use it until the Bureau of American Ethnology finally published an extensive index to it in 1954.

In contrast to Schoolcraft, Morgan's theoretical clarity helped to move Western thought to a new plane of international dimensions. For him, the history of all humans formed part of the same story, and all humans participated in a psychic unity of humankind. In this world history he included the tribal peoples of the Americas, Africa, and Asia in a synthetic and universal theory that had

profound impact on the second half of the nineteenth century.

Morgan was a true intellectual's intellectual, and he had a greater impact on other scientists and philosophers of the nineteenth century than any other American. Morgan met with Charles Darwin, who used his work, although he disagreed with some minor parts of it. Karl Marx studied Morgan's works carefully, and Friedrich Engels wrote about them extensively in *The Origin of the Family, Private Property and the State, in Light of the Researches of Lewis H. Morgan*. The German philosopher Johann Jakob Bachofen dedicated one of his books to Morgan for having given Bachofen a perspective on the reputed prehistoric era of mother-rule. A generation of classical scholars found in Morgan's work new insights on the tribal organization of the ancient Hebrews, Greeks, Romans, and Germans.

Even though Morgan's name has been forgotten by many, he continued to inspire thought around the world in the twentieth century. Through his influence on Bachofen, Engels, and Marx, Morgan became a staple in Soviet and Chinese thought. In America he survived mostly within anthropology, but in France he continued to exert a greater influence through Claude Lévi-Strauss.

In 1949, Claude Lévi-Strauss started modern French structuralism with his book *The Elementary Structures of Kinship*, which he dedicated to Morgan in recognition of the importance of Morgan's ideas in Lévi-Strauss's own work. Lévi-Strauss gave three reasons for this dedication: "to pay homage to the pioneer of the research method modestly adopted in this book; to honour the American school of anthropology that he founded . . . and perhaps also, in some small way, to try to discharge the debt owed to him, by recalling that this school was especially great at a time when scientific precision and exact observation did not seem to him to be incompatible with a frankly theoretical mode of thought and a bold philosophical taste" (Lévi-Strauss, p. xxvi).

Ethnological work such as that done by Henry Schoolcraft and his wife Jane Johnston Schoolcraft had a broad influence on other thinkers in the nineteenth century. Matilda Joslyn Gage, one of the major feminist writers and activists of that century, used the works of Schoolcraft to formulate her discussion of the importance of women in American Indian society. In *Woman, Church and State* (1893), a radical attack on nineteenth-century society, she quoted from the work of Schoolcraft and other ethnologists among the Indians.

Gate began her analysis with a look at the role of women in Native American society, with special attention to the League of the Iroquois. According to her analysis, American Indian society represented a more equitable society for women than did her contemporary American society. She held the Indians up as models and inspiration for women in the suffrage movement to move beyond mere attainment of a vote at the ballot box to a genuine sharing of power with men in all aspects of modern political, economic, and religious life.

Indians continued to play a crucial role in nineteenth- and twentieth-century anthropology not merely as passive objects of study but as active researchers and analysts, major contributors to the intellectual endeavor. Franz Boas shaped twentieth-century anthropology and linguistics more than any other person, and much of his work was done with, through, and by Indian collaborators and assistants employed or cajoled into working for him. Much of the work among the Kwakiutl of British Columbia for which Boas received credit originated with George Hunt, Boas's Tlingit-Scottish assistant. At first, Hunt acted as interpreter and collector, but after learning to write the Kwakiutl language, he began recording tales and myths. He came to New York, where he was instrumental in arranging the ethnological collection of the American Museum of Natural History.

George Hunt revised virtually all of the Kwakiutl language texts that Boas used, and he helped Boas to learn the language. Boas claimed most of the credit for this work, yet he sometimes blamed George Hunt for shortcomings. He frequently chastised Hunt in his letters, accused him of not working hard enough, and criticized him for making mistakes in the ethnographic and linguistic texts he collected.

The work pursued by Hunt among the Kwakiutl paralleled the work done by Ella Cara Deloria for Boas among the Dakota and Lakota. Her family called her Anpetu Waste, "Beautiful Day," after her birth at White Swan on the Yankton Sioux Reservation in South Dakota on the last day of 1889. As the daughter of one

of the first Dakota Episcopal priests, she received a good education in both traditional Sioux culture and in the mainstream culture. After high school she attended Oberlin College and Columbia Teachers College, graduating with a B.A. in science.

While at Columbia Teachers College, Deloria met Franz Boas, and began writing translations for him in 1915. For eighteen dollars a week, she translated texts collected in 1887 by George Bushotter, one of the first Sioux students to be educated at Virginia's Hampton Institute. With periodic interruptions, Deloria collected data and made translations for Boas until he died in 1942. Her work with him spanned a quarter of a century.

In addition to translating the entire thousand pages of the Bushotter collection, she translated the texts left by an Oglala Sioux, George Sword, around 1908, and the texts of a Santee Sioux, Jack Frazier, written in the 1830s. She also researched and completed a Sioux-English dictionary. In 1932 she published a bilingual book, *Dakota Texts*, in both English and Dakota. She wrote *Speaking of Indians*, which the YMCA published in 1944 to introduce a general audience to the complexities and diversity of Indian life. As she described her work in a 1952 letter, "I actually feel that I have a mission: To make the Dakota people understandable, as human beings, to the white people who have to deal with them" (Deloria, p. 236).

Many of Ella Deloria's works did not find publishers until after her death. These include a novel, *Waterlily*, that she wrote to show the life of Sioux women, since most writings about the Sioux concentrated on the colorful and macho activities of Sioux warriors in battle. Publishers declined to publish it during her life because they felt that a novel about an Indian woman in the nineteenth century would not attract enough readers.

Other members of the Deloria family had continued the intellectual pursuits of Ella and her parents. These include her brother's son, Vine Deloria, Jr., who wrote *Custer Died for Your Sins* (1969), *God Is Red* (1973), and *Behind the Trail of Broken Treaties: An Indian Declaration of Independence* (1974). Her niece, Dr. Bea Medicine, became an anthropologist and Ella's biographer.

Finding the correct way to credit the Indian voice in history, anthropology, and related disciplines has remained a problem throughout the twentieth century. As early as 1913, Paul Radin published a *Journal of American Folklore* article called "Personal Reminiscence of a Winnebago Indian" to stress the role of the Indians in creating his work. By 1926 he had published a biography called *Crashing Thunder*, but with the subtitle *The Autobiography of a Winnebago Indian*, which clearly shows the role of Crashing Thunder in creating the work. Radin also published a study of the Winnebago in 1950 in which he titled the book *Culture of the Winnebago, as Described by Themselves* to emphasize their role in the creation of the book.

In 1969 the anthropologist James P. Spradley removed himself one more degree from the creation of his book *Guests Never Leave Hungry* by listing himself as the editor rather than the author, and subtitling the book *The Autobiography of James Sewid, a Kwakiutl Indian.* Spradley left the text in the first person to emphasize that the words came from James Sewid himself. This marks a steady increase in the amount of credit given to Native Americans for their voices when appropriated into science.

Anthropology, linguistics, history, folklore, mythology, and literature have all borrowed heavily from Native Americans. Unlike the Pocola Mining Company that destroyed as much at Spiro, Oklahoma as it stole, the intellectuals have borrowed without destroying.

18

MIXED-BLOOD NATION

Lower Fort Garry overlooks Manitoba's Red River, which flows north to form the broad Lake Winnipeg. The fort rises up on a lonely, quiet stretch of the river, not too far from the geographical center of the North American continent. If one drew a large **X** on a map of North America, running one line from northern Quebec to Baja California in Mexico, and the other from Florida to the northwestern tip of Alaska, the lines would intersect in southern Manitoba, near Lower Fort Garry.

At only a little over fifty degrees north of the equator, Lower Fort Garry lies only a few hundred miles north of the halfway point between the equator and the North Pole. Despite this equidistance, the climate of the area seems markedly more regulated by the Arctic than the tropics. This part of Canada feels the full blast of the winter winds that blow in from the north and make the area a zone of transition between the agricultural prairie of southern Canada and the northern tundra.

Trees grow in this area, but they are small, stunted things, barely higher than the single-story houses that dot the fields. Few of them grow large enough for a person to wrap both hands around the trunk without being able to touch fingers. In most years, ice still covers parts of Lake Winnipeg in May.

The creamy limestone walls of the fort form a nearly perfect square, and the bastions built at each corner make it look, in fact, like a military fort. But since construction began on the fort in 1846, it always served as a trading fort of the Hudson's Bay Company in what the traders then called Rupert's Land. The bastion that seems to protect the fort actually served as washrooms, cookhouses, and storerooms rather than as shelters for cannons or sentries.

Because the fort occupies a high river bluff near a good limestone source, the typical visitor might assume that the builders of Lower Fort Garry had a major military, political, or perhaps economic reason for building it where they did. The fort seems to be the type that would protect the intersection of two great rivers, guard the crossing point of a traditional Indian trail, or serve as a northern boundary against attack.

Any of these could have been the reason, but cursory inspection dispels them all. The fort does not lie at the confluence of rivers or on the intersection of trails. It does not straddle an important boundary, and seems merely to divide one stretch of flat plain from another.

An older fort, the original Fort Garry, occupied a much better spot to the south at the confluence of the Assiniboine and Red rivers in the heart of what became the city of Winnipeg. Old Fort Garry to the south, and not Lower Fort Garry to the north, served as the crossing point of major trails and offered easier connection down to Lake of the Woods on the United States border, and from there into the Great Lakes and the cities of Ottawa and Montreal.

To find the reason why Governor George Simpson of the Hudson's Bay Company built Lower Fort Garry in 1839, we need to look beyond colonial policy, corporate interests, and economic accounts to Simpson's sex life. He built it because he had married a respectable white woman, his eighteen-year-old cousin Frances Simpson, and he wanted the fort to protect her. He did not need to protect her from the Indians or from the savage Americans to the south or the French to the east. Simpson built Lower Fort

Garry to protect his new bride from having to socialize with his Indian wives and children, who lived at *Old* Fort Garry.

Like virtually all the men who worked for the Hudson's Bay Company, Simpson had a succession of Indian wives. Unlike most of these men, who acknowledged Indian women as their "country wives" for at least a few years, and in some cases for life, Simpson led a debauched life with a succession of women whom he acknowledged as merely mistresses and "bits of brown." At least four Indian and mixed-blood women bore Simpson five children, in addition to two illegitimate daughters born of two white women before he emigrated from Britain (Newman, p. 260). Some estimates of the number of Simpson's illegitimate children have been as high as seventy, which led to his being called, insightfully, "the father of the fur trade."

To accommodate the flow of women in and out of his bedroom, Simpson insisted on a private entrance to his rooms. He dismissed these short liaisons curtly. Even Simpson's country wives who lived with him a long time and bore his children received scantily better treatment than the women hustled in and out of his special love door.

Simpson deserted one of his country wives pregnant and under the charge of his associate with the instruction to "keep an Eye on the commodity and if she bring forth anything in proper time and of the right color let them be taken care of but if any thing be amiss let the whole be bundled about their business." At another time Simpson gave the same associate instructions about another of his Indian women: "If you can dispose of the Lady it will be satisfactory as she is an unnecessary and expensive appendage . . . but if she is unmarketable I have no wish that she should be a general accommodation shop to all the young bucks at the Factory." If the wife could not be disposed of, Simpson instructed his associate that she be padlocked into a chastity belt to keep her from cavorting with men of lower class (Newman, p. 260).

By keeping his new white wife at Lower Fort Garry, Simpson sought to protect her from association with the racially mixed couples and their mixed-blood offspring who lived at Old Fort Garry and the nearby community of St. Boniface. The children of Indian women and Scottish or English men became known as half-breeds. The even more numerous offspring of French-Indian alliances became known as Métis, from the French word for "mixed."

The French colonial government of Canada never succeeded in stimulating massive immigration of French settlers to America the way the British did in the South. From earliest colonial times the French government and religious hierarchy encouraged intermarriage of French soldiers and traders with Indian women as a way of bringing the Indians into the power of the French state and the Catholic Church. As early as 1628, the charter of the New French Company, issued by Cardinal Richelieu, provided that any Indians who converted to Christianity "shall be held to be native Frenchmen." This enabled them to "inherit and accept gifts and bequests in the same way as subjects born in the realm and native Frenchmen" (Borah, p. 718). This acceptance of Indians as Frenchmen according to their religion (or culture) rather than a mythical or quasi-scientific notion of "blood" made the French much more accepting of intermarriage with Native Americans.

The contrast between French and British policy appeared clearly in early travel commentaries, such as that of Thomas Forsyth, who visited North America in 1818. According to him, the French Canadian men within one year of arriving in America "will eat, drink, sleep and be hail fellow well met with the Indians, will learn in the course of a few months the Indian language by which means the Indians become attached to the Frenchmen." He wrote further that most of the French villages consisted of men "who were married to Indian women and followed a life similar to that of the Indian themselves such as hunting, fishing & by which means the Frenchman's children were related to both parties." (Forsyth, p. 210).

The intermarriage of Frenchmen with Indians continued after Canada passed to British control. Britain encouraged Scottish immigration to America, and the Scots also intermarried frequently with Indians, although the English did so only rarely. Following American independence from Britain, many of the loyalist Scots from the south moved north, and they added to the number of mixed marriages in Canada.

With the shortage of white women in the western and northern British colonies in Canada, men practiced a lively commerce in female Indian slaves. Although not legally recognized by the government, men bought and sold women, or even leased them for a certain number of years. They trafficked in Indian and mixed-blood women for cash, to repay gambling debts, and in trade for horses and rum. They auctioned women to the highest bidder much the way Africans were sold at public auctions for Southern plantations. Sometimes Indian or mixed girls as young as nine or ten years of age were sold in this trade (Newman, p. 21).

After such extensive interbreeding through marriage, slavery, or casual relations, a large mixed-blood population emerged in western Canada. In the nineteenth century the Métis people formed a distinct ethnic group centered on the site of modern Winnipeg. They spoke Michif, a Cree-French creole, and adhered to a mixture of Catholicism and native spiritual belief. For subsistence they depended on the buffalo, which they hunted in annual maneuvers that approached the scale of a military operation complete with ranks and officers. The Métis formed annual caravans of two-wheeled ox-drawn carts that ventured south to St. Paul on the Mississippi River for supplies, which they hauled to Manitoba.

Métis culture combined elements of both Woodland and Plains Indian culture with European heritage. The men wore a bright red sash that readily identified them as Métis, and both men and women wore elaborate beaded patterns on their clothes. Because of their extensive use of floral motifs in their beadwork, the Dakota called the Métis "the flower beadwork people" (McMillan, p. 279).

While the Métis (Indian-French) controlled the buffalo hunt, the half-breeds (Indian-English and Indian-Scottish) worked as laborers for the Hudson's Bay Company and as small farmers along the Red River. They grew vegetables, potatoes, and grains for the local trade forts and for York Factory on Hudson Bay, where the growing season was too short even for garden crops.

This complex cultural and economic system of commerce and ethnic relations had been well established in the area for generations when Simpson arrived, but attitudes were changing. The new Victorian era of the nineteenth century looked with increasingly diminished tolerance on the interbreeding of whites with native peoples. New and supposedly scientific theories predicted dire consequences from race mixing: at best it led to criminal behavior and sexual wantonness; at worst it threatened to corrupt and eventually destroy the white European race and thus bring down the British Empire.

Because of Governor George Simpson's disregard for his own Indian wives, he broke up the traditional system of Hudson Bay men and their country wives. When he brought his white wife Frances to the Red River, he started a new tradition of higher-class men bringing white wives out to the Canadian west. For the first time in that area, men could no longer bring their country wives out in public. He forbade his men to bring their mixed-blood wives even to visit the new fort, much less to meet or in any other way interact with the minute collection of white women housed there.

As early as 1806, the North West Company, the fur-trading rival of the Hudson's Bay Company, tried unsuccessfully to stop intermarriages between its employees and Indian women by levying a fine of one hundred pounds for engaging in such unions (Newman, p. 23). As the century progressed, the pressures against mixed marriages increased across North America. Traders, officers, and men who had the slightest claim to being part of educated or polite society followed Simpson's example and yielded to social pressure and the newly stringent Victorian morals to withdraw from their Indian families. Three centuries of racial mixing in North America suddenly became shameful, unhygienic, unpatriotic, immoral, and in many places illegal.

The history of America is a history of racial and ethnic mixtures from the earliest contacts, and that mixture predates the arrival of European settlers. The Pilgrims, the first Europeans to make permanent settlements in New England, arrived in Massachusetts in 1620, but they found that other whites had already been there. They discovered this inadvertently while robbing Indian graves in search of goods they might use or trade. They were startled by one grave, which contained, in addition to all of the usual Indian goods next to the skeleton of a small child, the skeleton of a man with "fine yellow hair." This blond-haired man had many typical Indian possessions, but he also had some of the clothing and accoutrements of a European sailor (Cronon, p. 84). No one knew whether the sailor had been involuntarily cast up on the shore or whether he had voluntarily sought refuge among these people, but the grave made it apparent that he had lived among them for some time. It would be mere guesswork to speculate whether or not this particular blond man sired Indian children who lived, but such unions were common.

White settlers frequently deserted their own communities to live in the civilization of the Indians. White captives who lived among the Indians often refused to return to their own people, preferring to live among the Indians and raise their mixed children as Indians. This reluctance of whites to return created great theological and cultural problems for the settlers, who could not understand how a "civilized" Christian could possibly adopt the life and beliefs of "uncivilized savages." To combat such losses to the Indians, several colonies passed laws forbidding "Indianizing."

To help people resist the temptation to join the natives, colonial writers began a wholly new, American genre of literature in their "captive accounts" that depicted Indian capture of settlers in horrifying detail. These tales induced fear of Indians in the reader, but also helped serve as a guide and supposedly as Christian inspiration to the reader who might one day become a captive.

Despite the horrors described in captive accounts, a white trader among the Indians might find that his business thrived if he married an Indian woman. She gave him a status within the kinship organization of the tribe, and her relatives gave him a network of trading partners and helpers. Throughout North America we see evidence of such unions, and the children often attained positions of great respect within the native nations. Alexander McGillivray, the son of a Scottish trader and a Creek mother, became the Emperor of the Creeks in the southeastern United States. The Scottish Ross family produced many generations of leaders among the Cherokee nation.

Even within the white American elite, some important cases of intermarriage with Indians occurred, particularly during the early and crucial years of colonization. After the Virginia settler John Rolfe married Pocahontas, they had a son, Thomas Rolfe, whom Pocahontas bore in England. After his mother's death he returned to his maternal homeland, where he became a scion of the great families of Virginia including the Randolphs and Bollings (Robert, p. 9).

Ely S. Parker and his brother, Nicholson Parker, both married white women of prominent families. In 1867, Ely Parker married Minnie Orton Sackett, the daughter of a fellow general in the army. She was a popular socialite in Washington, and General Ulysses S. Grant gave her away at her wedding in the place of her deceased father.

In Alaska, unions of Russian men and native women produced many offspring to whom the Russians usually gave equal rights as Russian citizens and subjects of the czar. When the United States acquired these territories, however, officials sought to deny the mixed-bloods recognition as whites, and to force them into the ranks of Indians.

Some of the Founding Fathers openly encouraged such mixtures. Patrick Henry proposed to the Virginia House of Delegates that the state promote Indian-white marriages by exempting such couples from taxes. He further proposed that the state subsidize Indian-white marriages by offering money as an incentive for mixed couples and to supplement that marriage fee with additional gifts of money at the birth of each mixed-blood child (Johansen and Grinde, pp. 7, 10).

The bill failed to pass, but a similar sentiment was expressed in less monetary though far more ideal terms by Thomas Jefferson at a presidential reception for "Delawares, Mohicons, and Munries" in 1802 when he invited the assembled Indians to mix with the white settlers in every way. In a paternalistic manner he addressed them as his children and said that if they agreed to live under American law and understand private ownership of property, they would join white society.

Jefferson said, rather overoptimistically, "you will unite yourselves with us, join in our great councils and form one people with us, and we shall all be Americans; you will mix with us by marriage, your blood will mix with ours, and will spread, with ours, over this great island" (Padover, p. 503).

From the time of De Soto's arrival in Florida, Africans found refuge from European slavery by fleeing to Indian communities. Three of De Soto's slaves, two Africans and a Moor, became so enchanted with the land of the Lady of Cutifachiqui that they escaped from De Soto and found refuge with the Indians. They stayed on in Cutifachiqui, and according to one narrative account, one of the escaped slaves became the husband of the famed Lady of Cutifachiqui. Throughout De Soto's rampage from modern South Carolina to the Mississippi River, slaves of African descent escaped and intermarried with the local Indians, making these escaped slaves the first Old World settlers throughout much of the Southeast and the Gulf Coast.

Over the next three centuries, Indian groups throughout the Southeast provided a sanctuary for escaped slaves from the plantations. Some groups, such as the Choctaw and the Seminole, took in large numbers of slaves with ease. Other groups sometimes enslaved the runaways in imitation of colonial practices, but even in these cases the Indians often allowed the slaves to marry and become members of the tribe. The Seminole leader Osceola himself married an African-American woman of slave descent.

Indians and Africans also intermarried on the Southern plantations where both groups were enslaved. The slaveowners cared little which dark-skinned slave married which other dark-skinned slave. It quickly became difficult to tell Indian from African slaves, as is evidenced in many of the newspaper advertisements for runaway slaves. In New Jersey, a 1747 advertisement for a fifty-three-year-old man named Cohansie describes him as having "some Indian blood in him," and accompanied by an adolescent boy, Sam, who "was born of an Indian woman, and looks like an Indian." The advertisement continues to say that "they both talk Indian very well, and it is likely they have dressed themselves in the Indian dress and gone to Carolina (Forbes, p. 87).

Many of the African-Indians appear to us in history only in these rather anonymous forms. We have reports of them, but we do not know them by name or by any other information. One of the first African-Indians whose name was recorded in history was Cripus Attucks, who fell in the Boston Massacre of March 5, 1770, and thus became known as the first patriot to die in the struggle for American independence.

Although little is known about Attucks, he was probably in his early thirties when he died, and was of mixed parentage. He may have been an escaped slave from Framingham, Massachusetts. His Indian heritage is usually cited as Natick, but he is frequently called a mulatto in the historical literature. Attucks was described as a "stout" young man who carried "a large cord-wood stick" at the front of a crowd protesting on the Boston public square against British colonial policy. When the British soldiers fired on the crowd, Attucks dropped after the first volley, with two musket balls lodged in him. He died immediately, as did three other men. Of the eight other men wounded, two subsequently died as well. In the words of the poet John Boyle O'Reilly, published in 1889 to honor the men who fell in the Boston Massacre, Attucks had been "the first to defy, and the first die" (Quarles, p. 4).

People of African descent found their way into many groups of Indians in some of the most distant parts of the continent. When Henry Rowe Schoolcraft visited the Fond du Lac Ojibwa community near the eastern shore of Lake Superior on one of his early trips of "discovery" in 1820, he found that an African-Canadian had already found them. Bungo, a free African, had traveled through Canada with the British army in the War of 1812, and had married an Ojibwa woman with whom he reared four children at Fond du Lac before Schoolcraft ever arrived.

In colonial North America, intermarriage among Europeans and Indians occurred most frequently in Spanish-controlled lands, including Mexico, Florida, the Caribbean, and the western half of the United States. Like the French, the Spanish government sent soldiers to settle in America, but did relatively little to stimulate the emigration of women. Without European women around them, the soldiers married Indian women. The resulting mestizo class gradually became a majority of the population throughout most of the Spanish areas of North America.

Persistent prejudice in the Spanish colonies against Indian blood caused most people to obscure their Indian heritage and emphasize their Spanish blood. In this way, everyone strove to move up in the racial hierarchy. Indians who could speak Spanish and who wore Mexican clothing became known as mestizos, while many mestizos became white. The eighteenth-century Spanish colonial government sold "certificates of whiteness" to Indians who had mastered Spanish language and culture sufficiently to make enough money to buy such a certificate. Obviously white people, of course, needed no such document to vouch for their Europeanness.

In North America during the nineteenth century, the new social order of the modern industrial and scientific world had no room for mixed-blood and Métis. Excluded from Canadian society and losing their economic position, the Métis began to push for their own land. As pressures increased against them, and as the railroads simultaneously threatened their former livelihood, the Métis began to advocate independence from Britain. Because they were the New People born of both Indians and Europeans, they wanted to create a New Nation on the Red River with its capital at Winnipeg.

The quest for independence became even greater in 1869 when the Hudson's Bay Company gave its past North American holdings to newly emerging Canada. Known as Rupert's Land, this region included vast tracts of Indian territory. Under the Montreal-educated Métis Louis Riel, the Métis seized Fort Garry in revolt. The rebels established a provisional government in Winnipeg, and petitioned for admission to Canada as a new province. Even though supported by full-blood Indians and by many of the Anglophone mixed-bloods, Louis Riel and his New Nation failed. By 1870, British authorities had crushed their New Nation.

After the failure of his rebellion, Louis Riel fled to the United States while many of his followers dispersed through Manitoba and Saskatchewan, as far from colonial authorities as possible. Many other Métis also found refuge in Montana as well as North Dakota and Minnesota, but they did not surrender the dream of a new, mixed-blood nation that would include all Americans. Meanwhile, the Canadian government admitted Manitoba as a new, but non-Indian, province, whereupon the Métis repeatedly elected Riel to represent them in the Canadian parliament. But he was never seated.

It was a difficult time for Indians, but it was also a time for exaggerated hopes. The Sioux defeated Custer and his Crow allies at the Battle of the Little Bighorn in 1876, and this victory excited many Indian people with new hope for freedom and independence. Like the newly emerging Balkan nations, which had managed to throw off the yoke of Ottoman government, and like many European ethnic groups experiencing a growing sense of nationalism, the American Indians began to see themselves as a united group deserving better treatment.

When deprived of any hope of economic or political solutions to their problems, oppressed people often search for salvation in the spiritual realm. Just as the French had followed the mystic Joan of Arc in their struggle against English occupation, and just as the Spanish had liberated themselves from Muslim occupation by a fanatical Catholicism, Indian leaders in the nineteenth century often turned to spirituality as a means to redress their subjugation. In the United States, the Shawnee prophet Tecumseh led a religious and political movement. In the Southern states, the Red Sticks rose in rebellion under Chief Red Eagle. In the Yucatán, the Maya revolted while following a blend of traditional and Christian beliefs known as the Talking Cross.

Louis Riel also had a religious vision that he hoped would help his people to find salvation. Like many Catholics of the time, he resented the 1870 declaration of the Church proclaiming the infallibility of the Pope. He felt that the European Church, like the European governments, was out of touch with America. He favored a new religion for the New World, one that would be free of the Pope and would unite American Catholics and Protestants. Like the traditional Indians of his area, the new religion would allow polygamy, but it gave new rights to women, who would always be allowed to select their own mates and not be compelled by a father or anyone else to marry.

Riel showed a scholarly awareness of the hundreds of religious movements across North America during his time, and he borrowed or considered ideas from a variety of them. He thought of celebrating the Sabbath on Saturday as the Jews and the Seventh Day Adventists did. He accepted the Mormon teaching that the Indians of America were related to the Jews. He also supported the creation in Poland of a Zionist homeland for Jews that would be like the new Indian and mixed-blood homeland he wanted to create in America.

Riel wanted to create a pan-Indian confederacy, including all of the Indians and mixed-bloods of the central part of North America. This new nation would offer refuge to all the oppressed of the world, particularly to groups such as the Irish, who had suffered so severely under the British in much the same way that the Indians had suffered under British colonial rule. Riel's ideal Indian nation would also have close ties with the Indian peoples of Mexico and South America. He wanted to make St. Boniface in Manitoba an educational center that would teach children from throughout Latin America as well as Canada and the United States.

Although Riel hoped for assistance from the American government and repeatedly petitioned President Grant for support, he hoped to position his new nation as a counterweight to the United States, because it would keep the United States from dominating all of North America. Prophetically, he foresaw that Britain needed North America more than America needed Britain; he even predicted that Britain would need help in future wars with Germany (Flanagan, p. 169).

Riel traveled extensively throughout the United States and returned secretly to parts of Canada in pursuit of his mission. On one of his trips back into Canada, the Canadian authorities seized and imprisoned him in a Quebec insane asylum at St.-Jean-de-Dieu, outside of Montreal. In a preview of twentieth-century treatment of political dissidents, the forces of medical science and the newly emerging field of psychiatry were marshaled against Riel, and he was diagnosed as suffering from delusions of grandeur (Flanagan, p. 57). He spent much of his time in solitary confinement, tied by modern restraining devices. The authorities released Riel after he recanted his heretical political and religious beliefs.

In 1885 the Métis once again called on Riel for help, but this time the struggle erupted farther west, in Saskatchewan, rather than in Manitoba. The Métis had once taken arms against white settlers who wanted to take over the new farms the Métis had scratched out on the Saskatchewan plains after fleeing the Red River Valley in Manitoba. Knowing the importance of public and world opinion, Riel drew up petitions and wrote defenses of the creation of his new nation. He sought to solve the problem through diplomatic and political means rather than military ones, but that was not to be. This new revolt failed even more quickly than the first. Government forces rushed into Saskatchewan, dismantled the provisional government established by the Métis, and captured and imprisoned Riel. Despite the jury's plea for mercy toward Riel, the government hanged him on November 16, 1885, in Regina, the new city named for Queen Victoria and her new age of enlightenment and science.

After their crushing defeat, the Métis went through a long

period of decline during which most of them had to choose between being Indian or white. Many joined their Indian relatives as Cree or Ojibwa around the western Great Lakes and central plains of Canada and the United States. Many of the Métis families, especially those headed by French-speaking men, settled down to become farmers. They joined the white settlers moving in from Scotland and Eastern Europe. Other Métis moved east, where they joined French-speaking communities in Quebec, Vermont, and Maine.

The nineteenth century proved a hard epoch for North American Indians. In some ways it was the hardest of all since the Europeans had first arrived in America. During that century, white society tried in many ways to bar Indians and mixed-bloods from membership in the greater society; academic, government, and religious leaders tried to purge the white race and to undo three hundred years of race mixing.

Today the body of Louis Riel lies in a simple graveyard in St. Boniface, on the banks of the Red River, across from modern downtown Winnipeg. He lies in the graveyard of what was the Basilica of St. Boniface, but today the building is only a hulking shell, gutted by fire in 1968. The massive neo-classical façade stands hollow, deserted, and naked. The giant hole in the front left by the shattered stained-glass rose window stares out at the river like the blind eye of a giant cyclops. It seems ironically fitting that Riel should be buried before a destroyed church, since he spent so much time trying to rip the American church out of European hands.

Riel remains today as controversial a figure in Manitoba and Saskatchewan politics as he was in his own lifetime. Graffiti on odd walls around Winnipeg glorify or vilify him, and on radio stations the visitor can still hear songs dedicated to him. Riel symbolizes the rich mixture of cultures, genes, and ideas that created the modern population of North America. He also symbolizes the independent-minded people of the West who sought control over their own communities against the political, religious, and financial powers of the East.

English, native, and French musicians composed ballads, reels, and jigs in English and in French dedicated to Louis Riel and his quest for a totally new nation for the new mixed-blood culture that arose in North America. One such ballad, commonly available on cassette tape throughout Indian lands in the Canadian west, poses the question of who Louis Riel was, and answers that Louis Riel lives in all North Americans. The mixed-blood singers repeatedly emphasize their loud refrain, "It is we who are Louis Riel."

19

THE WHITE ROOTS OF PEACE

The Hiawatha Wampum survives as the oldest constitution in North America, perhaps the oldest in the world. The edges of the beaded belt have frayed slightly, but the skilled hands that made the purple and white beads from whelk shells, carefully tied each bead into its place. The Hiawatha Belt signifies the union of the nations of the Haudenosaunee, the Iroquois League, founded approximately six hundred years ago by Deganawidah and Hiawatha.

The wampum offers a simple message written in pictographs. The symbols depict four squares joined like the links of a chain, with a tree in the center of the belt. They represent the nations of the league united with one another by the chain of friendship. The tree signifies law and peace, and its branches represent the security and shelter given to humans by the law. Deganawidah named this constitution *Kaianerekowa*, "the Great Law of Peace," and he taught that peace and law had to be inseparable.

Before Deganawidah could make peace among the nations, he

needed to banish the Evil Mind that caused fighting and dissension. He persuaded the warriors to bring their weapons to him beside a great tree that grew over an underground cavern. He buried all the weapons deep inside the cavern beneath the tree.

With the Evil Mind destroyed, Deganawidah taught the new philosophy of the Good Mind based on Righteousness (*Gaiwoh*), Health (*Skenon*), and Power (*Gashasdenshaa*). *Righteousness* referred to relations between individuals and nations. *Health* referred to the condition of both the body and mind as well as to the social condition of peace. *Power* referred to the authority of law and custom that supported justice, and to the spiritual power that was inseparable from daily life (P. Wallace, p. 13).

When Deganawidah finally succeeded in bringing peace to the tribes, he planted a new tree to commemorate the alliance of friendship and to remind future generations of the precepts of the Good Mind. The tree had four large white roots, each of which grew in a different direction. Deganawidah prophesied that the roots of the tree would eventually grow to the far parts of the world, that in time the four roots would grow to include new nations of people not yet known. From many nations they would create one.

This story was already an ancient one when the first settlers came from Europe, and the native people shared their knowledge of the Good Mind with the newcomers. The new people came to live under the Great Tree of Peace, but they did not know its history. They did not know of the weapons buried in the earth, or of the white roots of peace that needed to be watered and nourished to help the tree grow.

In the bountiful life we have been given in America, we have not always remembered the law of the Good Mind. Sometimes we have reached out and taken an unfair share of the fruits of the tree. Sometimes we have enjoyed our place in the shade, but have not wanted to welcome others still suffering in the heat. Sometimes we have fouled the earth around the tree. We have spoiled the air and contaminated the water. In ignorance, we have even hacked at the roots of the great tree. But the tree has survived.

The great pine tree of peace is now more than half a millenium old. Some of the centuries have been harsh ones, but the tree has weathered the struggles between natives and settlers, an evil era of slavery, a bloody civil war, and heavy losses in foreign wars. Despite the hardships and cruelties of American history, the roots of that great tree have continued to grow, and new nations have found shelter under its branches.

The tree offered sanctuary to people of all cultures looking for a better life in a new world, to people fleeing from war, tyranny, poverty, oppression, famine, persecution, and genocide. The newcomers often had no water to give the white roots other than their own sweat, tears, and sometimes even blood. When they came without nourishment for the tree, the tree lived on their dreams and hopes, and it continued to grow.

We are the inheritors of a great American legacy: we are the children of Deganawidah. We are the children of Africa, Asia, Europe, the South Pacific, and all of the Americas, who have come to live under the peace of the great tree. We are the people who must uphold the Good Mind that our children may inherit this legacy of righteousness, health, and spiritual power. We are the people who now must nurture the Great Tree and water its white roots of peace.

BIBLIOGRAPHY

Armstrong, William H. *Warrior in Two Camps: Ely S. Parker, Union General and Seneca Chief*. Syracuse: Syracuse University Press, 1978.

Assu, Harry and Joy Inglis. *Assu of Cape Mudge*. Vancouver: University of British Columbia Press, 1989.

Axtell, James. *The European and the Indian*. Oxford: Oxford University Press, 1981.

————. *The Invasion Within: The Contest of Cultures in Colonial North America*. New York: Oxford University Press, 1985.

————. "Colonial America Without the Indians." In *Indians in American History*, edited by Frederick E. Hoxie. Arlington Heights, Ill.: Harlan Davidson, Inc., 1988.

Bakeless, John. *The Eyes of Discovery*. New York: Dover, 1961.

Barbour, Philip L. *Pocahontas and Her World*. Boston: Houghton Mifflin, 1969.

Barnett, Lincoln. *The Treasure of Our Tongue*. New York: Knopf, 1964.

Barlett, Michael H., Thomas M. Kolaz and David A. Gregory. *Archaeology in the City: A Hohokam Village in Phoenix, Arizona*. Tucson: University of Arizona Press, 1986.

Basso, Keith. "Ice and Travel Among the Fort Norman Slave." *Language and Society* 1 (1), 1972.

Bieder, Robert E. *Science Encounters the Indian, 1820–1880*. Norman: University of Oklahoma Press, 1986.

Bloomfield, Leonard. *Language*. New York: Holt, 1933.

Boas, Franz. *Geographical Names of the Kwakiutl Indians*. New York: AMS Press, 1934.

Bohannan, Paul, and Mark Glazer, eds. *High Points in Anthropology*. 2nd ed. New York: Knopf, 1988.

Bolton, Herbert E. *Coronado: Knight of Pueblos and Plains*. Albuquerque: University of New Mexico Press, 1949.

Borah, Woodrow. "The Mixing of Populations." In *First Images of America*, vol. 2, edited by Fredi Chiappelli. Berkeley: University of California Press, 1976.

Bourne, Edward Gaylord (ed). *Narratives of the Career of Hernando De Soto*. 2 vols. Translated by Buckingham Smith. New York: A. S. Barnes & Co., 1904.

Boxberger, Daniel L. *To Fish in Common: The Ethnohistory of Lummi Indian Salmon Fishing*. Lincoln: University of Nebraska Press, 1989.

Brain, Jeffrey. "The Great Mound Robbery." *Archaeology*, May/June 1988.

Brandon, William. *Indians*. New York: American Heritage, 1985.

Brose, David S., James A. Brown, and David W. Penny. *Ancient Art of the American Woodland Indians*. New York: Abrams, 1985.

Caldwell, Joseph R., and Robert L. Hall, eds. *Hopewellian Studies*. Illinois State Museum Scientific Papers, vol. 12. Springfield: Illinois State Museum, 1977.

Carnes, Mark C. *Secret Ritual and Manhood in Victorian America*. New Haven: Yale University Press, 1989.

Castañeda, Pedro. *The Journey of Coronado*. Translated by George Parker Winship. New York: Allerton Book Co., 1922.

Castanien, Donald G. *El Inca Garcilaso de la Vega*. New York: Twayne Publishers, 1969.

Ceram, C. W. *The First American*. New York: New American Library, 1971.

Chateaubriand, François René de. *Atala/René*. Translated by Irving Putter. Berkeley: University of California Press, 1952.

Chiappelli, Fredi, ed. *First Images of America: The Impact of the New World on the Old*. 2 vols. Berkeley: University of California Press, 1976.

Coe, Michael, Dean Snow, and Elizabeth Benson. *Atlas of Ancient America*. New York: Facts on File, 1986.

Cole, Douglas. *Captured Heritage: The Scramble for Northwest Coast Artifacts*. Seattle: University of Washington Press, 1985.

Cronon, William. *Changes in the Land: Indians, Colonists, and the Ecology of New England*. New York: Hill and Wang, 1983.

Crosby, Alfred W. Jr. *The Columbian Exchange*. Westport, Connecticut: Greenwood Press, 1972.

Davis, David B. *The Problem of Slavery in Western Culture*. Ithaca: Cornell University Press, 1966.

Deloria, Ella Cara. *Dakota Texts*. New York: AMS Press, 1974.

————. *Waterlily*. Lincoln: University of Nebraska Press, 1988.

Deloria, Vine Jr. *Custer Died for Your Sins*. New York: Macmillan, 1969.

————. *God Is Red*. New York: Grosset & Dunlap, 1973.

————. *Behind the Trail of Broken Treaties: An Indian Declaration of Independence*. New York: Delacorte Press, 1974.

————. "The Application of the Constitution to American Indians." In *American Indian Contributions to the Democratic Tradition and the United States Constitution*, edited by John C. Mohawk and Oren R. Lyons. Unpublished manuscript.

Driver, Harold E. *Indians of North America*. 2nd ed. Chicago: University of Chicago, 1969.

Drucker, Philip. *Indians of the Northwest Coast*. Garden City, New York: Natural History Press, 1963.

Dye, David H. "Death March of Hernando de Soto." *Archaeology*, May/June 1989.

Engels, Friedrich. *The Origins of the Family, Private Property, and the State, in the Light of the Researches of Lewis H. Morgan*. New York: International Publishers, 1942.

Ewen, Charles R. "Apalachee Winter." *Archaeology*, May/June 1989.

Fagan, Brian M. *The Great Journey: The Peopling of Ancient America*. London: Thames & Hudson, 1987.

Farb, Peter. *Man's Rise to Civilization: The Cultural Ascent of the Indians of North America*. New York: Bantam Books, 1978.

Farris, Glenn J. "The Russian Imprint on the Colonization of California." In *Columbian Consequences*, edited by David Hurst Thomas. Washington, D.C.: Smithsonian Institution Press, 1989.

Fenton, William N. "Lewis Henry Morgan: Pioneer Ethnologist." Introduction to reprint of Lewis Henry Morgan's *League of the Iroquois*. Secaucus, New Jersey: Citadel Press, 1962.

Fey, Harold E. and D'Arcy McNickle. *Indians and Other Americans*. New York: Harper & Row, 1959.

Fiedel, Stuart J. *Prehistory of the Americas*. Cambridge: Cambridge University Press, 1987.

Fitzhugh, William W., ed. *Cultures in Contact*. Washington, D.C.: Smithsonian Institution Press, 1985.

Flanagan, Thomas. *Louis "David" Riel: "Prophet of the New World."* Toronto: University of Toronto Press, 1979.

Folsom, Franklin, and Mary Eltin Folsom. *America's Ancient Treasures*. Albuquerque: University of New Mexico Press, 1983.

Forbes, Jack D. *Apache, Navaho, and Spaniard*. Norman: University of Oklahoma Press, 1960.

———. *Black Africans and Native Americans*. Oxford: Basil Blackwell, 1988.

———, ed. *The Indian in America's Past*. Englewood Cliffs, New Jersey: Prentice-Hall, 1964.l

Foreman, Grant. *Sequoyah*. Norman: University of Oklahoma Press, 1938.

Forsyth, Thomas. "The French, British and Spanish Methods of Treating Indians." *Ethnohistory* 4(2), Spring 1957.

Fowler, Melvin L. "A Pre-Columbian Urban Center on the Mississippi," *Scientific American*, August 1975.

Fundaburk, Lila Emma, and Mary Douglas Fundaburk Foreman, eds. *Sun Circles and Human Hands: The Southeastern Indians, Art and Industries*. Luverne, Alabama: Emma Lila Fundaburk, 1957.

Gage, Matilda Joslyn. *Woman, Church and State*. 2nd ed. New York: The Truth Seeker Company, 1893.

Gallenkamp, Charles. *Maya: The Riddle and Rediscovery of a Lost Civilization*. 2nd ed. New York: Penguin, 1981.

Galloway, Patricia. *The Southeastern Ceremonial Complex*. Lincoln: University of Nebraska, 1989.

Garcilaso de la Vega, El Inca. *The Florida of the Inca*. Translated by John and Jeannette Varner. Austin: University of Texas, 1951.

———. *Royal Commentaries of the Incas and General History of Peru*. 2 vols. Translated by Harold V. Livermore. Austin: University of Texas Press, 1966.

Geiger, Maynard. *The Indians of Mission Santa Barbara in Paganism and Christianity*. Santa Barbara: Franciscan Fathers, 1986.

———. *Juana Maria: The Lone Woman of San Nicolas Island*. Santa Barbara: Old Mission, undated.

Gibson, Arrell Morgan. *The American Indian: Prehistory to Present*. Lexington: D.C. Heath, 1980.

Gibson, Jon, *Caddoan and Poverty Point Archaeology*. Lafayette: Louisiana Archaeological Society, 1980.

———. *Poverty Point: A Culture of the Lower Mississippi Valley*. Baton Rouge: Louisiana Archaeological Survey and Antiquities Commission, 1985.

Grenfell, Wilfred T. *Labrador: The Country and the People*. New York: Macmillan, 1909.

Griffith, Benjamin W. Jr. *McIntosh and Weatherford, Creek Indian Leaders*. Tuscaloosa; University of Alabama Press, 1988.

Gudde, Erwin G. *California Place Names*. Berkeley: University of California Press, 1969.

Hall, Sam. *The Fourth World*. New York: Vintage Books, 1988.

Hamilton, Earl J. "What the New World Gave the Economy of the Old." In *First Images of America*, vol. 2. Edited by Fredi Chiapelli. Berkeley: University of California Press, 1976.

Harris, J. R., ed. *The Legacy of Egypt*. 2nd ed. London: Oxford University Press, 1971.

Harris, Marvin. *The Rise of Anthropological Theory*. New York: Columbia University Press, 1968.

Hays, H. R. *From Ape to Angel: An Informal History of Social Anthropology*. New York: Knopf, 1960.

Hecht, Robert A. *Continents in Collision*. Washington, D.C.: University Press of America, 1980.

Hobhouse, Henry. *Seeds of Change*. New York: Harper & Row, 1985.

Holbrook, Stewart H. *Burning an Empire: The Story of American Forest Fires*. New York: Macmillan, 1943.

Hoolinhan, Patrick, Jerold L. Collings, Sarah Nestor, and Jonathan Batkin. *Harmony by Hand: Art of the Southwest Indians*. San Francisco; Chronicle Books, 1987.

Horgan, Paul. *Conquistadors in North American History*. Greenwich, Connecticut: Fawcett, 1963.

Hosmer, J. K., ed. *Winthrop's Journal: History of New England 1630–1649*, vol. 2. New York: Barnes & Noble, 1953.

Hoxie, Frederick E., ed. *Indians in American History*. Arlington Heights, Illinois: Harlan Davidson, Inc. 1988.

Hudson, Charles M. "Tracking the Elusive De Soto." *Archaeology*, May/June 1989.

Iverson, Peter. *The Navajo Nation*. Albuquerque: University of New Mexico Press, 1981.

Jennings, Francis. *Empire of Fortune*. New York: Norton, 1988.

Johansen, Bruce E., and Donald A. Grinde, Jr. *Exemplar of Liberty: Native America and the Evolution of Democracy*. Unpublished manuscript.

Johnson, Elden. *The Prehistoric Peoples of Minnesota*. St. Paul: Minnesota Historical Society Press, 1988.

Johnson, John R. "The Chumash and the Missions." *Columbian Consequences*, vol. 1. Edited by David Hurst Thomas. Washington, D.C.: Smithsonian Institution Press, 1989.

Kopper, Philip. *The Smithsonian Book of North American Indians*. Washington, D.C.: Smithsonian Institution Press, 1986.

Krech, Shepard III, ed. *Indians, Animals, and the Fur Trade*. Athens: University of Georgia Press, 1981.

———, ed. *The Subarctic Fur Trade: Native Social and Economic Adaptations*. Vancouver: University of British Columbia Press, 1984.

Lauber, Almon Wheeler. *Indian Slavery in Colonial Times*. Williamstown, Massachusetts: Corner House, 1913.

Leach, Douglas Edward. *Arms for Empire*. New York: Macmillan, 1973.

Lévi-Strauss, Claude. *The Elementary Structures of Kinship*. Translated by James Harle Bell and John Richard von Sturmer. London: Eyre & Spottiswoode, 1969.

Liberty, Margot, ed. *American Indian Intellectuals*. St. Paul: West Publishing Company, 1978.

Lincoln, Kenneth, with Al Logan Slagle. *The Good Red Road*. New York: Harper & Row, 1989.

Lister, Robert H., and Florence C. Lister. *Those Who Came Before*. Globe, Arizona: Southwest Parks & Monuments Association, 1983.

Lowes, Warren. *Indian Giver: A Legacy of North American Native Peoples*. British Columbia: Theytus Books, 1986.

Martin, Calvin. *Keepers of the Game: Indian-Animal Relationships and the Fur Trade*. Berkeley: University of California Press, 1978.

Martin, Paul S., George I. Quimby, and Donald Collier. *Indians Before Columbus*. Chicago: University of Chicago Press, 1947.

Mason, Philip P., ed. *Schoolcraft's Expedition to Lake Itasca*. East Lansing: Michigan State University Press, 1958.

Mathews, Mitford M. *A Dictionary of Americanisms*. Chicago: University of Chicago Press, 1951.

Maxwell, James A., et al. *America's Fascinating Indian Heritage*. Pleasantville, New York: Reader's Digest, 1978.

Ray, Arthur J. *Indians in the Fur Trade*. Toronto: University of Toronto Press, 1974.

Read, Allen Walker. "The Evidence on 'O.K.'" *The Saturday Review of Literature*, July 19, 1941.

Reining, Priscilla, ed. *Kinship Studies in the Morgan Centennial Year*. Washington, D.C. The Anthropological Society of Washington, 1972.

Robert, Joseph C. *The Story of Tobacco in America*. New York: Knopf, 1952.

Rosenthal, Michael. *The Character Factory: Baden-Powell and the Origins of the Boy Scout Movement*. New York: Pantheon, 1984.

Sapir, Edward. *Language: An Introduction to the Study of Speech*. New York: Harcourt Brace, 1921.

Sauer, Jonathan D. "Changing Perception and Exploitation of New World Plants in Europe, 1492–1800." In *First Images of America*, vol. 2, edited by Fredi Chiapelli. Berkeley: University of California Press, 1976.

Saum, Lewis O. *The Fur Trader and the Indian*. Seattle: University of Washington Press, 1965.

Savage, Henry Jr. *Discovering America 1700–1875*. New York: Harper & Row, 1979.

Schoolcraft, Henry R. *Narrative Journal of Travels from Detroit Northwest through the Great Chain of American Lakes to the Sources of the Mississippi River*. Albany: E.&F. Hosford, 1821.

———. *Notes on the Iroquois*, New York: Bartlett & Welford, 1846.

Schoolcraft, Mary Howard (Mrs. Henry R. Schoolcraft). *The Black Gauntlet*. In *Plantation Life*. New York: Negro Universities Press, 1969.

Sherrod, P. Clay, and Martha Ann Rolingson. *Surveyors of the Ancient Mississippi Valley*. Fayetteville: Arkansas Archaeological Survey Research Series No. 28, 1987.

Silverberg, Robert. *The Mound Builders*. Athens: Ohio University Press, 1968.

Smith, Buckingham, ed. and trans. *Narratives of De Soto in the Conquest of Florida, by a Gentleman of Elvas*. Gainesville: Palmetto Books, 1968.

Smith, Bruce D., ed. *Mississippian Settlement Patterns*. New York: Academic Press, 1978.

———. "Origin of Agriculture in Eastern North America." *Science* 246(22), December 1989

Snow, Dean. *The Archaeology of North America*. London: Thames & Hudson, 1976.

Spicer, Edward H. *A Short History of the Indians of the United States*. New York: Van Nostrand Reinhold Company, 1969.

———. *The American Indians: Dimensions of Ethnicity*. Cambridge: Harvard University Press, 1982.

Spradley, James P. *Guests Never Leave Hungry: The Autobiography of James Sewid, a Kwakiutl Indian*. New Haven: Yale University Press, 1969.

Stafford, Kim R. *Having Everything Right*. New York: Penguin, 1986.

Steinbeck, John. *Travels with Charley in Search of America*. New York: Viking Press, 1962.

Stewart, George R. *Names on the Land*. New York: Random House, 1945.

———. *American Place-Names*. New York: Oxford University Press, 1970.

Stewart, Hilary. *Indian Fishing*. Seattle: University of Washington Press, 1977.

Struever, Stuart, and Felicia Antonelli Holton. *Koster: Americans in Search of their Prehistoric Past*. New York: New American Library, 1979.

Swanson, Earl H., Warrick Bray, and Ian Farrington. *The New World*. Oxford: Elsevier Phaidon, 1975.

Swanton, John R. *Indian Tribes of the Lower Mississippi Valley and Adjacent Coast of the Gulf of Mexico*. Smithsonian Institution Bulletin 43. Washington, D.C.: Smithsonian Institution, 1911.

Thornton, Russell. *American Indian Holocaust and Survival: A Population History Since 1492*. Norman: University of Oklahoma Press, 1987.

Tocqueville, Alexis de. *Democracy in America*, vol. I, translated by Henry Reeve. New York, Random House, 1945.

Toynbee, Arnold J. Foreword to Garcilaso de la Vega, *Royal Commentaries of the Incas and General History of Peru*, vol. 1., translated by Harold V. Livermore. Austin: University of Texas Press, 1966.

Trautman, Thomas R. *Lewis Henry Morgan and the Invention of Kinship*. Berkeley: University of California Press, 1987.

Truex, Faye, and Patricia Q. Foster, eds. *The Tunica-Biloxi Tribe*. Marksville, Louisiana: Tunica-Biloxi Tribe, 1987.

Turner, Frederick W. III, ed. *The Portable North American Reader*. New York: Viking, 1974.

Turner, Geoffrey. *Indians of North America*. Poole, Dorset: Blandford Press, 1979.

Underhill, Ruth M. *Red Man's America*. Chicago: University of Chicago Press, 1953.

United States Department of Agriculture. *Fact Book of Agriculture* no. 1063. Washington, D.C.: U.S. Government Printing Office, 1989.

Varner, John Grier. *El Inca: The Life and Times of Garcilaso de la Vega*. Austin: University of Texas, 1968.

Vogel, Virgil J. *This Country Was Ours*. New York: Harper & Row, 1972.

Waldman, Carl. *Atlas of the North American Indian*. New York: Facts on File, 1985

Wallace, Anthony F. C. *The Death and Rebirth of the Seneca*. New York: Vintage Books, 1972.

Wallace, Paul A. W. *The White Roots of Peace*. Philadelphia: University of Pennsylvania Press, 1946.

Warman, Arturo. "Maize as Organizing Principle." *Northeast Indian Quarterly* 6(1), 1989.

Waring, A. J., Jr. and Preston Holder. "A Pre-historic Ceremonial Complex in the Southeastern United States." *American Anthropologist*, 1945.

Waselkov, Gregory A. "Indian Maps of the Colonial Southeast." In *Powhatan's Mantle*, edited by Peter Wood, Gregory Waselkov, and M. Thomas Hatley. Lincoln: University of Nebraska Press, 1989.

Washburn, Wilcomb E., ed. *The Indian and the White Man*. Garden City, New York: Anchor Books, 1964.

Weaver, Muriel Porter. *The Aztecs, Maya, and Their Predecessors*. 2nd ed. New York: Academic Press, 1981.

Weeks, Philip. *The American Indian Experience*. Arlington Heights, Illinois: Forum Press, 1988.

Wenger, Gilbert R. *The Story of Mesa Verde National Park*. Mesa

Verde National Park, Colorado: Mesa Verde Museum Association, Inc., 1980.

Werner, M. R. *Tammany Hall*. New York: Doubleday, Doran & Co., 1928.

Willey, Gordon R. *An Introduction to American Archaeology*, vol. 1. Englewood Cliffs, New Jersey: Prentice-Hall, 1966.

Willey, Gordon R., and Jeremy A. Sabloff. *A History of American Archaeology*. 2nd ed. New York: W. H. Freeman & Co., 1980.

Williams, Ealter L., ed. *Southeastern Indians Since the Removal Era*. Athens: University of Georgia, 1979.

Winship, George Parker, ed. and trans. *The Journey of Coronado 1540–1542*. New York: Allerton Book Co., 1922.

Winsor, Justin. *Christopher Columbus: And How He Received and Imparted the Spirit of Discovery*. Boston: Houghton Mifflin, 1892.

Yenne, Bill. *The Encyclopedia of North American Indian Tribes*. New York: Crown, 1986.

ACKNOWLEDGMENTS

I owe the most to my family. My wife, Walker Pearce, traveled extensively for this project and served as a usually friendly critic. I also appreciate the encouragement and assistance of our children, Walker Pearce Maybank Buxton and Roy Pearce Maybank.

The publication of this book marks a decade of collaboration with my editor, James O'Shea Wade, and agent, Lois Wallace. With each year and each book, their guidance becomes more important and better appreciated.

I borrowed from many realms of academic thought, but I particularly appreciate the help of James Bodine, Rogert Buffalohead, Ray Fogelson, Bruce Johansen, William Leap, James Lenfesty, Nancy O. Lurie, John Mohawk, Allyn Stearman, Terrence Heath, and Catherine Warrick.

At Macalester College I appreciate the assistance of Robert Gavin, Diane Glancy, David Itzkowitz, Betty Ivey, Charlotte Johnson, David McCurdy, Anna Meigs, Paul Solon, Anne Sutherland, and the staff of the DeWitt Wallace Library.

For special help at the right moments, I acknowledge the contributions of Emigdio Ballon, Ada Deer, Kennon Dial, Tina Edwards, Ray Fadden, Evelyn Holt, Ramona Jones, Rochelle Jones, Chief Orin Lion, Phil Lucas, Freya Manfred, Ed Eagle Man McGaa, Tom Pope, and Jaune Quick-to-See Smith.

During the writing of this book, I received much appreciated financial assistance from the Dewitt Wallace Fund and a fellowship from the National Endowment for the Humanities.

INDEX

Noble, David Grant. *New Light on Chaco Canyon*. Santa Fe: School of American Research, 1984.

———. *Ancient Ruins of the Southwest: An Archaeological Guide*. Flagstaff, Arizona: Northland Press, 1981.

O'Connor, Harvey. *The Astors*. New York: Knopf, 1941.

Owen, Roger C. *The Anthropology of Native North America*. New York: Queens College Department of Anthropology, 1982.

Owen, Robert C., James J. F. Deetz, and Anthony D. Fisher. *The North American Indians*. New York: Macmillan, 1967.

Owsley, Frank Lawrence Jr. *Struggle for the Gulf Borderlands*. Gainesville: University of Florida Press, 1981.

Padover, Saul K. *The Complete Jefferson*. New York: Duell, Sloan & Pearce, 1943.

Page, Barbara. "Artifacts Reveal 12th Century Culture." *The Gilcrease Magazine* 3(3), July 1981.

Paz, Octavio. *The Labyrinth of Solitude*. New York: Grove Press, 1961.

Peattie, Donald Culross. *A Natural History of Western Trees*. Boston: Riverside Press, 1953.

Perlin, John. *A Forest Journey: The Role of Wood in the Development of Civilization*. New York: Norton, 1989.

Prufer, Olaf H. "The Hopewell Cult." *Scientific American*, December 1964.

Pyne, Stephen J. *Fire in America*. New Jersey: Princeton University Press, 1982.

Quarles, Benjamin. *The Negro in the American Revolution*. Chapel Hill: University of North Carolina Press, 1961.

Quinn, David Beers. "New Geographical Horizons." In *First Images of America*, edited by Fredi Chiappelli. Berkeley: University of California Press, 1976.

Radin, Paul. "The Personal Reminiscence of a Winnebago Indian." *Journal of American Folklore* 26: 1913.

———. *Crashing Thunder: The Autobiography of a Winnebago Indian*. New York: Appleton, 1926.

———. *Culture of the Winnebago, as Described by Themselves*. Bloomington, Indiana: Indiana University Publications in Anthropology and Linguistics, 1950.

McCrum, Robert, William Cran, and Robert MacNeil. *The Story of English*. New York: Viking 1986.

McFeat, Tom, ed. *Indians of the North Pacific Coast*. Seattle: University of Washington Press, 1989.

McGaa, Ed. *Mother Earth Spirituality*. San Francisco: Harper & Row, 1990.

McMillan, Alan D. *Native Peoples and Cultures of Canada*. Vancouver: Douglas & McIntyre, 1988.

McNeill, William H. *Plagues and Peoples*. New York: Doubleday, 1976.

Medicine, Bea. "Ella Cara Deloria." *Women Anthropologists*. Edited by Ute Gacs, Aisha Khan, Jerrie McIntyre, and Ruth Weinberg. Urbana: University of Illinois Press, 1989.

Meining, D. W. *The Shaping of America*, vol. 1. New Haven: Yale University Press, 1986.

Mencken, H. L. *The American Language*. New York: Knopf, 1937.

Milfort, Louis LeClerc. *Memoirs, or, a Quick Glance at My Various Travels and My Sojourn in the Creek Nation*, translated by Ben C. McCary. Savannah: Beehive Press, 1959.

Morgan, Lewis Henry. *League of the Ho-De'-No-Sau-Nee, or Iroquois*. Rochester: Sage & Brother, 1851.

Morison, Samuel Eliot. *Admiral of the Sea: A Life of Christopher Columbus*. Boston: Little Brown, 1942.

————. *The Great Explorers*. New York: Oxford University Press, 1978.

Mowat, Farley. *Tundra*. Salt Lake City: Peregrine Smith, 1989.

Mushkat, Jerome. *Tammany: The Evolution of a Political Machine 1789–1865*. Syracuse: Syracuse University Press, 1971.

Myers, Gustavus. *The History of Tammany Hall*, 2nd ed. New York: Boni & Liveright, 1917.

Nabokov, Peter, and Robert Easton. *Native American Architecture*. Oxford: Oxford University Press, 1989.

Nash, Gary B. *Red, White, and Black*. Englewood Cliffs, New Jersey: Prentice-Hall, 1974.

Newby, Eric. *The World Atlas of Exploration*. London: Michael Beazley, 1975.

Newman, Peter C. *Caesars of the Wilderness*. Markham, Ontario: Viking, 1987.

About the Author

Jack Weatherford's previous books include *Tribes on the Hill* and *Indian Givers*. His studies of Native Americans on both continents and their bridge building between the Old and New Worlds have taken him to fifty countries around the globe, and his works have been translated into five languages. He is an anthropologist at Macalester College in St. Paul, Minnesota.